Acclaim
for
Bipolar Disorder: Rebuilding Your Life

♦ *This book offers precious insight into the relationship of a man, struck by severe mental illness, to his church, his congregation, and his God. Stout writes elegantly about the turmoil he lived through while coping with manic depression, his experience magnified by a disrupted career in an institution where, according to the author, many of its leaders still believe that mental illness came from demonic possession.*

— Robert K. Lundin, Publication Manager, Recovery Press
The University of Chicago Center for Psychiatric Rehabilitation

♦ *Rev. Stout has done an excellent job of honestly sharing his personal story in a way that makes it helpful for anyone trying to deal effectively with this unpredictable and baffling disorder.*

— Mary Ellen Copeland, M.S., M.A.
Mental Health Educator

♦ *This remarkable story of a courageous man who overcame adversity after adversity to reinvent his life is the best autobiography by a person with bipolar disorder I have read.*

— Max E. Dine, M.D., F.A.C.P.

♦ *Dr. Stout has given us a gripping account of his victory over the haunting memory of childhood abuse by a mentally ill mother and the challenge of his own bipolar disorder — a victory enabled by strength gained from a loving family and friends, and faith in God's constant presence.*

— Gunnar E. Christiansen, M.D.
Former President, NAMI California; Co-chairman, FaithNet NAMI

bipolar disorder:

rebuilding your life

A Bipolar's Story that Includes
Practical Strategies, Techniques
& Tips for Managing Moods

Rev. Dr. James T. Stout

Cypress House

BIPOLAR DISORDER: REBUILDING YOUR LIFE
Copyright © 2002 by Rev. Dr. James T. Stout

For information, or to order additional copies, please contact:

Cypress House
155 Cypress Street
Fort Bragg, California 95437
800-773-7782
Fax: 707-964-7531
http:\\www.cypresshouse.com

Cypress House books are available for special promotions, premiums and bulk discounts.

Cover Design: Gopa Design and Illustration

Library of Congress Cataloging-in-Publication Data

Stout, James T., 1942
  Bipolar disorder: rebuilding your life / James T. Stout.-- 1st ed.
  p. cm.
  ISBN 1-879384-44-2 (pbk. : alk. paper)
  1. Manic-depressive illness--Popular works. 2. Manic-depressive illness-Religious aspects--Christianity--Popular works. 3. Depression, Mental-Popular works. 4. Depression, Mental--Religious aspects--Christianity--Popular works. 5. Stout, James T., 1942-
6. Manic-depressive illness--Patients--United States--Biography. 7. Depressed persons--United States--Biography. I. Title.

RC516.S795 2002
616.89'5'0092--dc2l   2001054828

[B]

2   4   6   8   9   7   5   3

First edition

Printed in Canada

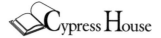
Cypress House

ORDER FORM

BIPOLAR DISORDER: REBUILDING YOUR LIFE
by Rev. Dr. James T. Stout

☞ **No. of books ordered @ $18.95 each**	**SUBTOTAL** ☞	
○ *Please put me on your book catalog mailing list.*	7.25% sales tax (CA residents only)	
Shipping & handling charges: $3.00 USPS or $5.00 UPS or priority mail, plus $1.00 for each additional book.	Shipping & handling	
Name	**TOTAL**	
Address	Ship to	
City State Zip	Address	
○ Check enclosed *Charge to:* ○ VISA ○ MasterCard	City State Zip	
Card Number		Expiration Date
Authorized Cardholder Signature	Daytime Phone Number	

SEND YOUR ORDER TO:

Cypress House
155 Cypress Street • Fort Bragg, CA 95437
or call **1-800-773-7782**
You can also fax your credit card order to 707-964-7531
or visit our website at www.cypresshouse.com

About The Author

Dr. James T. Stout is an ordained Presbyterian minister. He has pastored five churches: three as a senior pastor and two as an associate. His ministry experience includes working with college and graduate students at Miami, Harvard, MIT, Boston and Northeastern Universities, social work with Young Life's outreach to teenage gangs in New York City, and being student chaplain to the men's violent ward at Danvers State Mental Hospital in Massachusetts. Dr. Stout has taught and written on stress, burnout, depression, manic depression, job/career/educational transition, marriage enrichment, parenting, work fulfillment, and refocusing for the second half of life. He has spoken in such diverse locations as college campuses, professional football and baseball locker rooms, executive boardrooms, camps, retreat centers, and churches. Since 1965 he has career counseled more than 7,000 individuals. He has organized and led support groups for men, women, mentally ill persons and their family members, high school, college, and graduate students, teenage gang members, athletes, and people in career transition. Dr. Stout was given the NAMI California's "Distinguished Clergy Award 2001" for his efforts on behalf of those affected by mental illness. He is listed in Marquis' *Who's Who in the West* and Marquis' *Who's Who in Religion* and in the 1973 volume of *Outstanding Young Men of America*. He has been married to the former Leah Ann Hayden since 1967. They have two sons, Jim, Jr. and John.

◆ ◆ ◆

If this book has been helpful, or if you are interested in other articles and books written by Dr. Jim Stout or in scheduling him for a speaking engagement, please call 949-631-7040.

To Leah, Jim, Jr. and John,
with deepest gratitude for your love,
faith, encouragement, patience and prayers.

Permissions

Author's Notes

THIS BOOK WAS BORN FROM personal experience and strengthened by numerous resources. I have researched the topics covered extensively, and have gleaned information from family memorabilia as well. These pages have been reproduced, of course, from my memory and assorted sources such as interviews with relatives, friends, hundreds of mentally ill people and their families, and dozens of mental health professionals. While many recollections of past events are clear, I don't claim to have a photographic memory; I've reconstructed quotes and dialogue as accurately as possible to capture their essence. Having participated in and led support groups for those living with damaged minds and those close to them has also provided many insights.

Gender equality is important to me, but for brevity, in most cases I use "he" or "she" rather than the longer "he and/or she."

The information in this book is intended to complement, not substitute for, the advice of your physician, psychiatrist, psychologist, or other mental health professional, whom you should consult about your unique needs.

Contents

Introduction

O N A COOL NIGHT IN MAY 1989, I sat on a motel bed, counting lethal dosages of medications. Nearby lay a fifth of rum to wash them down, and a .357 magnum pistol. The alcohol would more than double the pills' effect; the bullet would be instant. I pondered which to use. Either way, my self-inflicted death would be painless, almost comfortable!

I'd researched the least painful, most effective suicide methods, reading several books that describe the common lethal medications and dosages. I studied them slowly, pen in hand, underlining my choices, debating which to use. My first choice was overdosing on medication. I'd just go to sleep and never wake up. Second, a pistol — it would all be over in moments. No slipups, no pain.

Other methods had been eliminated: slitting my wrists, hanging myself, carbon monoxide poisoning, and speeding my car into a concrete abutment. Those and others were too painful, or could fail. Either way, my unbearable mental pain would soon end. Permanently!

I was emotionally hemorrhaging from past and recent wounds inflicted by others. The pain was so awful I could no longer bear it. The future only appeared to hold more unfair treatment and no solution. The final straw had broken the camel's back. I was so upset by all the criticisms, abandonment, and betrayals of youth and adulthood that my mind screamed to escape any more pain. I no longer wanted to live. I, the lifelong fighter, had given up.

Many times during the previous six months, I'd contemplated ending my life, and reflected on the effects that would have on others. Those reflections were painful, frightening, depressingly lonely, and guilt-laden. I envisioned the reactions of my family, relatives, friends, and fellow church members. It seemed unreal to be planning my own funeral. As horrible as my suicide would be

for those who cared about me, my anguish was so bad that I no longer cared. I just wanted out of life; out of any more torment. I dearly loved my wife, Leah, and my sons, Jim, Jr. and John. But even my Christian faith and my love for them weren't enough to stop my suicide plans.

When I began my ministerial career in 1969, there wasn't a clue that my biggest battles were ahead. I loved being a pastor, because it meant using my gifts for what I believed God created me to do. However, after years of successes and conflicts, my fast-paced life finally came to an abrupt halt.

Previously, I'd served four other congregations: one in Florida, as an associate pastor, and three others as senior pastor. Then, in August 1986, we moved to California, where I had accepted the position of "Minister of Evangelism and Family Life" on the staff of the 4,500-member St. Andrew's Presbyterian Church in Newport Beach. I was in the prime of my life and ministry. Everything I did there flourished. Until I hit the wall.

September 1988, nine months earlier, marked the kickoff for the year ahead. It was the beginning of my second year. Fall programs were being launched. Although an incredibly busy time, everything was going splendidly, except for some unforeseen stressors that soon would turn my life upside-down.

I considered myself a good counselor. During twenty years of professional ministry I'd counseled all sorts of people: laypersons, professional athletes, pastors, psychologists, psychiatrists, and physicians. Year after year, I'd probably intervened in four or more potential suicide situations every month.

I was fairly well read on psychological issues and thought I knew myself. I had taken graduate-level counseling courses that included a six-month seminary clinical pastoral education course working in the men's violent ward of a large state mental hospital near Boston, Massachusetts.

As a pastor, I'd successfully guided and consoled others. Now I stood on the other side of the counseling fence! Ironically, the teacher-giver was now the learner-receiver. On November 11, 1988, at age

forty-seven, my life fell apart. I, who'd helped so many others, spent five agonizing months in a psychiatric unit. Almost three months after that, I entered another mental hospital for almost a month.

Those six months of hospitalization initiated me into a strange, scary new level of others' psychic pain, plus my own major depressive episodes, extreme manic agitation, and ongoing suicide thoughts, plans, and botched attempts. My diagnosis was "bipolar disorder," which is often called "manic-depressive illness," a life-threatening condition involving extreme mood swings: elated or agitated manic "highs," and despairing, suicidal "lows."

Bipolar disorder is one of the major mental illnesses. The psychiatrists also identified me as a "rapid-cycler," one whose moods shift four or more times a year. My emotions could undergo extreme changes weekly, daily, sometimes hourly, from high energy and agitation to no energy and suicidal thinking.

Why would a successful Christian leader want to end his life? What would make a husband and father, athlete, scholar, senior pastor of three churches, and respected minister on the staff of a large, influential church want to kill himself?

Many who have a mental illness come from happy, "normal" families. I didn't. All along, I was aware of having been raised in a dysfunctional home, but I never realized how deeply the emotional injuries from my childhood and several church-related traumas had scarred me. Like dormant California fault lines that suddenly erupt into devastating earthquakes, my inner cracks finally gave way.

Through much pain, counseling, and self-education, I discovered the probable causes of my mental illness:

♦ Growing up in a terribly dysfunctional family

♦ Abandonment by both parents at different times

♦ Severe emotional abuse by my mother, father, and grandmother

♦ Years of sexual abuse by my mother and grandmother

- Brutal treatment from three of the five churches I pastored

- A twenty-five-year history of working sixty-plus hours a week

- A genetic predisposition for mental illness

- A chemical imbalance in my brain

Truly, it is a miracle of God's grace that I'm still alive and sharing my story.

For years after my discharge from the second hospital in 1989, I led a roller-coaster existence. My family and I were kept continually off balance by my changing moods. A number of suicide plans between my two hospitalizations were thwarted. I came close to killing myself many times during the next nine years. Sometimes I was strong enough to seek aid; other times, too weak. But somehow God intervened with help: a phone call or unexpected visit by someone, a book or other source of rescue. I was plagued by conflicts with my insurance company. Those upsets often precipitated severe agitation or serious depression.

I tried thirty-seven different medicines; thirty-six of them had no lasting positive results. Time and again I got my hopes up for a pill that would work, only to endure intolerable side effects, including several errors that could have killed me.

While losing a number of "friends" due to my illness, I've built stronger relationships with old friends and new ones. I've fought debilitating emotional swings, toxic medication reactions, loneliness and stigmatization. Progress has been one step backward, two steps forward. In spite of setbacks, I've rebuilt my life, refocused my energies, and applied my faith in new ways. For years I believed I'd never again feel good or hopeful.

Yet despite nine years of off-and-on difficulties, the past four years have been my best. Now I'm happier, more at peace, and as productive as ever. Although I still experience occasional mild manias and depressions, I continue using my skills and experience in helping others. While recuperating, I've started several successful ministries that have impacted hundreds.

My mind is once again focused on accomplishing personal, family, and professional goals. I still occasionally preach, teach, and conduct weddings and funerals, but the kind of people I serve and the type of pastoring I do has changed. It's truly exciting to anticipate future opportunities to make my life count!

I'm living life in a fuller way than I ever imagined, and want to pass on some of what I've learned. I hope that my fellow sufferers and those who care for them will derive helpful information, encouragement, and inspiration from these chapters.

The theme of this book is that every person can cope with or overcome his or her background, tragedies, and mental illness (with its stigmas) by using the experiences and tools in these pages. This is a survival manual designed to help bipolars, depressives, and their loved ones navigate the minefield of these serious afflictions. The pages ahead have a threefold purpose:

1. To show how devastating and potentially deadly clinical depression and bipolar disorder are;

2. To provide practical, helpful information on restructuring a life shattered by these disorders; and

3. To inspire people affected by these mental illnesses (and their families) to move beyond a mere endurance-survival mode to enjoy wellness and productivity.

The resources in the appendices provide a summary of *practical* information. Appendix A suggests strategies, techniques, tips, and tools for patients/consumers living with bipolar disease and depression. Appendix B offers simple ways that loved ones and friends can give help and hope to mind-damaged people. Appendix C mentions doable things your faith community can do to help the mentally ill and their families. Appendix D lists support, information, and advocacy organizations you can contact for your specific needs.

Would that there were a quick fix for recovering from a severe mental illness. Obviously, that's not the case. Neurological disorders are far too complex in their causes, symptoms, and treatments

to be solved by a prescription or treatment that fits everyone. Each person must find his own path. We can, however, learn a lot from what others have gone through. In addition to a lot of technical reading about causes, symptoms, and treatments, I've benefited much from reading the stories of people who've overcome great odds and succeeded. I've researched what worked for others who've recovered from depression and manic depression and are living well. Many have shared what they were like, what happened to them, and how they got better. Personal stories are not statistics, or case studies or theories, and I hope that after reading this book you'll be able to say, "If he could recover and rebuild, a happier, more meaningful and productive life, so can I!"

Bipolar Disorder: Rebuilding Your Life is the true story of my life and my ongoing recovery from past traumas, depression, and bipolar illness. These pages describe the pilgrimage and, perhaps most importantly, the battle for my mind and soul. It has been a long fight. I've chronicled some of my struggles with emotional and sexual abuse, work and insurance conflicts, and my ordeal with serious, chronic mental illness. Some of this story was painful to write, but I felt compelled to do so. This is a "how it is" book as well as a "how-to" book that describes the tools I've found helpful in healing and rebuilding my life.

You might not agree with everything you read in these pages, but I hope you'll find encouragement and be stimulated to think, pray, and act in ways that will revolutionize your life. I don't wish to offend anyone who might consider this self-revealing account in bad taste, but I believe that only by disclosing our problems can others identify with us, find hope, and get help. So I'm willing to take the personal and professional risks of candid disclosure. I don't want to hide behind my title, degrees, or accomplishments.

I've been told by some that this book will be "too religious" for secular people and "too honest" for Christians. I must admit it's humbling and a bit scary to publicly acknowledge what I've been through, and my need for ongoing medication, counseling, and support groups. It squashes my pride knowing that some will see

my suicide plans, depressions, manias, and other actions as weak, neurotic, or sinful, and categorize me as unstable, unreliable, or crazy. But if my experiences can help guide some into recovery, it's worth the risk of a "tarnished" reputation.

Hopefully, my vulnerability will help give you or your loved ones the courage to:

- Keep seeking effective treatment and support

- Speak out about your struggles

- Empathize with the mentally ill, whether they're unshaven and wearing grubby clothes or dressed in power suits

- Work for better treatment of mind-handicapped people by faith communities, government, insurance companies, and society as a whole.

I pray that you and your loved ones can benefit from the many healing tools that have helped others and me to rebuild happier, more meaningful lives.

Do not go gentle into that good night.
Rage, rage against the dying of the light.
— Dylan Thomas

Part One

Childhood: Ongoing Family Strife and Sexual Abuse

We have suffered terror and pitfalls, ruin and destruction...
— Lamentations 3:47

Chapter 1

Surviving in a Dysfunctional Family

I'VE BEEN IN DR. PHIL SUTHERLAND'S OFFICE several hundred times over the past eleven years. It's comfortable, non-threatening, lots of brown colors softened with dim lighting, and a wooden desk and bookcase. Phil's in his early sixties but could easily pass for a forty-year-old. His jogging, golf, and trout fishing keep him tanned and trim. He never wears a tie, just a shirt or sweater and slacks as he slouches in his orthopedic chair, feet propped on a brown leather footstool.

You get the feeling Phil really cares what's happening with you. He always speaks softly, doesn't use big words to impress. You'd never guess he's got the equivalent of two Ph.D. degrees, one in psychology, the other in research and measurement. Or that he's written a couple of books. Or that in addition to his psychotherapy practice he's mentored numerous clinical psychologists. You don't need to be around him long to realize you're in the presence of an authentically humble mind healer, who's a skilled, seasoned, effective, wise practitioner in healing wounded emotions. Like many others, I owe my life to him.

I drape my two hundred eighty-five pounds over the brown leather couch across from him. Peering through wire-rimmed glasses, he grins and asks, "What's going on with James this week?" Another session begins. I start with a report on my latest stresses and victories.

Near the end of our time together, Phil shakes his head, repeating what he's said several dozen ways over the past decade, "Jim, you've come from one of the most damaged home backgrounds I've seen in all my years of counseling. The fact that you're not psychotic, or haven't spent your life in a mental institution or prison is

truly a miracle. That you've not killed yourself or others is incredible. But far more awesome to me than all these are the accomplishments you've made despite your scars!"

Were my parents and significant others the blame for my difficulties? To some extent, but not entirely. Every parent messes up; no parent does it perfectly. I'm sure my mom, dad, and grandparents did the best they could, given their flaws. A father of two sons, I certainly know what it's like to make ample mistakes.

Few, if any grow up in an ideal home. Each of us bears some bruises from our family background, no matter how good a job our parents tried to do. Regardless of the inadequacies of my parents' nurturing, I too share responsibility for the choices I've made along the way.

On the wall of my study is a framed a large photo-poster of Muhammad Ali. Beneath are words that describe what a boxer does: he fights, struggles, battles. Those descriptions symbolize my life: constant combat. As far back as I remember, life has been a constant fight for emotional survival. I've had to contend with wrenching injustices, conflicts, criticisms, rejections, betrayals, and terrors. Most of the time I've felt like a salmon swimming upstream against the current, or a boxer brawling with a stronger opponent.

My birth, on February 20, 1942 brought genuine joy to my parents and both sets of grandparents. Old black-and-white photos show them holding me, smiling with pride. A few years later, photos of my mom and dad reveal the loss of their initial happiness, their faces etched in sadness or anger.

Growing up and navigating through my teens and into adulthood, there were fun times: toys, sports, vacations, trips, and accomplishments. Despite those instances, I didn't have a joyful, carefree youth, nor did I experience the happiness I usually projected. For me, life has been scattered moments of gaiety mixed with long periods of struggling with disappointments, fears, and pain.

Reflecting on my youth, the overall feeling I get is a haunting loneliness. In fact, most of my recollections of growing up are tainted with deep sadness. Today, I understand why those melancholy

reflections are so strong. Our upbringing affects our self-esteem, relationships, ministry, in fact, our whole life.

One of my earliest memories of childhood was a situation when Mom was putting my "sleepers" on me. She seemed hurried, angry. I recall her holding me roughly, trying to change me. It felt like she was upset with me, that I was a burden to her. Dad watched from about six feet away. Somehow, he seemed intimidated. Maybe he was unsure of how to change me. From that time on, I never had a feeling of safety, comfort, or security with anyone. I grew up believing I could count on no one, not Mom, Dad, grandparents, relatives, friends. One central thought became my mental life preserver: *If Jimmy's going to survive in this big world, he'll have to fend for himself. He can't rely on anyone.*

I can still summon the fear I felt when Mom held or carried me. She seldom kept me close to her, protectively, snugly. When sitting, she held me loosely against her chest or laid me across her knees, with barely a hand on me to guard against my falling. She toted me carelessly at her side, as one might a football. On the other hand, even though I intuited that Dad wasn't confident of how to handle me, he always cradled me, awkwardly, but gently.

Contrasting with Mom's casual ways of supporting me, photos from family albums show Dad, my aunt and uncle, and all four grandparents carefully holding me close to them. The pictures show Mom propping me loosely, away from her body. Even now, I can sense that childhood terror of being dropped. I'm afraid of Ferris wheels, roller coasters, ladders, cliffs, and other heights.

Mom read stories to me starting when I was a preschooler. Dad did, too, though less often. Those were cozy, safe times. Mom was gentlest when she sang soft lullabies. I appreciate the many "Mom" things she did with me: baking cookies, making handicrafts, teaching me to swim, being my Cub Scout den mother, buying me ice cream cones, candy, and toys, and doing dozens of special "mother-son" activities.

My sister, Betsy, and brother, Bob, and I grew up with our parents in State College, Pennsylvania, a small town and the home of

Penn State University. Dad was a professor of economics at Penn State; Mom was a homemaker and later worked as a teacher and secretary. Betsy is two years younger than I, and Bob five years younger.

State College excelled as a place to raise children. Serious crime was minimal. While classes were in session, university buildings and downtown sidewalks teemed with students. But on holidays and during summers, it looked like a ghost town. In the autumn, the town and campus trees looked like an artist's palette — a breathtaking sight. Our area provided an ideal environment for year-round hiking and hunting. As a result, from the age of ten or so I became an avid outdoorsman.

Outwardly, we looked like an all-American family: a dad, a mom, sister, and two brothers. Inwardly, our home life was embroiled in chronic tension. Very few photographs showed any of us smiling! While many in our community knew my parents had a rocky marriage, I doubt anyone ever guessed the degree of marital discord and child abuse that occurred in the Stout family.

Awakening each morning was like getting up to go to war! The friction between Mom and Dad exuded a silent anger that spilled over and infected us kids like a toxic chemical. Mealtimes were verbal battlefields, with Mom doing most of the attacking. Nearly every day she'd bring up a controversial subject to goad Dad or us kids. I never knew when an argument between them might explode, or when she'd tee off on me. Consequently, I was always on guard while eating meals, watching TV, or on family outings, waiting for her next barrage of criticism, betrayal, humiliation, and unreasonable orders.

Everyone lived continually on edge. For us three kids, home was a boiling cauldron of stress. We never knew quite what to expect, but we could usually predict some kind of daily emotional explosion. Betsy, Bob, and I hadn't a clue what the words "safe," "haven" and "refuge" meant.

In the midst of the chronic tension there existed a seesaw battle between Mom's dictatorship and her permissiveness. She made 98

percent of the rules — bedtime, curfew, chores, and homework — but changed them on a whim. On the rare occasions when Dad tried to set a restriction, Mom overrode him.

I resented that fact that she, not Dad, did the rule making and punishing. Dad rarely spanked us, and then only after Mom had goaded him into action, repeatedly hounding him, "Do something, Randy."

Punishments were arbitrary at best. The boundaries we grew up with were always in a state of flux. Since Mom and Dad were usually quarreling, we kids had to make decisions for ourselves for the most part. But, like dogs on leashes, we could go only so far before Mom yanked us into line.

Starting at age three, I wet my bed almost nightly. Gram Stevenson, my maternal grandmother, went ballistic over my "baby behavior," constantly telling Mom, "Punish Jimmy when he does that." Of the two women, Gram dealt the severest verbal punishment for my nightly "accidents." Many times, she told Mom, "Jimmy's rebelling against us. He's deliberately disobeying us. He'll be scarred for life if he doesn't quit. You've got to stop his terrible behavior."

I was horribly embarrassed about my inability to control myself. I tried everything to stop, and prayed repeatedly, "Dear God, please help me stop wetting my bed." But nothing ever worked. Often, Gram and Mom scolded, "You're such a bad boy, Jimmy. When are you going to quit this baby stuff?" But try as I would, I still wet the bed, almost nightly, until I was fourteen.

Whenever Gram and Grandpa Stevenson visited us, everything revolved around Gram. She smiled, scowled, barked orders, made threats, and generally took over our household. A few of their winter visits took place during some of Pennsylvania's coldest months, many nights recording sub-zero temperatures.

I remember being four years old and waking up in a wet bed in the middle of an icy winter night. *I can't let them see my damp sheets and pajamas. Gram and Mom will surely punish me some way. And they'll just embarrass me more.*

So, I draped my pajamas and sheets to dry over the two radiators in the bedroom, and went back to bed, naked, shivering myself

to sleep. Often I got away with the cover-up, but sometimes they discovered the still-damp, smelly sheets, and then the retribution, verbal and otherwise, began.

In addition to bedwetting, I defecated in my underwear several times a week. Playing with neighborhood friends, I'd put off going to the bathroom until it was too late and I'd pooped in my pants. Mom got enraged. She did her best to humiliate me into changing that awful habit: "You're such a bad boy, Jimmy. Why do you keep disobeying me?" Like wetting the bed, I tried and prayed, but was unsuccessful most of the time until I was nearly fourteen. I felt like a miserable failure, always afraid others would find out my secret "baby habits," and tease me, and then stop playing with me.

The main "players" influencing my formative years comprised a web of convoluted, and at times very scary, relationships. Mom, the central character who shaped me, was far too heavy; always twenty-five pounds overweight throughout my early years. Then, during my adolescence, she gained about a hundred pounds. She personified complexity, flip-flopping between dictator and martyr.

Mom had some wonderful strengths: spontaneity, expansive thinking, pioneering spirit, and generosity. Yet, despite her virtues, she was an unhappy, angry woman. Her blue eyes seldom twinkled. Usually, they either blazed with fury or, more commonly, appeared dull blue, staring at me with the saddest, most pitiful expression I've ever seen. When Mom looked at me, it was as though her eyes cried out, "Jimmy, do something. Help me." After turning twelve I could no longer stand to look her in the eyes. They made me feel too guilty for not being able to improve her circumstances.

At other times Mom exuded self-confidence, projecting an image of absolute knowledge, strength, and toughness. She spoke with authority on almost every subject. Even when she tried to show tenderness, she seemed rough, almost masculine, rather than displaying a sensitive, motherly gentleness. In her best times, she came across as detached and preoccupied.

Few of her mannerisms seemed feminine. Even in a dress, Mom appeared very "mannish." Her movements and gestures looked more like a man's than a woman's. Her fingers were nicotine-stained, because she'd chain-smoked cigarettes all her life. Because of this, she had an incessant, raspy cough that grated on me. Her voice sounded rough, like a man's.

Most of the time, despite wearing perfume, Mom's clothes and breath smelled of tobacco. But worse was her offensive body odor. She seldom bathed. You could smell her the moment she entered a room. What bothered me most was the habitual way Mom blew her nose into her cupped hands rather than using a handkerchief. Afterward, even in public, she licked the mucus off her hands. I didn't realize it then, but surely those were symptoms of her deteriorating mental condition.

How I longed for a mom like most of my friends had — gentle, warm, comforting, encouraging, attractive, and fun to be around. I felt terribly disloyal to Mom, and guilty for being repulsed by her domineering personality, physical appearance, and noxious hygiene.

Sometimes she bubbled with effervescence. Most of the time, though, she came across as cold, emotionally distant. Always preoccupied with problems about Dad, finances, and other concerns, it seemed that she didn't have time to listen to mine. Even in first grade I felt that she wasn't really there when she was with me. Mom never seemed to display happy, caring emotions. When she spoke, it came across as mouthing a rehearsed "mother's script" rather than speaking from her heart. Her hugs and words seemed robotic; her displays of affection contrived. Inwardly, I writhed when she gave me her mechanical hugs and kisses. Outwardly, I stood still and held my breath, partly because of her odor, partly because it felt as if she was doing the "motherly thing" rather than expressing genuine warmth for me.

I'm sure Mom praised me for things, but I don't remember her saying more than a few times, "I'm proud you drew such nice pictures" or "Your printing is so good, Jimmy." Her best attempts

at affirmation usually included a criticism: "Nice job helping your brother and sister with their coloring books. Why can't you *also* stop wetting your bed and obey me better?" While she probably said, "Jimmy, I love you" plenty of times, I can't recall a single one. Still, I'm grateful for the many ways she attempted to express her love for me: toys, gifts, letters, money, vacations, and other demonstrations of affection.

I remember feeling confused and guilty because she always seemed to be upset about something. I'd think, *Why is Mom so unhappy? It must have been something I did or said.* Rarely did she initiate fond gestures like kissing or hugging. She would stand, arms open, waiting for us to come to her. I don't remember her ever coming forward and reaching out to us like Dad did. We always had to approach Mom.

Conversely, Dad radiated warmth and affection. His hugs and kisses were almost too generous at times. It made me feel glad for his attention, but uncomfortable. He was about five feet seven inches tall, and built like a muscular fullback. I outgrew him by sixth grade, but always respected his strength. Dad was an only child, doted on by his mother. He grew up on his parents' mid-western farm, no stranger to hard work. After high school he attended Illinois College, Northwestern University, and the University of Pittsburgh. He made outstanding grades and eventually earned his doctorate. Then he became a college professor and married Mom.

Dad lived as a quiet intellectual. I hardly ever saw him without a *Wall Street Journal, U.S. News and World Report, The New York Times,* or some economics book in hand. He epitomized a hard-working, honest man. While he was myopic about some aspects of life, I always respected his work ethic and intellectual acumen.

I believe he was not so much an introvert as he was socially inept. Apart from discussing economic and farm issues, Dad couldn't carry on a meaningful conversation with anyone other than his best friend, a fellow professor at Penn State, and a few others. That was probably why he had only a few friends among his professional colleagues and even fewer outside his academic sphere.

Dad's strengths were his hugs and kisses, and his appreciation of the beauty in flowers and animals. In our family, he functioned alternately as naive optimist or victim, steadfastly refusing to discuss anything negative. He seemed unable to talk about feelings, especially emotional pain, and chose to focus only on life's positives. Yet Dad was quick to comment on his appreciation of life's little things: gardens, cornfields, cattle barns, a home-cooked meal, the texture of a coat. He came across as a harmless, kind, gentle, even naïve, person who worked hard. You couldn't imagine him harming an ant.

Tragically, he and Mom were ruled by their mothers, catering more to their wishes than to each other's. I doubt that either of them ever made a significant decision without consulting their parents. While Mom ran the show at home, she rarely acted without first checking with Gram. They talked at least once a week by phone. Just as Gram dominated Mom, so Mom tried to control Dad and us kids. Mom learned her lessons well from her mother, and became a carbon copy of Gram. As much as Mom verbally assaulted Dad, Gram Stevenson, her mother, railed at her with equal vehemence. Likewise, Dad capitulated to his mother's desires.

I remember thinking, *Mom and Dad sure do give in to their parents a lot. Why can't Mom and Dad hash out these things with each other? Why do they always need to talk with their parents? Aren't Mom and Dad grown-ups who can make their own decisions?*

They were opposites in just about every way. We kids were about all they had in common. He was passive and indecisive; she was aggressive, domineering, and opinionated. I'm not sure what held them together apart from us three kids. They differed on raising children, politics, socializing, vacations, and, especially, spending money. Dad was overly cautious and miserly; Mom spent liberally, sometimes frivolously.

Money was the central theme of their fights. Mom incessantly complained, "We need more money, Randy. You've got to buy this, we need that..." Sometimes in tears, other times in a rage, she griped, "Jimmy, your father won't give me enough money to run

the house. I can't pay the bills, buy enough food, or buy you kids the clothes you need." A month didn't go by without her complaining about money and asking me to intervene with Dad — even when I reached adulthood and had my own family.

Unfortunately, whenever I spoke to Dad about Mom's money issues, he replied angrily, "Jimmy, I'd never ask *my* father those kinds of questions. They're none of your business. It's between your mother and me. But since you asked, I'll tell you exactly what I've been giving her." Then he explained how much money he'd given her and what it was to be used for, concluding, "Now, go tell your mother what I said."

I never really knew whom to believe regarding finances, but Dad's answers usually sounded better. I never could figure out why Mom was always grumbling about not having enough money — especially since she bought huge amounts of candy, soft drinks, pastries, and other nonessentials.

Mom was always buying us "things," often with conditions: "This is yours if you clean up your room. I'll buy you that toy if you treat your sister nicely." Her generosity was also a way of exposing Dad as an uncaring skinflint: "See, Jimmy, I buy you toys; your father never does. He's too stingy." Yet, despite those motives, I believe that most of the time Mom bought us things as a genuine attempt to show her love.

Dad was a homebody, his vision seemingly limited to the borders of State College and the university. He was content never to leave our town to vacation: "Why should we go anywhere else? Our area has all anyone would want — libraries, sports, plays, farms, flower gardens, and a host of activities." His contentment came from walking through the Penn State cow barns and flower gardens, and occasionally attending university events.

Mom had bigger ideas. I'm glad she carped at Dad until he agreed to take our family on vacation to the New Jersey seashore and other places. I appreciated her attempts to socialize with others outside Dad's professional realm.

Mom's parents, Gram and Grandpa Stevenson, and her brother,

Uncle Jim ("Unc") lived five hours away in Pittsburgh, Pennsylvania. We visited them at least every other month, and several times a year they came to stay with us. Actually, in many ways Gram and Grandpa Stevenson did a better job of parenting me than did Mom and Dad.

Like most people, Gram Stevenson was a study in contrasts: happy and angry, loving and prejudiced, kind yet vicious. She had a devout prayer life but remained blissfully ignorant of a lot of basic Bible teachings. Her rotund figure, wide, toothy smile, and extroverted nature displayed friendliness and caring. Her friends viewed her as a giving, fun-loving person, a spiritual giant. To her children and grandchildren, she was both an awesome Christian who lavished gifts, and a bigoted, vengeful despot. She told us kids that she hated, "niggers, kikes, micks," and anyone who drank liquor or gambled. Gram lectured us frequently on the evils of "those other people who aren't our kind."

Gram's life profoundly affected three generations both constructively and destructively. Her deeds and words encouraged her children and grandchildren in a host of positive spiritual ways, but her cruel words and actions also caused great harm.

On one hand, she participated in church activities, teaching Bible studies and helping others in all sorts of ways. I was a recipient of Gram's spiritual values, and will always be grateful for her Christian influence. She taught me to pray, and bought me Christian books and Bibles. She rewarded me with turtles, goldfish, candy, and other "prizes" for memorizing Bible verses. On the other hand, she could be obstinate, mean, and manipulative. Her ready smile could become a furious scowl in a split second. Dad, Mom, and us kids felt the sting of her sharp rebukes hundreds of times.

Gram was a matriarch in the fullest sense of the word. She loved to talk, and relished gossiping. Inevitably, she monopolized every conversation, thrilled at being the center of attention at social gatherings. She loved giving orders, controlling, and seemed to enjoy attacking others with her acid tongue. Gram could cut someone to shreds with a saintly smile on her face!

Frequently, her and Mom's words seemed to be compliments, but actually were accompanied by censure. First the pat on the back, then the knife went in there. As a little boy I craved their affirmation and believed their seemingly flattering words, only to discover a few minutes later I'd been hit with a "velvet-covered brick." Frequently, a sadistic "but" was attached to many of their compliments: "Jimmy's a nice boy. He always says, 'Thank you.' *But* he wets his bed a lot." Even though Gram used "zingers," she was lavish with praise, both privately and in public; Mom rarely praised me anywhere.

Both seemed to take sadistic glee in causing trouble. Gram excelled at playing one family member against another: us kids against Dad or against each other, Mom against Dad. Gram taught me, "Honor your father and mother," even though she did everything in her power to undermine my respect for Dad.

Gram bossed everybody, especially Mom, whom she continually criticized and gave blunt advice like, "Alice, you're too fat. Stop eating so much. You shouldn't smoke. You have to quit. You should bake Christmas rolls and cookies for all your neighbors. You've got to get Jimmy to stop wetting his bed, pooping his pants, and breaking his toys." She never stopped hounding, criticizing, and directing. It seemed like Mom couldn't do a thing right in Gram's eyes. I don't ever recall Gram complimenting her except when Mom complied with Gram's wishes.

Just as Gram Stevenson was the spiritual giant for us grandchildren, Grandpa Stevenson was our athlete-medical hero. Grandpa had been an all-American football player. He was a big man who awed people with his sheer muscular size and authoritative position as a doctor. Though he was soft-spoken and didn't say much, Grandpa never came across as a wimp. Whenever he spoke, everyone listened. Strangely, he usually let Gram run the house and their social obligations. Unlike Mom and Gram's incessant verbal bombardments, I don't remember Grandpa ever criticizing me beyond the occasional gentle admonition, "Get your father to shape up and not be so stingy."

Of all my relatives, Grandpa Stevenson was the most affirming. His compliments about my athletic abilities fueled me with inspiration for months. I idolized him and wanted to be an athlete and doctor like him. He taught me about football and told fascinating sports stories. I always looked forward to hunting and fishing trips with him.

Unc, Mom's younger brother, owned a successful real estate and insurance company in Pittsburgh. He'd been a college football player and enjoyed athletics of all kinds. He was large and imposing, but overweight. I envied his sense of humor and decisiveness.

It thrilled me whenever Unc invited me to go hunting with him and his two sons. He took us to Pitt-Penn State football games, Kenneywood Amusement Park, circuses, and other fun outings. He was generous to me in every way. Even though he shared the same intimidating characteristics of intolerance and control as Mom and Gram, he provided strong male role modeling for me.

As a youngster, it was obvious that "control" was the name of the game for the "Big Three," Gram, Mom, and Unc. It never ended. Sometimes they tried getting their way by bribing with gifts, or they intimidated with threats. They acted like they were the authorities on everything. Each had a mean streak and didn't hesitate to use cruel words or act vengefully to get their way. Gram, Mom, and Unc constantly maneuvered to sway Dad, Betsy, Bob, and me to bend to their wishes.

Compromise was seldom an option; they refused to take "no" for an answer. You had to "go along to get along." If their "opinions" weren't taken, they scowled in anger or looked hurt, as if seriously offended. To buck them meant paying a price: being shunned, bad-mouthed, or humiliated by public criticism. All three were quick to verbally bash those who displeased them. They carried grudges and were adept at revenge. I never saw anyone stand up to Mom, Gram or Unc, and win.

For the most part, Dad was helpless against their strong wills and persistent arguments. I resented the extremes to which they went to foist their plans on him. It disgusted me, too, when he

allowed them to walk over him like a doormat. *Why can't Dad have the guts to stand up against them? Why doesn't he just tell them off?*

My bedwetting and defecating in my underpants was an ongoing issue. Mom and Gram habitually teased me in front of Betsy and Bobby. "Jimmy, you're supposed to be a big boy. Even your younger brother and sister don't wet their beds. Neither do any of your friends. If you don't stop, we'll tell your friends what a big baby you are." It wasn't long before they began mentioning my "problem" to their friends and some of my classmates.

I never knew whom Mom would tell, or when, or in what kind of detail, or if she was just trying to scare me into reforming. It made me afraid to be around my fellow students, terrified they'd say something like, "Hey Jimmy, are you still wetting your bed? Why don't you grow up?"

When Gram visited, she or Mom often discovered my pooped pants and forced me to strip naked in the middle of the living room. Then they marched me to the bathroom and ran cold water in the sink. One of them held the underwear in one hand and shoved my nose in it with the other, snarling, "What a bad boy you are. You're doing this just to spite us. After all we do for you, you should be ashamed of yourself treating us this way, Besides, you're too old to be acting like this. Big boys, good boys, don't behave this way. If you do this again, we'll tell all your friends and teachers." To my utter embarrassment, Betsy and Bob saw and heard everything.

Never once did Dad criticize me for my bowel-control problems. One of the few times he confronted Mom and Gram happened after an episode. When Gram and Mom started to punish me, Dad lit into them: "Jimmy's just a kid. He's trying the best he can. He'll grow out of it. Just leave him alone." He took me by the hand, led me away, and hugged me, saying, "Jimmy, you're not bad like they say. You'll stop wetting the bed and pooping in your pants when you're ready. I love you." I gushed tears of relief, of gratitude, that someone understood my plight and believed in me.

Starting when I was about seven, every fall, Mom and Gram warned, "Jimmy, Christmas is coming. You'd better be a good boy or Santa will give you ashes instead of presents." Needless to say, I made extra efforts to toe the line as Christmas neared.

One of the earliest Thanksgivings I remember took place in second grade. Mom, Dad, Betsy, Bob, and I made the long drive from State College to Grandma and Grandpa Stevenson's house in Pittsburgh. In future years, Dad attended only one or two of these annual clan gatherings, because of the criticism heaped upon him by Mom and Gram. I don't blame him for avoiding those barrages, but I always wished he'd come with us, for the sake of family unity.

Over the Thanksgiving weekend, Gram took Mom, Betsy, Bob, and me shopping in Pittsburgh's big department stores. During that buying marathon, Gram always took me aside and said, "Jimmy, your father's a cheapskate. Grandpa and I are buying these clothes for your mom and you kids because your father doesn't give her enough money. I want you to talk with him when you get home. See if you can convince him to give your mom more money to buy clothes and run the house. I know Betsy and Bob need more guidance. They certainly aren't getting it from either your mom or dad. I want you to supervise them and spend time with them." I always answered dutifully, "I'll do my best, Gram."

After our last store, Gram and Mom took us to see Santa. I recall long waits in line and the combined feelings of excitement and stark terror. Just before I stepped up to sit on Santa's lap, one of them rattled off a lengthy list of my shortcomings, saying loudly enough for all the children and parents in line to hear, "Santa, this is Jimmy Stout. He's a nice boy, but this past year he's done a lot of naughty things: He's wet his bed nearly every night, pooped his pants often, broken his toys, lost his temper, and disobeyed his mom. If he shapes up, will you give him presents this year?"

I remember turning red-faced at being so publicly shamed, fully expecting him to say, "Sorry, Jimmy, your bad behavior means I'll only bring you ashes this Christmas. Try harder to be a good boy next year." However, as I climbed on his lap, his words weren't

as bad as I'd dreaded. He mumbled something like, "Jimmy, I hope you'll work at being a nicer boy next year and mind your mom and grandmother better. You'll be good won't you?"

Flushing even more, I stammered weakly, "Yes, Santa." His words gave me a thin hope that I might still be able to get some Christmas presents if I "behaved." From then on, I both anticipated and dreaded every Christmas. Each holiday, I sighed with relief when Santa had somehow overlooked my wrongs and left so many gifts.

Excluding my anxieties, Christmas was the highlight of my year. Of all the times of the year, it brought our family the closest. It was a welcome respite from yearlong family tension because it offered a temporary cease-fire from Mom and Dad's ongoing conflicts. As an adult, it's still my favorite time. Something about Christmas carols and the sentimental trappings of the holiday strikes a nostalgic note deep within me.

Chapter 2

Coping with Sexual Abuse

AS A YOUNGSTER, I'd only had mild previews of the escalating emotional mistreatment and sexual abuse to come. Anyone who's been sexually violated by an older, trusted caregiver, can readily understand the on again-off again feelings of disbelief, fear, horror, rage, self-hatred, and betrayal. My insides were all too often torn up by those emotions, because starting when I was four, Gram, and especially Mom, repeatedly desecrated me with inappropriate sexual behaviors. I won't go into specific details of their actions during my youth. Even now, I'm not sure which ones had the worst effects on me. I'm still discovering the extent of my

inner damages and have begun to heal. In my attempts to find solutions for my difficulties, I've learned some sobering facts about child sexual abuse.

There are numerous definitions of it; legal wordings differ from state to state. The essence of most interpretations is, "Any act perpetrated upon a minor by a significantly older person with the intent to stimulate the child sexually and to satisfy the aggressor's sexual impulses. This includes exposure of genitalia, fondling, intercourse, oral sex and pornography." Some quibble over the fine points of what is and is not sexual abuse. The majority of experts seem to agree that emotional harm can result as much from fondling as from intercourse.[1]

Statistics for the frequency of sexual abuse vary. Most studies conclude that it's alarmingly high and increasing. The book, *Child Sexual Abuse,* estimates that one out of every four girls will be molested before she is eighteen, and one out of every eight boys will also be victimized.[2]

It is reported that the average age of abused children is eight,[3] and that most perpetrators are not strangers, but people the victims know and trust. [4] Studies also show that sexual victims are at least twice as likely to attempt suicide as those who were never abused.

For a long time I didn't remember a lot of the details of being sexually victimized. Although I'd known that Mom and Gram had behaved in "bad" ways over the years, I either forgot or blotted out their deeds. Until I was hospitalized at age forty-six for clinical depression, I'd never made the connection of how destructively their maltreatment had impacted me. Now I'm aware of the many negative effects it has had over most of my lifetime.

For years I carried the guilty belief that *I* was the instigator of sexual activities with Mom. Much counseling and reading has freed me of the awful burden that it was *my* fault. *She* was the perpetrator; I was entirely the victim. There is no way a youngster can stop a grownup. A minor is absolutely no match for an adult molester's deceitful manipulations, clever words, bribes, or

threats. A child's mind can be completely against a sexual experience, but his body automatically becomes aroused, even against
his will.

All the doors in our house had locks: front, back, basement,
bedrooms, and bathroom. It didn't matter, though; there was never any privacy, no safe refuge. Mom rarely knocked before entering
through a closed or locked door. She always had a key. Her room
invasions continued all through my college and seminary years.
Almost daily, she'd barge into the bathroom or bedroom, unannounced. It was the same with Gram. Their actions made me feel
awkward, uncomfortable, trapped and, at times, silently outraged.

In September I entered third grade. About that time, Dad was
offered a job working in Illinois alongside Governor Adlai Stevenson. He accepted, and wanted Mom and us kids to join him there.
Mom refused.

Preceding his yearlong absence, Dad and Mom fought daily. I
remember constant arguments over his decision. She didn't want
him to leave, and stubbornly refused to take us and join him for
the year. I thought he'd probably never come back because of their
sour relationship. Those twelve months were when she most seriously violated me.

Mom and Gram often groused, "Jimmy, why can't you talk some
sense into your father and get him to stay? He doesn't love you
kids. If he did, he wouldn't take that Illinois job. Get him to change
his stubborn mind." I felt solely responsible for Dad's leaving,
and cringed inwardly. *I can't dissuade him. I'm to blame for his
leaving. Gram and Mom will really be mad at me. I guess she'll
divorce Dad.*

I was torn between showing loyalty to one parent or the other.
It was obvious how angry Mom was at him. When we drove Dad
to the train station, they barely talked. Their silence in the car and
at the station was deafening. Dad hugged and kissed us kids good-
bye. I held on to him for dear life, believing that he and Mom
would divorce and I'd never see him again. I choked back tears,
believing my crying would antagonize Mom and show her I was

on Dad's side, so I stuffed my feelings. She gave him a quick, sullen kiss before the train left. The year ahead would be tumultuous.

Mom constantly criticized Dad and his decision in front of us children, growling, "Kids, your father's deserting you. He doesn't love you or he'd stay here with you." Almost daily I overheard her angrily talking on the phone with Gram, Grandpa, and Unc about Dad's leaving us.

When he left, I was eight, Betsy six, and Bob three. Every chance Mom and Gram got they painted terrible pictures of Dad. I turned their words over and over in my mind. *Does Dad really care about Mom and us? If so, why's he leaving? Is he going to Illinois because his job requires it? Does he no longer love Mom, Betsy, Bobby, and me?*

That year of Dad's absence, the parent-child roles reversed in our family. Mom pressured me to be her surrogate husband and a substitute father to Betsy and Bob. Later that day she took me aside and said, "You're going to have to be the man of the house now. Your father's never spent any time with you kids or disciplined you, so you've got to make up for that, Jimmy. Sure hope you can do better than he did." To my eight-year-old mind, it was a heady experience at first.

From then on, I felt Dad was angry with me because he was jealous of the attention I got from Mom. I felt I was usurping his place as husband and head of the family, but I was helpless to do anything about it.

Some therapists consider that when a woman develops a relationship with her child that is more important than the one she has with her spouse, it constitutes "emotional sexual abuse" or "covert incest."[5] I wasn't aware of it, but Mom was forcing me into an emotionally destructive relationship with her, as I became the object of her special attention.

She turned to me as her confidant and complaint hearer, positions I was required to hold not only that year but for the rest of her life. Almost daily she griped about the marital problems she and Dad were having. Hundreds of times I muttered under my

breath, "I wish Mom would stop telling me about her loneliness and all the bad stuff about Dad. It's none of my business."

At first, it was flattering when she treated me like her "little husband." Soon, I churned with anger at being constantly put in the middle between her and Dad, always having to solve their problems. I despised Mom's dictatorship, her constantly changing rules and unfair punishments. I pitied Dad for being so mistreated, and resented him for his spinelessness.

In third grade, I was indoctrinated to be a compulsive caretaker by Mom and Gram, who saddled me with adult responsibilities from that year on. They treated me like a "little adult," rather than the child I was. In order to gain their approval, I was compelled to neglect my own needs so as to meet my family's. I took over much of the parenting role, and from then on became the nurturer, encourager, homework helper, teacher, and disciplinarian for Betsy and Bob. Unfortunately, too often I acted like a drill sergeant to them.

In addition to all the usual stresses most kids face while growing up, I encountered crisis after crisis that I was expected to solve. Gram told me it was *my* responsibility to keep my parents together, that it was *my* duty to raise my brother and sister.

The seeds of workaholism were planted as I attended to Mom's, Dad's, Betsy's, and Bobby's needs at the expense of my own. That, I think, birthed a lifestyle of working hard at helping others and pleasing key adults in an ever-increasing workload. As a result, I've sacrificed for others much of my life, trying to give them what I wished had been given to me. I suppose that many of my achievements were, in part, attempts to get the approval from others that I so rarely got at home.

I felt like an object rather than a person, and mused, *Who cares for me other than for what I can do for them? Why's it my responsibility to keep my family together? I'm just a kid. Why do I have to spend all my time refereeing between Mom and Dad, instead of playing with my friends? Why is it always up to me to solve their problems?*

At times, thinking back on childhood still makes my skin crawl. As an innocent third-grader, I was deliberately and regularly seduced

during Dad's yearlong absence by an adult woman whom I trusted: Mom. I shiver remembering my childhood terrors of being alone in the dark. Falling asleep was difficult. Most nights I lay awake, listening for Mom's footsteps, for the familiar creaks in the wooden floor as she approached my room. Sometimes I'd hear her coming and I'd turn on my side to face the wall, feigning sleep, hoping she'd leave.

Falling asleep has been difficult all my life. I've always slept lightly; even little noises have awakened me. Until a few years ago, I was plagued by nightmares: being chased, shot at, cornered, captured. Many were filled with terrifying tableaus of bloody violence, monsters, and snakes. Most mornings I awoke exhausted from such scary dreams.

In the years ahead, I lived in mute fear that someone would discover my "big secret." I felt I was a dirty, disgusting, and far worse person than any of my peers were. I was convinced I was a sexual deviant. *After all, I've been such a bad boy. Besides, I can't stop being curious about girls. My lustful thinking proves I'm twisted and bad to the core.*

I often wondered whether, besides her sexual behavior with me, Mom also instigated "special times" with Bob and Betsy. I asked them a couple of times and they implied that nothing had happened. I never had the courage to ask them again. But, according to some studies, an offender seldom transgresses only one time.[6]

I was afraid to tell anyone else about my secret. *It might mean I'll be taken away and locked up in reform school, or Dad will be so angry with Mom that he'll divorce her.*

I desperately wanted to talk with someone about my awful feelings, but I had no good options. There was little information about sexual abuse available. No "800-Abuse" hotline to call. Neither could I tell an adult. If I reached out for help, who'd believe me? Our family wasn't very active in the local Presbyterian church, so phoning the pastor or a church member wasn't a choice. Confiding in my teachers or scout leaders didn't feel safe; I was convinced that they wouldn't believe me and I'd get into trouble for accusing Mom of such bad things.

What good will it do to tell Dad? He's oblivious to what's been going on. Why doesn't he intervene? How could he not know? Is he just plain gutless? Doesn't he care about my welfare? I thought about telling my closest friends, but decided against it. *They'll think I'm weird or they'll tattle to their parents. Then I'll get in trouble.* I abandoned the idea of approaching either set of grandparents or Unc. *They'll never believe me and I'll get punished for lying about Mom.*

All along, Mom acted like nothing had ever happened between us. Sometimes I doubted my sanity. *Maybe nothing ever happened and I'm just making all this up.* Somehow, I couldn't convince myself of that, but, like Mom, I pretended nothing had occurred. Nonetheless, I condemned myself for being a "bad boy."

Mental health experts disagree on the extent of damage done by child sexual abuse. Some are convinced that sexual mistreatment causes no more harm than other traumas.[7] Others strongly disagree, and believe that childhood sexual abuse causes serious, insidious, pervasive repercussions lasting into adulthood.[8] In fact many therapists argue that there is no such thing as "mild" sexual molestation, that childhood sexual abuse is always traumatic, and that, indeed, every incident of childhood sexual abuse can devastate a life.[9] The book, *No More Secrets, No More Shame,* reports that sexual abuse victims are at least two times more likely to attempt suicide as those who were never abused.[10] Some mental health professionals believe mother-son incest is the most damaging of all forms of incest, and that men can suffer even more long-term harm than women can.[11]

What damages have I suffered as a result of Mom and Gram's sexual behavior? I'm still unsure. Perhaps I'll never know whether some of my adult emotional damages were caused by their wrongs or were simply the effects of growing up in a severely dysfunctional home and other life difficulties. Reading and counseling have shown me there's a strong possibility that both sexual traumas *and* childhood family life have been major contributors to my emotional struggles: my explosive temper, my need to be on guard all the time, distrust and fear of authority figures, need to be in

control, driving need to achieve, sensitivity to criticism, fear of rejection and abandonment, life-threatening depressive episodes, and other internal battles.

How did I cope with those awful sexual offenses? Perhaps the same ways as survivors of other traumas. People who go through a job loss, divorce, major health crisis, or some other trial commonly use comparable coping tools. One way of dealing with my inner pain was to *numb out my inner chaos through addictions.* The book, *Faithful and True,* explains that the worse someone has been abused, the more likely he will be to have multiple addictions. [12]

Feeling a desperate need for relief from stress and pain, I turned to food and sports and became dependent on both. I was a skinny little boy until Dad left for Illinois and Mom's "serious" aggressions started. Suddenly, at age nine, I puffed up into a pudgy little fourth-grader — a phenomenon many experts say is one of the symptoms of sexual abuse. The photographs from our family albums are proof of my weight change soon after Mom's more blatant actions occurred.

Another survival mechanism I used was *denying the reality of what had happened to me.* I'd always known about my mother and grandmother's "less serious" sexual conduct. For years, though, my recollections were only that "something" happened. I guess I shoved those memories under my mental carpet, refusing to admit their reality.

Then, at forty-seven, those shadowy memories resurfaced, one fragment at a time. Still, I often questioned the reliability of my memory. *Did those things really happen with Mom? Did I make them up as a way of getting revenge on her? Was I influenced by my therapist or by what I read? But they never once initiated anything about my molestation — I brought the details to them.* However, after research into old family photos, albums, letters, birthday and Christmas cards, and much self-analysis, I'm certain that my incest did take place.

Another way I dealt with the molestations was by *compartmentalizing my life.* I put the past on my mind's back burner and moved

on as if nothing wrong had occurred. This worked until my life started falling apart. During my hospitalization and afterward, those long-shelved memories came to the fore; I couldn't avoid them any longer.

I also escaped what could have been overwhelmingly destructive emotions by rationalizing Mom and Gram's behavior, justifying their seductive actions. *They didn't really mean anything sexually offensive. I shouldn't read so much into it.*

For years I excused Mom's sexual conduct, reasoning that I should accept her attempts to demonstrate love, as inadequate as they might have been. I excused her and Gram's actions and blamed myself.

Also, to endure the sting of betrayal, I *minimized* the harms done to me, underrating those sexual traumas. *They weren't so bad. Many have gone through worse. That was then; this is now. The past is past. Leave your childhood behind and get on with your life. Stop dwelling on those things. Besides, as a Christian, you've got to forgive, forget, and move on.*

Maybe someday a clearer understanding of the insidious effects of their molestation will surface. One thing I'm certain of is that what my mother and grandmother did to their innocent, trusting little boy has had some devastating effects, no matter what conscious or unconscious reasons they may have had! Unfortunately, this wasn't the end of my sexual abuse.

Chapter 3

An Emotional Orphan on the Battlefield of Key Relationships

I WAS NINE WHEN DAD RETURNED from Illinois. It didn't take long for Mom to unleash the resentments she'd nursed against him for his lengthy absence. She resumed her verbal assaults almost immediately. Her nagging intensified daily, as though she was determined to make his life as miserable as possible so he'd capitulate to her every whim or else leave the family.

She told Betsy, Bob, and me frequently, "Your father deserted you kids and me last year. Now he'll pay. Just remember who's really taken care of you." Every week I thought one of them would get fed up and initiate a divorce. *It's scary, but it would be a welcome relief from the nonstop conflicts and from having to choose sides all the time.*

From that point on, Mom outdid herself to demean Dad as a person and as a man. She repeatedly pledged to me, "I intend to make your father's life as miserable as I can." Besides her attacks on Dad, I never knew when she'd turn on me as well.

It felt unsafe sharing anything meaningful with Mom and Dad. At best, they were poor listeners. I remember yearning to get polio or become blind. *Maybe then I'll get at least some kind of reprieve from Mom's incessant verbal assaults and more positive attention from Dad.*

Increasingly, both parents and Gram relied on me, pushing me further into the roles of substitute spouse and family leader as Dad relinquished more and more of his authority. It was an awkward, lonely position for me. I was also afraid to share anything about my home life or my feelings with teachers, coaches, scoutmasters, and others, lest my words get back to Mom and Gram,

the "queens," and result in punishment. I felt like an emotional orphan living in a spiritual desert. No one, not Mom or Dad or my relatives, seemed to genuinely listen to me or care about my needs.

To survive the emotional duress at home, I learned to "read" people, especially those who could possibly harm me: Mom, Gram, Unc, Dad, teachers, coaches, and classmates. I desperately wanted to please them, so I tried anticipating and meeting their needs before they mentioned them. I became acutely aware of their moods. If I thought Mom was angry, I tried to placate her. When Gram was upset with how Dad was treating Mom, I tried to intervene. If I saw Dad or Mom upset, I stepped in to soothe their feelings. Until their deaths, I labored under a weighty sense of obligation to "fix" them. I never felt I could please them. Ever.

I envied kids who had parents who were nice to each other. My friends appeared to live without the constant fear, guilt, anger, and insecurity I felt. I often daydreamed about being adopted into a family where smiles were the norm, hoping my home would someday be happy. *What would it be like to escape the daily criticism, parental fighting, and sexually tainted behaviors?*

Mom sure knew how to smother anyone's enthusiasm: "Jimmy, you're selfish to spend so much time playing football. Why are you always going to the gym? You should be doing homework, or cleaning the garage, or mowing the lawn." Because Mom and Dad were usually fighting, I felt guilty about having any kind of fun at home. In fact, laughter seemed almost sacrilegious. When we kids cracked a joke or pulled a prank, Mom and Dad rarely laughed. She usually put some kind of sarcastic spin on our attempts at humor, so whenever we were having fun, I waited for the inevitable criticism ... or for some kind of disaster to happen.

Mom's sadistic sense of humor tainted all our levity. Veiled judgement usually accompanied her humor. As she joked, she'd add a caustic comment, putting one of us kids down with a lilt to her voice and a smile on her face, nearly always criticizing, teasing, or embarrassing. Instead of evoking laughs, I often felt frightened. On the other hand, Dad's serious demeanor was broken up

by his sporadic jovial quips. Sometimes he laughed with abandon about something that seemed almost childish to us kids.

Not only depressing, living at home was like tiptoeing through a minefield, never knowing when you'd set one off. Family life was tense, like a stretched rubber band ready to snap at any moment. Threatening, ridiculing, belittling, frightening, teasing, or humiliating, were commonplace. Most of the time, I never knew why Mom boiled with anger. She always seemed upset, hurt, or furious about something. It was a welcome relief when she wasn't upset, manipulating, coercing, or criticizing. It felt like I was under continuous emotional assault.

Mom was quick to tattle our misdeeds to Gram or Unc or our friends, but she'd usually let infractions slide with only a harsh glare or sharp words. As a result, we never knew when she'd follow through on a punishment. Most of her punitive actions were capricious and rarely fit the offenses. As the oldest child, I received the most penalties. The youngest sibling often gets away with more than the older children do. Bob usually slid by, barely reprimanded by Mom. I got nailed for the slightest violation.

Dad refused to discuss school difficulties and sports problems. He brushed aside all talk of conflict or emotional pain, saying, "I don't want to discuss that. Life has too many good things happening. Let's not talk about the sad or bad things." Then he'd invoke a list of blessings for which we should be grateful: "We live in a nice house. You kids have three good meals a day. Look at all the toys you have. You're far better off than most kids in the world."

At other times, those upbeat words contradicted his typical avoidance-of-pain mentality. I recall him pointing his finger and warning me hundreds of times, "It's a hard, cruel world out there, Jimmy. There are plenty of mean people waiting to harass you. They'll mistreat you any way they can. You don't know how good you've got it here at home. Just wait till you leave and start slugging it out in the big bad world. You've got to be tough and not let them get to you."

This was an unusual negative from Dad, our family's self-designated optimist. It usually came when explaining some of the rough times he'd endured at Penn State or, more frequently, the battles he fought with the "anti-Dad Team" of in-laws.

In a similar fashion, the "big three" repeated *their* threat-prediction countless times before I entered college: "Jimmy, you're a bad, evil boy, a selfish, uncaring son, and a poor big brother. Your father won't discipline you, so you've got to obey your mother. If you don't, we'll have nothing to do with you. If you continue misbehaving, you'll end up in reform school, then prison, and the electric chair by the time you're twenty-one." In the years ahead, whenever I was with Mom, Gram, or Unc and we passed a police officer, police station, reform school, jail, or prison, they'd recite that familiar warning. It became their mantra.

As the eldest son, I was accorded all the privileges of rank: later curfews, new clothes and toys and other advantages. Mom, Dad, and Gram deferred to me ahead of Betsy and Bob in most decisions. In reality, we kids were just pawns for Mom and Gram, sources to prop up their egos, carry out their strong-willed plans, and vehicles to use in attacking Dad.

As a third-grader, I started playing other roles than surrogate husband, messenger boy/mediator, caregiver, and eldest son. In any given week, I was coerced into wearing one or more of those titles, or assumed them out of a need to bring peace to our family. By the time I turned ten, Mom and Gram had conscripted me as the messenger boy to carry their never-ending demands to "shape up your Father" in some way. They habitually assigned me tasks that would set me at odds with Dad.

I became the family's official black sheep. It seemed I was always the center of controversy, always getting into trouble at home because I didn't fulfill everyone's expectations or comply with all their demands. Twice, Mom called a neighbor to our house "to quiet Jimmy down, since his father can't control him."

Week after week Mom whined, "I don't know what to do with you, Jimmy. After all the good things I've done for you, you still

treat me like this. You've made my life miserable. You have no kind feelings toward me, or you'd behave differently. Your father won't discipline you so others will have to do it. I've talked with Grandma, Grandpa, and Uncle Jim about your misbehaving. We've talked with the police about you. If you continue misbehaving we'll have you arrested. You'll be sentenced to a reform school for boys who disobey their parents. After that, you'll be sent to prison."

A number of times, one of the "Big Three" phoned the State College police. How extremely scary to look up at two tall policemen with guns. They were courteous, but always warned me, "Your relatives called us about you. We hope you'll start acting right. We don't want to come back and have to take you to reform school, so start behaving."

It was embarrassing beyond words to know that the neighbors and many of my friends were watching as the cops drove up to our house and came inside. After each incident, I had to make up a story to explain the policemen's visit. From fourth grade on, I lived in terror of the cops coming to get me. I never could really relax, knowing they could show up any time I had a disagreement with Mom.

Whenever I lost my temper and cursed, or smashed a lamp, or put my fist through a cabinet, or yelled at Mom or Dad, I dreaded the sound of a knock on our door from the police. Those fears grew into an ongoing fear of authority figures. Even now, my stomach tightens when I'm in the presence of certain authorities.

Day and night, waves of anxiety troubled my mind. When the obligations of refereeing and caretaking became too onerous, or the stings of criticism and shame smarted too much, I numbed my hurt feelings by overeating or playing with friends. As I grew older I added other anesthetics: sports, hunting, fishing, helping others, workaholism, and an increasingly serious eating disorder.

The times when I felt closest to my family while growing up were watching TV, vacations, Halloween, Christmas, Easter, and birthdays. Mom made extra efforts to prepare, decorate, bake, and cook for each special occasion of the year. At Halloween, she bought

big pumpkins and lots of candy. It was fun carving scary faces with Dad. Like most youngsters, I loved having him go trick-or-treating with me from house to house. Birthdays were also exceptional days. I guess mine were special because the cake, ice cream, and presents were tangible assurances of being loved.

Christmas was my favorite holiday of all, even though I feared Santa might give me ashes instead of presents. Mom decorated the house and baked cookies and sweet rolls. It was exciting to go with Dad to pick out a tree. I could barely sleep the night before Christmas: the curiosity over what gifts I might receive grew almost unbearable. I don't know whether it was the presents or the family closeness, but Christmas morning was the most wonderful time of the year.

No child likes to see his parents unhappy or fighting. Over and over I asked myself, *What did I do to make Mom and Dad so unhappy and fight so much? What can I do to make them stop quarreling and get along? When will they divorce?*

Even when things between them were at their best, they showed little affection for one another. At times Dad would reach out to hold hands, or hug or kiss Mom, but she would stiffen like a board when he put his arm around her. I don't recall ever seeing her initiate any affection toward him. When she did kiss him, her kisses were quick "pecks" that looked like token responses.

It was obvious that Mom had no respect for Dad. She was engaged in an ongoing personal vendetta against him, oozing bitterness. Her vitriolic attitude infected our home life, poisoning all joy around her. If we kids disagreed with her or "sided" with Dad, we received the same verbal hostility.

Usually, it seemed that Mom had to belittle Dad into spending time with me. I had to beg him to play catch, watch me ride my bike, drive me to the Penn State Creamery for an ice cream cone, or take me fishing. Once in a while he would. It was somehow reassuring to be with him, yet there was often a letdown, because the times were so brief. It always seemed that no sooner had we started to play catch, or kick the football, than he'd say, "I'm tired, Jimmy, let's call it quits."

Many times I questioned, *Why does Dad always get tired so fast? Does he really like being with me? Maybe there's something wrong with me. Maybe he doesn't like me 'cause he thinks I'm loyal to Mom by letting her buy me things.* Nevertheless, while times with Dad were few and far between, they were special, treasured events.

Dad was beset by a wrathful wife and spiteful mother-in-law. All his married life, he existed under continual emotional siege of verbal attacks by the "Queens." Though he couldn't do a thing to please them, Dad managed somehow to get on with his life, remaining committed to Mom and us. Perhaps he saw no alternative to staying married to her.

Tragically, he lived his life submitting to his mother, Mom, and Gram's demands. He became Mom and Gram's psychological punching bag, a victim of their tireless antagonism. Dad seldom defended himself or struck back. I watched time and again as they ground him down until he no longer put up any opposition. He probably realized it was useless to fight them, and resigned himself to enduring their never-ending onslaughts.

Most men I know would never have put up with the abuse Dad took. I vowed never to be weak and indecisive like him when I grew up. Yet, I always wondered, *Does he passively tolerate Mom's attacks because he's weak, or because he realizes she's mentally ill and placates her, or to "keep peace" in the family for the kids' sake?* Regrettably, Mom rarely reciprocated his patient suffering with her. Instead, over the years, she kept driving wedges between us kids and him, weaving us into her possessive web, isolating us from Dad as much as she could. I pitied him, and I felt guilty for not respecting him as a man.

I don't know how Mom and Gram's vitriolic words affected Dad, Betsy, or Bob, but they stung me to the core. Each time they teamed up to disgrace Dad, my stomach tightened, my head flushed. Inwardly, I vowed, *I'll never be a doormat like Dad. I'll fight back against them any way I can. They'll never beat me down and destroy me like they're doing to him. I'll be a man's man, like Grandpa Stevenson.*

Whenever I obeyed the Queens' shifting agendas, they'd simply pour on more and more demands, as though intent on provoking me to rebel. In retrospect, I believe if I'd surrendered to their strong-arm tactics, they'd have smothered my personality and killed my soul.

One way Dad avoided Mom's ranting was by absenting himself from her as much as possible. Unfortunately, that also meant being away from us kids a lot. After dinner, he usually retreated to his study in the back of our house. Many Saturdays he went to his campus office to "work." I didn't blame him for wanting to escape.

Mom's attacks on Dad were far more than the occasional venting of frustrations; they were deliberate attempts to undermine all trust we had in our father. She put him down in front of us or disagreed with him at every opportunity: about allowances, curfew, clothes, discipline, school, vacation decisions, and most everything else. I couldn't believe anyone could be so cruel as to humiliate her husband in public, let alone before his children. She relentlessly degraded Dad, seeming to delight in vilifying him. I felt sorry for him. It was embarrassing to watch a man being verbally castrated by his wife. I choked back anger at him for not having the guts to stand up to Mom and Gram. They attacked him to his face: "Randy, you ought to spend more money on your family. You shouldn't be content just being an underpaid college professor. You're too stubborn. Why don't you spend more time with your family?"

They cut him down behind his back to us and to anyone who'd listen: "Your father's got no ambition. He doesn't care for you or he'd get a higher-paying job in the business world. He's not respected among his peers. He's a lousy father: never plays with you; never spends money on you; never gives your Mom enough money. You poor kids go around wearing hand-me-downs all the time."

Never once did Mom or Gram hold Dad up to us as a role model. They loved to zero in on his defects: "Don't be like your father. He's a poor excuse for a man and a father. Be like your Grandpa. He treats his family like a caring father should."

Whenever I defended Dad to the Queens, they put on hurt expressions or blamed me: "Jimmy, how can you dare stand up for him? Can't you see we've got the contacts to ruin your reputation at school, on the football and wrestling teams, with the Boy Scouts, and all your friends? We'll tell them what a bad, ungrateful, uncaring son you are."

I spent the next thirty years trying to figure out why Mom and Dad were attracted to each other in the first place, what they had in common, why they stayed together, and who was most to blame for their marriage problems. I arrived at some acceptable answers: Both were deeply wounded human beings; unconsciously, each acted out prewritten scripts given to them by their parents and others. Nevertheless, I believe that Mom and Dad share equal responsibility for the failure of their marriage. They did the best they could to be good parents. Nonetheless, I believe that both were responsible for their harmful omissions and commissions as parents.

Through years of counseling, reading, and involvement in recovery groups, I've come to understand them in a different light. I see how they injured me and some of the terrible effects of their actions. They often aroused extreme anger in me. Now I ache with sadness over what is unrecoverable, and I mourn the happy childhood I might have had, but missed. Had I simply glossed over their wrongs, and quickly "forgiven" them, I think I would still be consumed with anger, resentment, and depression. Now, I bear no more resentment toward Mom, Dad, Gram, and Unc. I accept them with their flaws and strengths. I have a peaceful inner calm now, despite the awful memories that surface from time to time.

Hundreds of times over the years I've pondered whether we kids would've been better off had Mom and Dad divorced and we had lived with one or the other. Time and again I found that keeping score of their failings proved a frustrating, guilt-inducing exercise. I'm still not sure whether Betsy, Bob, and I would have been better off living with one parent. There would have been many tradeoffs, none of them ideal.

I remember a scene that was repeated untold times during my childhood. The only thing that changed was the circumstances. Gram introduced me to her friends by first complimenting me, then shredding me: "Jimmy's such a nice boy. *But* he still wets the bed, breaks his toys, and disobeys his mother." Each time, like a robot, I nodded affirmatively, burning with inner resentment at being shamed in front of others.

Compared to Dad, Mom was lavishly generous with money and gifts to Bob and me. For some reason, she gave us the most gifts; Betsy always got the least. Mom used natural sibling rivalries to fire jealousy among us, seemingly taking sadistic delight in fueling animosity. She'd buy me an ice cream cone or a toy and say, "Jimmy, don't tell your brother or sister that I bought this for you." Then, astonishingly, the moment we arrived home, she gleefully blabbed to Betsy and Bob about what she'd just bought me. She played these dissension "games" until I was in my college years.

To entice us to do her bidding, Mom frequently offered cash, toys, food, and privileges as rewards for house chores, errands, or whatever she defined as good behavior. Other than Christmas and birthday presents, I don't recall more than a few gifts she ever gave without some condition attached.

I learned I could never believe what she said, or count on any of her promises. Frequently, I planned on taking part in Boy Scout outings that Mom had agreed to. But if I had a blowup with her over some small "infraction," she canceled my participation. All the while, Dad stood by meekly, saying nothing.

When I was in fifth grade, Mom convinced him that us kids should be given allowances. But in less than two months she canceled them. From that point on, I never could depend on any kind of steady income. My earnings from then on came primarily from working for neighbors and other people, mowing lawns, spading gardens, shoveling snow off sidewalks, and selling Christmas wreaths and other items I made.

Mom prodded, "Save your money, Jimmy. You spend too recklessly. You should open a savings account."

"If I put my money in the bank, and then decide I want to buy something, can I get it out whenever I want?"

"Of course you can, Jimmy. Trust me." So I opened an account, and for several months deposited my earnings from various after-school and weekend jobs. Then I saw a model airplane I wanted to buy. It took hours of lawn work for neighbors to earn enough for it, only to have Mom change her mind: "That plane's a waste of money, Jimmy. You can't buy it."

I stiffened. *Mom promised I'd be able to take my money out whenever I needed it. Now she's double-crossed me.* So I just left my money in the bank, and never took Mom at her word again.

The Queens meted out nearly all of the discipline I received. The intention was usually to drive me into submitting to their wishes and theirs alone. Once I reached ten, they realized spankings didn't work. Instead, they'd slap me in the face, or grab a spatula, wooden spoon, yardstick, or broom and hit me anywhere they could. It wasn't hard to dodge them, but they'd merely wait and catch me off guard, then slap me.

If those punishments didn't do the job, the Queens bullied us kids, Dad, and others with lengthy "silent treatments." For hours, days, or even weeks, they refused to speak to me when I didn't go along with their wishes. They treated me as though I didn't even exist, walking past me, not even looking at me. Their muteness hurt more than their harsh words or physical punishment. I still wince with the sense of utter rejection I felt so often. The only way to end their emotional exile was capitulation to their directions.

But in my teenage years, I fought back when they waged silent warfare, giving them silent treatments of my own that lasted much longer than theirs. My shunning chafed Mom far more than it did Gram, often driving her to tears. I couldn't treat Gram the same way — she was tougher than Mom. Once, I retaliated against Gram's mute spurning with my own silent punishment. She became incensed and threatened to call the police. After that, I never tried to out-silence her.

Chapter 4

The Beginnings of an Eating Disorder

To endure the constant emotional upsets at home, I fought for survival using any method I could. One tool I used was dividing my life into a public "nice guy" and a private "bad guy." Our family knew me as hot-tempered and foul-mouthed, while at school I was seen as a fun-loving, friendly boy. Because of my two-sided personality, I suffered terrible guilt over being a "phony." It was like having a Jekyll-and-Hyde personality, but it helped me endure.

Another escape mechanism I used at home was my temper. Angry outbursts enabled me to express some degree of individuality. Mom's unfair punishments, betrayal of confidences, and protracted silences made me seethe. I could bottle things up only so long, then took revenge. Often, a minor event triggered a violent temper explosion. Enraged, I threw lamps and chairs across the room, put my fist through doors, and splintered kitchen cabinets. Sometimes, in exasperation, I swore at Mom, and I even slapped her a few times.

Most children rebel occasionally, none is perfectly obedient. Apart from "normal" youthful rebellion, any attempts I made to be independent from the ever-changing, unremitting demands of the "Big Three" authority figures in my life were met with subtle or outright harsh rebukes.

Mom, Gram, and Uncle Jim tried their best to keep me under their thumbs with threats that began when I was in third grade and continued through my college years. Their warnings hung over me into my forties. Often, the last thing they said to me when parting was, "Be good." Those words always hurt due to the tacit implication that I was bad, deserving of the "prison-to-electric-chair" mantra I would hear into my thirties.

As I entered junior high, the Queens had already sullied my reputation with my peers as well as with the adults whom I respected. I was known to friends, neighbors, church members, relatives, and scoutmasters as a "bad boy," an incorrigible youth, an uncaring, disobedient son.

I recall, as a fifth-grader, Mom thundering, "Jimmy, if you do that again, I'll leave you and the family and move where nobody can find me. And should you locate me, I won't let you visit me. I'll never again help you." In the coming years, she, Gram, and Unc followed through on these and other threats.

Whether it originated in Mom and Gram's sexual misconduct, or in an extremely dysfunctional home, I started numbing my emotions, soothing myself more and more, by compulsively overeating. It worsened as I spent after-school hours buying candy, hamburgers, cokes, ice cream cones, and other junk foods. I shifted back and forth from no control over what I ate to absolute control, gorging for days, then starving myself. I desperately wanted to lose weight, to look trim and muscular, to stop the binge-starve cycles. By fifth grade, I was caught up in the beginnings of a serious compulsive eating disorder. Time and again I agonized, *How can I stop? Willpower and prayers don't work.*

Chapter 5

How a Dysfunctional Family Communicates

OUR FAMILY HAD UNSPOKEN RULES for communicating: "Don't talk; don't tell; don't feel." I couldn't have defined them during my youth, but now I see how they influenced our family dynamics. In healthy families, parents talk about what's going on at school, after school, at home, and in the neighborhood. They encourage sharing thoughts and feelings, and listen to their children.

Such communication barely existed between Mom and Dad, let along between them and us. When I asked my parents a question, it was often ignored or evaded, rarely answered directly. When I tried to express pain or anger about a teacher's comment, or a classmate's betrayal, they shifted the conversation, diminished the severity of my problem, or accused *me* of causing the difficulty.

Frequently, it was difficult to decipher what Mom and Dad really meant behind their words. They said one thing, but their body language often said the opposite. Most of the time I had to guess. I very rarely felt really listened to and understood by either of them. It was as though their own inner agenda framed their every response.

In the Stout household, *don't talk* meant that all conversations had to be limited to small talk about inane subjects. It was impossible to have a normal, meaningful conversation with Mom and Dad. It always felt like we were on different wavelengths, speaking unrelated monologues, rarely a dialogue.

Don't tell demonstrated our family's "code of silence," strictly enforced by the Queens. They cautioned us kids time and again, "Don't tell your Sunday school teacher, your coaches, your teachers, your scout leaders, your friends, or anyone else about your family. It's none of their business. What goes on at home stays

here." But their secrecy rule never applied to *them*; they never hesitated to broadcast my bedwetting, temper outbursts, and disobedience.

Don't feel showed our family's deficiency in dealing with emotions. I believe Mom and Dad always genuinely cared about us, but they were so overwhelmed by their own difficulties that they couldn't see anyone else's needs. Whenever we kids tried to bring up a difficulty, they simply couldn't respond to it with empathy. Since Mom and Dad couldn't respond to my feelings, I felt like an "it," an invisible, nonexistent person. Sadly, after a while it just became too painful for me to bring up either a happy or hurtful situation only to have it ignored, discounted, or explained away, or be made the guilty party. Knowing that my celebrations, questions, and distresses fell on ears that were incapable of responding, I learned to shelve my excitement, ignore my pain, keep quiet, and go on smiling. Since no one listened to me, I was forced to become a listener to the successes and problems of others.

I remember bubbling with enthusiasm about a Valentine's Day party my fourth-grade teacher had organized. Mom squelched my jubilation, rasping, "I certainly hope you paid attention the rest of the day. Make sure you do your homework after dinner." Always a negative response. Dad, on the other hand, missed the whole point of my excitement, rambling on for the next ten minutes about Penn State's business school.

I recall another fourth-grade instance when, in tears, I whimpered to them, " I'm awfully discouraged. I'm just not as good at math as most of the class. It's no use trying any more. I guess I'm just stupid." Neither offered comfort or reassurance. Dad replied, "Jimmy, you shouldn't feel discouraged. You live in a nice house, you have warm winter clothes. Tough it out. Be strong. You can do it. We need you."

Characteristically, Mom barked, "You're flunking math, Jimmy. You should've studied harder. This is what you deserve. Now we'll have to pay to get you a tutor. You'd better shape up and put your mind to it."

Surrounded by such dysfunctional parents and relatives, I was, of necessity, a solitary child. The word "lonely" took on new meaning. I never had a sense of really belonging anywhere, whether at home, at school, on teams, or with friends. Even while immersed in school, sports, and scout activities, I felt like an outsider looking in on classmates, indeed on the human race.

My friendly, smiling appearance hid utter misery. I had plenty of "friends," but hung out mostly with three, and I wasn't really close even to them. There was literally not a person in the world with whom I felt safe enough to confide a problem. I joked and played, but mostly listened to everyone else's troubles and aspirations, rarely divulging my own.

Mom increased the frequency of her threats to leave us: "Jimmy, if you don't start obeying me better and get your father to straighten up, I'm going to leave. After all, none of this family cares about me, anyway." By the time I graduated from seminary, Mom moved out a dozen times or more, and lived by herself for months or years at a time.

Chapter 6

Good and Bad Spiritual Influences

OUR FAMILY NEVER GOT ACTIVELY INVOLVED in a church, but we attended a Presbyterian church in State College semi-regularly. I remember attending Sunday school, then sitting in the worship service with Mom and Dad. Both Sunday school and worship bored me to death. Once, we went to a church Christmas play and potluck dinner. I felt terribly out of place because I didn't know most of the people. Also, in those days, divorced persons bore a big stigma. Though my parents hadn't taken that route, most people knew they fought frequently. I felt judged. It was also an uncomfortable evening because Mom had badmouthed me to my Sunday school teachers and some of the kids in class, and I felt extremely self-conscious.

My knowledge of Christianity was shallow at best. I knew the golden rule, and that Jesus was supposed to have been a kind man who helped people. I had been taught in Sunday school that He died on a cross alongside two other men, but I didn't understand why. I never understood anything about the people the Sunday school teacher talked about: Paul, Timothy, Matthew, and others. That was the extent of my biblical knowledge until my first year of college.

From age ten to thirteen, I spent a number of weeks each summer with Gram and Grandpa Stevenson in Pittsburgh. They were more strict, but fairer than Mom and Dad. In most ways they did a better parenting job than my parents. Every visit meant that I was required to go to church with them.

I believed that there was a God, a Higher Being to whom I could pray about my concerns. Yet, as often as I prayed for Mom and Dad to reconcile, those prayers weren't answered, so I figured I was just

too bad a boy for God to pay attention to or to grant favors.

Gram and Grandpa continued exerting a strong spiritual influence on me. They prayed and read the Bible with me, bought me Christian books, and paid for me to attend First Presbyterian Church summer camp in Ligonier, Pennsylvania. Each visit with them also meant nightly prayers with Gram.

Our family sometimes vacationed for a week in Wildwood or Atlantic City. I loved our times at the beach: building sand castles, swimming and riding the waves, walking the boardwalk, fishing off docks, eating lots of fresh cantaloupe and honeydew melons. Mom and Dad's flare-ups were more moderate, but they still argued a lot. At the time, I didn't realize most families didn't have such incessant battling. I guess I just got used to living in a volatile atmosphere.

Entering fifth grade was a big deal. In good weather, I rode my bike over a mile to the redbrick elementary school, and on winter days I walked through the snow. Most of my friends headed home right after school. Some hung around local pool halls or played pinball in a popular store. I avoided going home after school at all costs. I went to afternoon movies, worked out at the Rec Hall (the university's main gym), hunted and fished — anything to stay away from criticism and seduction at home.

Mom and Dad allowed me to ride my bike to Sunday school. On the way to church, I often stopped and, with my slingshot, hunted squirrels, rabbits, and chipmunks on the Penn State campus. One fateful morning I made the mistake of taking a dead chipmunk in my pocket to my fifth-grade Sunday school class. When the offering plate was passed, I dropped its brown-and-white-striped body onto the plate. Immediately, girls shrieked and boys howled. The teacher escorted me out to discuss my devilish deed with the superintendent. After a thorough chewing out, I was allowed to return to class, but that was the last time I ever attended Sunday school. From then on, I worshiped only with our family, and that was just a few times a year.

Chapter 7

Dire Predictions

MOM SEEMED TO CARE LESS AND LESS about her appearance. Her hygiene became so terrible that I was horrified to have my friends come near her. I abstained from most foods she prepared, and ate mostly what I fixed or bought at a store. Soon I avoided hugging or kissing her, and cringed when I had to. I felt awful for not wanting to eat the food my own mother cooked and for not wanting to touch her. Mom seemed to grow more and more detached. She seldom expressed gratitude for my efforts at chores, helping with Betsy and Bobby, or giving her gifts. Sometimes she'd offer a perfunctory, "Thank you, Jimmy," but her words sounded hollow.

Many of my fifth-grade school friends had frequent sleepovers. I went to only four during my entire childhood. All were at a friend's house. His parents were close friends with mine. Each time, Mom brought the thick, brown rubber sheet to cover the mattress, in case I wet the bed. When I did, fortunately, my friend and his parents didn't make a big deal over the "slip."

When I was eleven, we visited Gram and Grandpa during Easter vacation. One overcast morning, Gram said, "Let's go have your pictures taken, kids. Your mother and I want a photo of the three of you." She marched us off to a photography studio a few blocks away. A huge, black camera and tripod stood in the middle of the room, surrounded by clutter: empty boxes, a broken chair, two stools, and assorted camera equipment. After what seemed like an hour, the photographer finished having us hold still in various poses.

The day before we had to leave for home, Gram cheerfully suggested, "Jimmy, let's you and I go get the pictures. You can help me pick out the ones for your mom."

She asked the photographer, "Could I see my grandchildren's pictures?" He handed her a packet. She smiled, thanked him, and said, "We'll be back in a few minutes after we've made our selections." Gram and I walked to a grassy hill nearby. She sat on a three-foot-high brick wall; I sat on the grass next to her.

She set the photos aside and pointed at my head, saying, "Everybody knows that all redheads have bad tempers. Your red hair proves it." Her sobering assessment continued as she stung me with the reform school-prison-electric chair mantra.

Suddenly, Gram's serious look changed to a wide grin, and she said, "I know you can do better, Jimmy. You're my oldest grandchild. I want to be proud of you. Don't break any more of your toys. Your mother and I only want what's best for you. Try harder to please your mother." As she spoke, I shut down inside, but automatically promised, "I'll do better, Gram."

That summer, someone gave me a homing pigeon pen, which I kept in the backyard. I saved money and bought four other "homers;" how proud I was of my new pets. Tenderly, I carried the box inside to show Betsy, Bob, and Mom. Betsy and Bob giggled, "They're so cute. Can we pet them?" Mom's response was, "You sure wasted your money on those birds. They have diseases. They cost too much to feed. Don't expect me to lift a finger to help you clean their cage or feed them."

One fall afternoon when I was twelve, I came home from school to find Mom dressed inappropriately. "Hi Jimmy. Glad you're home from school." I flushed with embarrassment, boiling with anger inside. *What's going on here? Is she trying to seduce me again?*

That wasn't a one-time event; it happened regularly. After that, the few times I came home before dinner, I always peeked nervously before entering the living room, incensed at her brazen behavior. Mom never talked about those incidents, and I was mortified to bring them up. I was afraid to be alone with her, and terrified to invite friends home because of what they might see, so I seldom came home directly from school or team practices.

One Saturday morning, I exploded with swear words at Mom

because, on the spur moment, she'd changed a major chore as-
signment. I ran to Dad to complain about her unfairness. He said,
"Jimmy, you've got to realize that's what your mother's like. I'm
tired of fighting with her and your grandmother. They simply
refuse to listen. I can never please them, and neither can you.
They'll wear you down. So don't even try to fight them. It's no
use. Let them have their way. Don't waste time arguing, just move
on with your life. You've got friends, sports, fishing, and other
things to occupy you."

Dad's life revolved around taxation issues and Penn State. He
spoke repeatedly about the university, delighted with its athletic
teams, new buildings, growing student enrollment, and cultural
events. As I grew older, it was a special treat once in a while to go
with him to Penn State basketball games, gymnastic and wrestling
meets, and boxing matches.

Other than economics and the college, his conversation remained
extremely limited. I wondered, *Why can't Dad talk about my school
or baseball or fishing? He turns every conversation to one of his
topics. Doesn't he care enough to ask questions about my friends, my
classes, my hobbies, my achievements, or respond when I share my
hurt feelings?*

The college sponsored year-round sporting events. I attended
many. From sixth grade on, I became a "gym rat," and Rec Hall
became my second home. My friends and I wrestled and played
handball and basketball after school, evenings, on weekends, and
school vacation breaks.

At twelve I left Cub Scouts to join the Boy Scouts. My troop
leader and his assistant were terrific. Each week's meeting offered
a fresh adventure. Learning first aid and survival techniques in
the outdoors, and taking hikes were my favorites. I had mixed
emotions about overnight campouts. They were fun, but I dreaded wetting my sleeping bag and having my fellow scouts find out
about my "baby" behavior. I drank nothing after dinner and stayed
awake as long as I could so I wouldn't have an "accident," but
inevitably I slipped. So I avoided most overnight camping trips

due to fear of embarrassment. As a result, I never got beyond earning my Star badge. Nevertheless, scouting was one of the few highlights of my adolescence until seventh grade, when football and wrestling took its place.

The summer between sixth and seventh grades, our family traveled cross-country by train to southern California. It was a bittersweet time. The idea originated with Gram Stevenson. As usual, she coaxed Mom to convince Dad that we ought to take the trip. He dragged his feet about going. Finally, after Gram offered money to help with expenses, he grudgingly agreed.

It was thrilling to see Indian reservations, the Grand Canyon, Yellowstone Park, authentic Indians, real buffalos, and dozens of other wonders. However, being aware of Dad's reluctance tainted what could have been a much more enjoyable vacation.

One of the fascinating spots we visited in southern California was Knott's Berry Farm. Before leaving there, Mom pointed to the western jail on the main walkway. She said, with a twinkle in her eyes, "Look, Jimmy, a jail. Better watch out! The police might put you in there." As we approached, a convict mannequin inside growled, "Hey there, Jimmy Stout. I know you. You'd better start obeying your mother better or you'll end up in here with me." *How could he know about how I behave?* Gawking tourists surrounded us. The combination of his words and Mom's raucous laughter made me want to crawl in a hole and die. Dad was silent. Betsy and Bobby looked scared. Once more, a delightful outing was blighted by public humiliation, guilt, and fear inflicted by Mom, the expert terrorist.

A more frightening incident happened that fall. Unc stopped by to see us, saying he'd driven to State College for a business meeting. After a cup of coffee, he asked, "Jimmy, how'd you and your mother like to go for a drive with me? We can see Fisherman's Paradise and some other places."

The three of us slid into Unc's big Buick. He pulled out his wallet and showed me a deputy sheriff's badge, saying, "This helps me whenever I get stopped for speeding." A few minutes into our drive, he casually mentioned, "Because I'm a deputy sheriff, I get

some special privileges. You know the state penitentiary, Rockview, a few miles from here? Want to see what a prison looks like up close? I've asked one of the warden's assistants to take us on a tour."

Instantly, my body stiffened. Something was very wrong. Unc hadn't just "accidentally" driven five hours to visit with us. Somehow, I knew he and Mom had plotted this penitentiary "tour." I felt trapped and betrayed. Yet, despite my anxieties, I was curious about what it was like inside. Besides, I couldn't refuse Unc. No one turned him or Mom or Gram down.

Our family had driven past Rockview many times. We'd been told it was one of the official execution sites in Pennsylvania. Each time we passed by, Mom had intoned her too-familiar reform school-prison-electric chair song.

Unc and Mom chain-smoked the whole way to the prison. We drove up the grass-covered hill to the gray stone buildings surrounded by high walls and fences. Unc talked with some official who walked over, introduced himself, and began describing the huge dining hall and the large areas where prisoners stood around in groups or played baseball. Then he soberly intoned, "See that building over there? It's where the death row inmates are executed in the electric chair." Unc and Mom whispered, "That's where you'll end up if you don't start being good, Jimmy." Everyone chuckled, including me. But my insides tightened. All I remember after that was getting back into Unc's car and driving home.

On into high school, college and adulthood, I believed the "Big Three" about my violent, criminal future. Those dire predictions saturated me with a near-inescapable feeling that I was rotten through and through and deserved nothing but the punishment that would come sooner or later — it was just a matter of time. Their words made me feel like a trapped animal, destined for slaughter. My past temper outbursts over Mom's unfair treatment confirmed all that they had said; I was certain I was under a curse, branded a criminal, soon to be a vicious killer. Only in recent years, through much counseling, reading, and involvement in various twelve-step

support groups, have I begun to change that despicable bad-boy-headed-for-the-electric-chair self-image.

How did I make it through my first twelve years? Dr. Phil Sutherland, my psychologist, as well as other therapists say it was a miracle. I suppose I detached from the pain of home life by playing pickup softball, football, racquetball and handball, fishing, hanging around Rec Hall, making model planes, working at odd jobs, and numbing my loneliness with compulsive overeating and thinking about girls. Would things change in junior high?

Part Two

Finding Guidance in Education, Career and Marriage Decisions

For waging war you need guidance,
and for victory many advisors.

— Proverbs 24:6

Chapter 8

Bulimia Begins

ENTERING JUNIOR HIGH EVOKED both excitement and anxiety. Being a lowly seventh-grader was a bit overwhelming, but being on the football and wrestling teams meant new friends and the elevated social status that athletes enjoyed.

Registering for courses each year from then through college could have been a positive experience; instead, it was always tense and disappointing. Mom and Dad seldom agreed on which classes I should take. When seeking advice, I invariably received conflicting views. If I took Dad's suggestions, Mom intervened: "It won't work out, Jimmy. Your father doesn't know what he's talking about. You'll be sorry. Listen to me." Dad usually shrugged his shoulders and said, "Listen to your mother. You'd better do it her way."

I never could trust that they were looking after my best interests, so I always looked for the motives behind their words. Since I couldn't rely on my parents for unbiased guidance, I sought direction from friends and teachers. From then on, asking Mom and Dad for help was merely a token gesture.

The following summer, I stayed with Gram and Grandpa and worked on the outskirts of Pittsburgh at the new cemetery that Unc and Grandpa had bought. I mowed the lawns with a tractor, dug ditches and graves, and cut wood with chain saws. That fall I earned money by parking cars on a neighbor's spare lot during Penn State home games.

As youngsters, we got accustomed to our parents' arguing and tried to make the best of those times. I deeply appreciate Mom's widening my range of experience and broadening my horizons. Were it not for her and Gram, and Grandpa Stevenson, I believe I'd have ended up with no vision for college or beyond.

Beneath my jovial, easygoing outer appearance lay a fragile self-image, but being a "jock" propped up my deflated self-esteem. Starting in the seventh grade and continuing through college, my athletic accomplishments, albeit limited, were my primary source of affirmation.

I'm sure that to schoolmates and others I appeared to be enjoying myself, but I couldn't truly "feel" many emotions other than anger and sadness. It was like being dead inside except for feeling a deep sense of loss. In the midst of some of life's funniest situations, hilarious jokes, and sentimental situations, my emotions were numb. To survive the constant wounding at home, I'd shut down inside.

Feeling nothing was better than endless pain. I continued to delay coming home after school — any diversion would do. One way to escape my loneliness, hurt, and anger was practicing bulimia. I started bingeing and vomiting food I'd bought at stores and restaurants. I don't know how this gorge-purge habit originated; at the time, I thought it was because I wanted to avoid classmates' comments about my pudginess, maintain a good wrestling weight, and have a better physique.

I also anesthetized difficult feelings with sexual fantasy. As an adolescent I had a precocious interest in the opposite sex. Reading an occasional *Playboy* magazine provided escape from criticism at home. But my compulsive behavior convinced me that I was over-sexed, indeed a disgusting boy, just as the "Big Three" had so often said. I can see now how bulimia and preoccupation with sexual thoughts were external pacifiers, substitutes for feeling loved.

I wondered whether having been sexually exploited by Mom and Gram had robbed me of normal youthful sex exploration. I concluded that my loss of sexual innocence had blunted the excitement of discoveries about women. When classmates giggled about girls' figures or what it might be like to have sex, I laughed with them. Inwardly, however, I tensed with sadness, knowing I'd already experienced a lot of what they'd been talking about.

Mental health specialists note that one of the lesser consequences of being sexually molested is that most abused children grow up

believing that they are *bad*. I suffered an irrational fear of being exposed as a fraud: *If you knew the real me, the one whose mother had done sexual things with him, you'd never want me as a friend.* I worried constantly that someone might discover and reveal my "secret." I continually felt I was hiding something about myself: a deep, awful, indefinable stain; finally, in junior high, I realized that it was mainly the sexual abuse by my mother. I yearned desperately to tell someone about my "badness," but I was terrified of rejection. It was exhausting having to pretend I was a nice guy while thinking I was really a phony. Guarding this enigmatic inner badness was hell — and terribly lonely.

I felt that Mom's unhappiness and deteriorating health were my fault. Time after time she blamed me for all that was wrong in her life, manipulating me into feeling guilty so I would help her. I think she actually enjoyed making me feel responsible for her problems, and marinating in the role of self-pitying martyr. "See this lump in my neck, Jimmy? The doctor says it's probably cancer. I'll have to have surgery soon, but you and your father don't care what happens to me. You're both stubborn and selfish. If this is cancer, it's because of all the heartache you've brought me. I hope you'll get what's coming to you someday."

It was never clear how real her injuries were. *Is her lump really a cancer, or is she exaggerating or lying again to get my sympathy? Why's she always blaming me for her problems? I'm not old enough to drive her to the hospital. I can't make Dad pay more attention to her. What can I do?*

In addition to the dozens of times Mom whined about Dad's cheapness and what a poor father he was, through my college years, she threatened to kill herself a number of times, saying things like, "Jimmy, you and your father have driven me to the end of my rope. I can't take it anymore. Since no one cares what happens to me, you'll be better off without me. I don't want to live like this. When I'm gone, then you'll wake up and see how much I've really done for you, and how little your father has. You'll soon see how selfish you've been. Then how will you feel?"

She switched from threatening to tell my friends, coaches, and others about my shortcomings to actually telling them. I never knew whom she told or what she'd said. Periodically, a classmate or an adult would ask, "Hey Jimmy, still causing trouble for your mother?"

Her comments to others induced me to withdraw from my classmates, coaches, and teachers. Apart from classes and sports practices, I associated mainly with the same three friends, but I was on guard even with them, in case Mom's words had soured them on me. As a result, I spent more and more free time alone, solitude my closest companion.

Since I got no allowance, I picked up odd jobs to earn spending money. In spring I spaded gardens for neighbors. In summer I mowed lawns, caddied at the Penn State Golf Course, and sold lemonade I'd made and golf balls I'd found (and sometimes stolen). During the fall, I raked leaves off people's lawns and collected soft-drink bottles for money at Penn State football games. In winter I shoveled snow from walks and driveways.

In eighth grade I took up ham radio as a hobby and read several books and magazines on it. I built a receiver and transmitter, installed a twenty-five-foot-tall antenna in our backyard, and asked Mom and Dad for permission to buy a newer receiver if I earned the thirty-eight dollars. Both agreed. I was thrilled and worked hard after school and weekends. Finally, with the full amount in hand, and proud of my accomplishment, I showed them the money.

Mom glared. "No, you certainly can't buy that radio. It's too expensive. You don't know enough about them. You'll probably just get mad and break it like you do all your toys." As usual, Dad caved in, mumbling, "Jimmy, you know how useless it is to argue with your mother. Just use your money for something else." Another broken promise.

At last, when I turned fourteen, I stopped bedwetting and defecating in my pants, which had been a source of endless embarrassment for me. Many experts believe these behaviors stem from either

sexual abuse or a severely dysfunctional home. In my case, it was probably both.

Betsy received as much negative treatment and verbal abuse from Mom and Gram as I did, maybe more. The Queens bugged her to develop a hobby: "You need to keep busy with some kind of activity, Betsy. Why don't you try sewing? We'll help you." After much badgering, Betsy decided to try it. Gram and Grandpa bought her a new Singer sewing machine and paid for her to attend a special sewing class. Betsy seemed pleased at the attention showered on her. She sewed beautiful dresses, skirts, and blouses. Initially, Mom and Gram paid for the fabrics and other items. Soon, Betsy began paying for almost all her projects.

Then, the "Twin Critics" dripped their poison: "You shouldn't be tackling such advanced patterns. You're spending far too much money on fabrics, and squandering our money and yours. You ought to be ashamed for being so self-centered. You're wasting too much time sewing when you could be helping your mother around the house."

Like Dad and me, Betsy couldn't win with those two angry women. Even when we tried to play by their rules, they'd change them. *Nobody* could please Mom or Gram except, perhaps, Bob; most of the time he could do no wrong, probably because he was the youngest.

That summer, Mom browbeat Dad into vacationing in Florida. This was exciting news. In Pennsylvania, you had to be sixteen to get a driver's license. Florida's laws lowered the age, so I was eligible! After passing the driver's exam, I flew out the door, temporary license in hand. Mom let me drive most of the rest of our trip. I was thrilled, but only for a short time. Sadly, my newfound accomplishment was stained by her exhorting Dad to sit in the back seat with Betsy and Bobby while she or I drove: "You drive too slowly, Randy. You're like a little old lady. You'll cause an accident. We'll never make good time with you driving, so Jimmy and I will drive."

I cringed at Mom's disrespectfulness of Dad in front of us kids. She seemed so cruel, disdain for him seeping out of her like sewage from a broken pipe. I hurt for him and wished he'd tell her off

or even slap her face. I thought, *Where are your guts, Dad? Don't take that. Put her in her place. Make her treat you with civility. Force her to show you respect, especially in front of your kids.*

During the spring of eighth grade, Mom's verbal attacks on Dad intensified. I was awakened many nights by their arguing. Finally, around May, Mom announced to us, "I've had it with your father. I can't stay here any longer." Then she said to Betsy and Bob, "As soon as school's out, I'm taking you to live with me in Pittsburgh. We'll rent a small apartment in the basement of your Uncle Jim's office building. I'll get a job teaching at an elementary school nearby."

Then, half-pleading, half-seething, her eyes piercing mine, she hissed, "I suppose you'll want to stay here in State College with your father, Jimmy. You've always sided with him. I can't control you; maybe he can, but I doubt it — he can't make a decision about anything. But if you'll promise never again to misbehave, you can come with me and your brother and sister. What do you want to do?"

I winced like someone who'd been punched in the stomach. It felt like she had already decided to reject me. My mind whirled with confusion, sadness, anger, and guilt. *I've finally blown it. I've failed to get Dad to give her more money. My actions, my temper, have worsened their marriage. Now Mom has written me off as her enemy and given up on me for good.*

The only answer I could give her was, "Let me think it over, Mom. I want to talk with Dad first." When Dad trudged home from work, I cornered him in his study.

"Mom says she's leaving you this week and taking Betsy and Bob with her to live in Pittsburgh. She wants me do decide whether to go with her or stay here with you. What do you want me to do?"

"Your mother's been threatening this for a long time, Jimmy. It breaks my heart that she feels she has to do it but there's nothing I can do to stop her. You know that when she makes up her mind about something she won't let go of it. Obviously, she'll need you there to help with Betsy and Bob. But I need you too. If you stay with me, we can cook, take hikes, and go to football games together. I'll understand, though, if you decide to go with her."

Then he hugged me and convulsed into loud sobs. I didn't know what to do, so I just stood there helplessly and hugged him. "It'll be OK, Dad. Everything's going to work out all right." He kept sobbing.

"I can't abandon Dad. He needs me, Mom."

"OK, have it your way, Jimmy."

I remember phone conversations with Mom and Gram, both of them trashing Dad and trying to persuade me to go with Mom. In the end, I decided to remain with him, mostly out of pity because he was the underdog.

Once I made my choice, however, I got "both barrels" from Mom's side of the family. Grandpa said little, but Gram and Unc gave me their disappointed looks and guilt-inducing words: "Jimmy, you know you're breaking your mother's heart by choosing to stay with your father. How can you do this to her, to your brother and sister? After all she's done for you, how can you turn on your own mother?"

All I could do was mumble to Mom, "I'm sorry, but I've got to go with Dad to help him. I can still visit you and Betsy and Bob."

During my talks with her on the phone I got the same angry accusations. "Very well, then, have it your way," she replied stiffly. "After all my sacrifices you've chosen to stay with your father! You've made your bed, now lie in it. Don't expect any kind of support from me ever again, or from Unc, or your grandparents. I've tried so hard to keep you out of trouble, out of reform school, out of prison. You know your father won't be able to control you. You'll be sorry. You're just an ungrateful son. I give up on you!"

Later that summer I took a bus to Pittsburgh to visit Mom, Betsy, and Bob. As arranged, Unc met me at the downtown bus station. "Hi Jimmy. I need to make a brief business stop. It's only a few miles out of our way. Won't take but a few minutes. Do you mind?" The next thing I knew, he'd tricked me into going with him to meet with a social worker at an Allegheny County juvenile court facility. He took me to one of the upper floors where, with two armed policemen outside the office door, a caseworker lectured

me. "I understand you're a real hell-raiser at home, and the main cause of your family's problems. Were it not for you, your parents might not be split up. Your relatives say they've given up trying to control you, that you're incorrigible."

I felt absolutely abandoned, sold out, by Unc, Mom, and Gram. The ache of having everyone give up on me was like an icicle stabbed through my heart. Now they'd pulled out all the stops and called in the cops to put me in reform school. I was on my way to prison, just as they'd predicted.

Behind my mask of teenage bravado was a terror-stricken, enraged kid in a one-hundred-eighty-pound body. My mind whirled, *What a set-up! I thought Unc cared about me. Why'd he betray me like this? Mom and Gram must have conspired with him. Could Dad be in on it too? I'll never trust any of them again. Will they try to lock me up in this place? How can I get out of here?* I tried to foresee what might happen. I squinted, looking for exits and stairs. My hope gone, I mentally rehearsed what I might have to do in the next few seconds.

"Consider this your last warning, young man. Next time I hear you've messed up, I'll have police officers come to arrest you. You'll be taken from your family and sentenced to a reform school till you're eighteen. Then, if you haven't turned around, it'll be prison. Understand me?"

I nodded, hoping he and Unc and the cops wouldn't see my panic and white-hot rage. The policemen just stood there, never saying a word. I was lightheaded. My legs turned to rubber as Unc and I walked out to his car. No mention of what had just happened, other than, "Those people really mean business, Jimmy. You'd better watch your step from now on." Then our conversation turned to fishing, hunting, and football. He added, "If you decide to stay here with your mom, brother, and sister, you can work part-time for me, cleaning up around my offices and mowing our lawn at home. Let me know."

I thought, *They're right. I'm as bad as they say. I know I misbehave, but I really do try to be good. God, where are You? I can't feel*

You here. Why don't You speak to me? Why'd You birth me if You knew I'd be such a mean person? Have You given up on me, too? Are You out to get me? I guess so, 'cause You certainly could've stepped in and prevented this from happening.

When we arrived at Mom's basement apartment, Gram was there too, Mom unsmiling, Gram's face a disgusted scowl. Neither reached out to hug me. I had to take the first steps toward them. Both stood rigid as fence posts when I hugged them; they didn't even kiss me.

For the next three days, the Queens repeatedly chastised, "How spiteful you are, Jimmy. Staying with your father has hurt us and your grandpa and Uncle Jim terribly. We don't think we'll ever forgive you for the hurt your disloyalty has caused us. Don't you ever think of anyone but yourself? Don't ever come to any of us for anything again." That evening I told them I still intended to stay with Dad. After that, they barely talked to me the rest of the time I was there. For months to come, their coldness was evident in our phone conversations.

In addition to taking Betsy and Bob to live in Pittsburgh for a year, Mom left at least ten more times during and after my high school years. She always told Gram, Unc, and others that Dad and I were the reason for her being "forced to leave." In the years ahead, she lived a martyr-like existence by herself in New York, Florida, South Carolina, and elsewhere.

That fall, school became bearable, thanks to football, which began in late August, and wrestling in November. I started as a tackle on the junior high football team. Things seemed to become somewhat amicable between Mom and Dad, so he and I took the bus to Pittsburgh to share Thanksgiving with Mom, Betsy, and Bob.

That year I prayed over and over for God to get Mom and Dad back together. One afternoon, I was walking along some snow-covered streetcar tracks on the hill across from Gram's place. God seemed very close. I thanked Him for finally reuniting my parents. Unfortunately, the awareness of His presence was short-lived, as the truce ended within a few months. We children knew that Mom and Dad were patching things up merely for our sake. Mom

soon resumed her quarreling with Dad, and from then until I was in my thirties, they continued their on-and-off warfare.

By the time I entered my sophomore year at State College High School, I'd exercised off most of my adolescent chunkiness, and started at tackle for the junior varsity football team. The recognition was great for my delicate ego. Yet, despite my status as a football player, I still hung around with only a few friends. I lacked confidence talking with girls, thinking I wasn't handsome or clever like most of the class leaders.

Chapter 9

Guidance Issues

GRAM AND GRANDPA STEVENSON REMARKED several times how detrimental they thought our home situation was for me. Because my grades were only B's and C's, and my parents battled constantly, they felt it would be best for me to leave home and go to a military prep school. They began the task of convincing Mom, then Dad.

I'm sure they were thinking of my best interests in extricating me from domestic conflict. They also wanted to halt my "troublemaking," and prepare me for a career. It would mean big financial sacrifices on their part to pay my school expenses. They persuaded Mom, then hounded Dad to concur. At last, against his will, they coerced him to go along with their plan for me to attend Admiral Farragut Academy in St. Petersburg, Florida for my last two years of high school.

They thought Betsy didn't need a private-school education, but felt that Bob and I, as males, should be equipped with good study

habits if we were to succeed in college and afterward. Like most people of that era, Gram and Grandpa believed that the only career for a woman was to be a teacher, nurse, or secretary.

I had mixed feelings about the decision. There wasn't a single impartial adult with whom I could discuss my concerns, because I was afraid people would go back on their word and tell Mom or Gram of my misgivings. Few of my classmates knew anything about private or military schools, so, had I asked them, they would probably have advised me to remain in State College.

It bothered me to leave Betsy and Bob in the sour home environment. I was anxious about whether they could cope with Mom's ranting at Dad. The thought of leaving my friends and having to make new ones was scary. *What will the students at Farragut be like? Spoiled, cliquish rich kids?* I'd worked hard to improve at football and wrestling, and looked forward to being a starter on the State College High School varsity football and wrestling teams. Farragut didn't even have a wrestling team. *Will I do well in football there?*

I hated pretending to be excited about going to Farragut, when in fact I felt strong-armed into transferring, but once Dad surrendered, I realized it was useless to battle everyone. I began shifting gears for the upcoming life change.

In August, at the start of my junior year, I left my family, friends, and familiar surroundings to ride a bus nearly twelve hundred miles south to St. Petersburg. I arrived for fall football practice several days before classes started. Leaving State College wasn't as difficult as I'd imagined. Actually, it was a welcome relief to get away from Mom's criticism and the disharmony at home. A fifty-pound sack fell off my sixteen-year-old shoulders; never once did I get homesick! Almost from my first day at Farragut, I felt at home. What a reassuring experience to live with fair, firm rules, something I desperately craved.

I'd always believed Dad loved me, but since his return from Illinois I felt he also resented me. Each summer, when I left State College to stay with Gram and Grandpa Stevenson or attended church camps, I'd sense his displeasure, which he confirmed by

his facial expressions and comments.

With hard work, I earned a starting position at tackle, but I had no respect for the head coach's knowledge of the game and his coaching style. Paradoxically, I idolized his two assistants, who were just the opposite of him and felt the same way about him as I did.

One assistant coach had retired with forty years' experience in head coaching jobs. The other had taken the job at Farragut as an interim position while looking for a top coach opportunity. Both had encyclopedic football knowledge. They taught and lived with integrity, and the whole team liked and respected them.

My self-esteem skyrocketed due to the recognition I got from players, students, and teachers. Academically, my grades were in the B range. I studied just enough to get by, was selected to be a low-ranking cadet officer, and enjoyed the popularity of being elected class secretary. I loved my two years at Farragut, except for the daily inspections and parades and the loneliness I endured. I hate to think where I would be had I not gone there. It wasn't an overly strict military school as such places go, and it offered solid academic preparation. Farragut was a genuine period of restoration for me.

Dad didn't attend my graduation. What could have been a landmark occasion for me was again tainted with sadness, regret, and shame, because I knew that in attending Farragut I'd sided with Mom and her relatives against Dad. As usual it was a no-win situation, another bittersweet experience.

In retrospect, I think my mood swings started at Farragut. Most teenagers experience fluctuating emotions. I had a pattern: every four to six weeks I'd feel energized, cheerful, and extra-friendly. The whole world seemed wonderful; my brain raced from one thought to another, one plan to the next. During the "gusto" weeks, I accomplished three times as much work as during my "off" times. Oddly, on even my best days, when everything went right athletically, in the classroom, and with friends, I had a sense of impending calamity.

Then, predictably, I'd crash — no energy, no enthusiasm, just blah. At the time, I was aware of these regular occurrences, but

figured it was normal, how I functioned best. Regrettably, those cycles were the beginning of worse to come.

I stayed close to Farragut throughout the school year, except for going home at Christmastime. Gram and Grandpa Stevenson left the cold Pittsburgh weather in November to live in an apartment in downtown St. Petersburg until late April. Their place was a half-hour bus ride from Farragut. I usually spent weekends and other holidays with them, or alone, working out at the YMCA, going to movies, or jogging on the beach. Since my finances were minimal, I couldn't go to most of the restaurants and other places my classmates went. Once again, I existed as a lonely stranger in the crowd.

All my life I had disliked my body, believing I was overweight even when I was, in fact, trim. In weightlifting rooms or in pickup basketball games, I rarely went without a shirt. I wore my sweat suits and other clothes baggy rather than a regular fit. Some therapists thought this was due to my having been molested. That summer, against Dad's wishes, Mom bought me my first car, a beat-up old green Plymouth. This would normally be a big deal for any high school student, but Dad's opposition diminished the fun and replaced it with a sense of having betrayed his wishes.

Early in my junior year at Farragut, I found temporary relief from stress and boredom by bingeing and purging again. Far from home, isolated, and spending much of my spare cash on food, I gorged at every opportunity. I hid the habit well, doing it at least once a day and many times on weekends. Feeling full and not wanting to gain weight, I hid in the bathroom of my dorm room, and restrooms of restaurants, department stores, or wherever else seemed safe. Then, I stuck my finger down my throat until I gagged and vomited.

Often, I'd repeat this a dozen times in a half-hour period, until my stomach felt empty, then I'd go right out, eat more, return, and vomit again. Except for a few weeks, I probably binged and purged eight or more times a week over the years. I kept up this practice until I was forty-three years old. I'd never heard of the serious eating disorder, bulimia, until well into my ministerial career. At

that time only a few Hollywood celebrities who struggled with it had gone public.

My mischief more than made up for Farragut's military strictness. I short-sheeted classmates' beds, filled their shoes with shaving cream, put popcorn and peanut shells between their bed sheets, rolled marbles down the aisles in physics class, put live goldfish in the commandant's water pitcher, and pulled numerous other pranks.

During visits home, Mom appeared to be in a sad, detached fog much of the time. Increasingly, she seemed to be pulling into herself and withdrawing from everyone. It felt extremely awkward, even disgusting, to be around her, because her body odor got so bad that I literally had to hold my breath to hug her.

Any time I complimented her, she'd either say nothing or change the subject. When opening the gifts I gave her, she responded in an automatic monotone, "Well, thank you. That's very nice" or, "Oh, you shouldn't have done that." All my attempts to reach out to her, to express love, seemed to hit brick walls.

I worked out hard in the summer before my senior year, looking forward to my last year of high school football. I'd been elected team co-captain. Various sportscasters had picked me as a probable Florida all-state player. Lamentably, in one of our early fall practices, I injured my right knee and was out for the entire season. The injury shattered my hopes of all-state recognition and ended my dreams of playing for a major university of my choice.

Numerous colleges that had previously contacted me learned of the extent of my knee damage and withdrew their football scholarship offers. My options kept shrinking; remaining opportunities were Miami of Ohio, Baylor, Miami in Florida, and Penn State University. I decided against Miami of Ohio because it was too small, Baylor and Miami in Florida because of the hot, humid weather.

In the midst of my decision making, there was another family feud. Dad wanted me to attend Penn State. The "Big Three" wanted me to go to the University of Pittsburgh because Grandpa and Unc had gone there. They also believed that doing my undergraduate work there would make it easier to get into Pitt's medical

school. I'd long dreamed of being a pediatric surgeon.

I would have loved to go to Penn State, but fearing that sooner or later Mom would start badmouthing me to the coaches, I turned it down. The University of Pittsburgh seemed like the best option. It had a fine medical school and, because Grandpa Stevenson had gone there, I believed his influence might help me get accepted.

I was offered only partial financial aid. I weighed the pros and cons and finally opted to attend Pitt, believing I could quickly prove myself and earn a full scholarship after the first football season. In fall of 1960 I entered Pitt's pre-med program. Our freshman football team was loaded with talent and went undefeated, but having missed my senior year of high school playing experience, my confidence was shaky and my performance reflected it.

Chapter 10

A Spiritual Awakening

DURING THAT FIRST SEASON AT PITT, Bob Long and two other football players invited me to Fellowship of Christian Athletes (FCA) meetings. Different speakers came to a large dorm room each week and talked about their faith in Jesus Christ. I had never heard anyone speak about Him the way they did. Being a skeptic, I read a dozen books on Christianity and other religions. Some months later I decided to open my life to Jesus and accept by faith that He had been executed for my wrongs. I asked Him to take over leadership of my life. That was the start of my spiritual awakening. No goose pimples, no dramatic feelings of religious euphoria, but I noticed a gradual shifting of my attitudes, priorities, and self-esteem. For the first time, I began to like myself and to see

meaning and purpose in events.

As a new follower of Christ, I had limited knowledge of Christianity. Undaunted, I began teaching a Bible study for a few of my fraternity brothers. I also taught a Sunday school class of Afro-American fifth-graders in a small storefront church in the Hill District of Pittsburgh. As a new Christian, I believed my life could be best used to help people by being a doctor, so I continued in the pre-med program.

Also that September, my brother Bob was sent to Farragut, and Betsy enrolled at Penn State. Bob attended there from seventh through twelfth grades, excelling academically and athletically, and he avoided many of the damaging effects of living in our "house of horrors" during his six years away. Betsy lived at home all that time and couldn't escape the debilitating environment.

After freshman football season ended, I began working out in a nearby gym and noticed a man coaching a fighter in the upstairs boxing ring. I watched, intrigued. This could be a great way to stay in shape for spring football. I introduced myself and asked, "Would it be OK if I used your heavy bag for a while?"

"Of course." After I'd pounded at the bag for a few minutes, he introduced himself and asked, "Jimmy, how'd you like to fight in some Golden Glove tournaments coming up this spring? You've got good speed and power, but you've got a lot to learn about boxing. I'd love to be your manager."

"Thanks, but let me think about it." Two days later, I decided to try boxing as a conditioning method for football. Some weeks later, he had me sparring with seasoned amateur fighters as well as professionals.

My manager provided the technical know-how and inspirational stories from his professional boxing career as a light-heavyweight contender. He inundated me in affirmation. Even before the tournaments began, he started encouraging me to turn pro. He had met with ten influential businessmen and several key politicians who would back me financially if I did. They knew I wanted to remain in college and go on to medical school, so they wanted to

bill me as "The Fighting Medic." They planned to pay all my education expenses and give me a salary and a sizable cut of my winnings.

That winter, I went undefeated and won Golden Glove novice heavyweight championships in Steubenville, Ohio, and Pittsburgh. A number of my opponents had fought many more fights than I had, and later turned pro.

After the Golden Glove fights, my manager wanted to groom me for the professional ranks. He stepped up the workouts and sparring sessions with pros and experienced amateurs in the Pittsburgh area. After winning at the Pittsburgh Golden Gloves Tournament, my next fight was AAU-sponsored (Amateur Athletics Union). He, and Bob Long, and Unc were my corner men. Unfortunately, my undefeated record ended with that fight; I lost the bout in a close decision. Still, this didn't slow down my manager's or my eagerness to pursue a professional boxing career while I studied to be a doctor.

Bob Long became my best friend. He lived across the dorm hall from me, and played end on the football team. In the coming years, he became my companion in fun times and comforter in bad ones. For two college summers we worked with teenage gangs on New York City's Lower East Side and in Harlem.

Pitt football players were assigned alumni sponsors who acted as mentors and provided encouragement. Mine was a general surgeon. He invited me to "scrub" with him, holding instruments and assisting in a wide variety of surgeries. I assisted him and his team two days a week for nearly two years, in dozens of operations — every pre-med student's dream!

After a few months, however, the initial excitement of participating in surgery wore off. I discovered I needed to interact with people on a more personal level. At the same time, I found that even with my best efforts, I had a rough time with chemistry. As I looked to my future, I began wondering whether I really wanted to put up with all the hours required to get top grades for medical school admission, much less the amount of study needed to stay current in a medical practice.

I decided to forgo spring football practice in my freshman year to concentrate on extra training for another AAU fight scheduled for May. Several factors influenced me: my performance in freshman football was mediocre, and because I wasn't on full scholarship, I felt I wasn't given the attention that full-scholarship players received. I was extremely disappointed and saw a limited football future at Pitt. And, I had a lucrative offer to pay for my education by boxing professionally, so I wouldn't need football's financial help.

One afternoon in April, Unc took me to lunch. "Jimmy, you've done a great job in all your fights, but let's face it, you're still inexperienced. There are a lot of fighters who could whip you. Your mother, grandmother, grandpa, and I don't want to see you get hurt. You could be permanently brain damaged. We want you to quit. Why risk it when you've got a medical career ahead of you? Cancel this next match and end this boxing fancy of yours right now or you'll never get a penny of support from us. Nor will you get any of Grandpa's backing for medical school. Think about it. We only want what's best for you."

I felt like I'd been sandbagged yet again by someone close to me who didn't believe in me. "I'll have to think about it, Unc."

The next few days, I bounced my options off my manager and others. Finally, I gritted my teeth and phoned Unc. "I guess you're right. I'll put medical studies ahead of boxing."

"Congratulations. I knew you'd come to your senses and do the right thing."

Over the years, I had met only a few people who really listened to and affirmed me, but I couldn't open up to them. After all, those closest to me had repeatedly misunderstood, maligned, threatened, and betrayed me. To keep from being emotionally destroyed, I always had to be on guard, looking for others' hidden agendas. I couldn't take people at face value. My experience with Mom and Gram's sexual betrayals and Mom's track record of broken promises had left me wary. I was an outgoing person who made friends easily, but the trust was one-sided: others could rely on me, but I

couldn't truly trust them. The word "trust" was purely an intellectual concept to me.

Up to this point, only six people had given me solid encouragement: a junior high football coach, two high school assistant coaches, Dad's best friend, my scoutmaster, and Bob Long. Each knew of my rocky home situation and offered support if I needed it. Moreover, they routinely affirmed my strengths both as an athlete and a young man. But as much as I liked and respected them, I was afraid to discuss my home situation, lest my words would be misunderstood and I'd be rejected.

For Phys. Ed., I was taking a wrestling class taught by the head coach of Pitt's nationally ranked wrestling team. After the second class, he approached me. "Stout, I like your moves. You'd be a great addition to our team. How about joining us? If you do well, I can get you some scholarship help."

That week I started practicing with the team. I loved the conditioning, the contact, the moves, and the strategizing. For not having wrestled on a team since ninth grade, I did far better than I could have imagined. By the end of the season, though, it was obvious that while I could start at many major universities, my wrestling talent wasn't of the tops-in-the-nation caliber of many of my teammates.

In the spring of my sophomore year, I phoned one of my Farragut assistant football coaches. Previously, he'd tried to persuade me to go to his alma mater, Miami University, in Oxford, Ohio. He'd repeatedly told me, "Jim, I know you've got offers to play at larger colleges, but Miami plays topnotch football too, including one or two Big Ten teams each season. Miami's known as the 'cradle of coaches.' You'll easily make their varsity. I know you're headed for medicine, but I think you'd make an excellent coach. What better training could you get than at Miami? You can definitely get a scholarship there. Why not try it?" While at Farragut, I'd turned down his advice because I'd wanted to play at a big "name" college.

He listened attentively as I poured out my frustrations about football and boxing. Then he repeated his wish to see me attend

Miami of Ohio. "Jim, if you're open to it, I'll call Miami's head football coach to see if they want you to play there." I agreed. The next evening, Miami's head coach phoned, offering me a football scholarship starting that fall. I accepted.

NCAA (National Collegiate Athletic Association) rules required all transferring athletes to sit out a year before becoming eligible for varsity sports. The coach wanted me to play with the freshman team that fall to learn his system. I started several games, but injured my right knee in practice. A week later I had surgery and was out for the season. The next year, the coach resigned and a new one was hired.

The summer following my junior year at Miami, I did volunteer work with Young Life, a Christian organization that specialized in reaching high school students who were non-churched, that is, unaffiliated with any church. Bob Long and I joined several others to do social work, coach a football team, and lead Bible studies with teen gangs on New York City's Lower East Side. We lived in a tenement apartment with several gang members. Day and night we hung out with tough young men, going to movies, playing stickball, basketball, wrestling, and boxing with them. At the end of summer, I returned home ready to relax for a week, then head off to fall football camp at Miami of Ohio.

A few minutes after arriving, Mom dropped a bomb on me. As was her custom, she stood waiting for me to come to her. As I hugged her, she stood rigid. Immediately, I knew something bad was about to happen. She greeted me with a sarcastic, "Glad you've finally come home. I hope you feel proud of yourself for leaving me here with your father and Betsy and Bob. You certainly haven't shown any responsibility, going off with your friends to have fun in New York City, not earning a cent this summer.

"Since I'm no longer wanted at this house by you or your father, I'm leaving this week. I've got teaching offers from schools in Utica, New York and several other places. I'm not sure where I'll go. It doesn't matter to you, anyway. You'll not know where I'm going or how long I'll be gone. Maybe someday you'll see what

suffering you've caused your mother."

Suddenly, I lost all feeling. My mind raced, *Mom gave me permission to work with those gangs. If she really wanted me to stay home, why didn't she just say so? Besides, what more could I have done for her this summer, other than remain in State College to hear her complaints and referee between her and Dad?*

Wrongfully accused, deeply hurt, I smoldered with resentment. I began making plans that night not to return for Miami's fall football camp, and to drop out of school for a year and get a job. Since Mom had written me off and had badmouthed me to everyone, I decided not to tell anyone about my decision. The next morning, I awoke early, packed, and left the house, telling everyone I was going back to school.

For the next two months, I lived off my savings, traveling to Cleveland, Ohio by bus. I landed a job selling life insurance for a national company. All the while, I was depressed, angry, guilty, and terribly lonely.

Somehow, Unc found me. He confronted me in the bank where I'd gone to withdraw money to buy a car for my job. "Jimmy, if you drop out of school, I'll never back you in anything again. Don't ever come to me for help if you leave Miami. Think about it."

I knew he loved me, but as usual it was "my way or else." Then he added, "How about talking over your decision with your Grandma's minister? You've attended his church many times. I'm sure he'll give you some good advice." I nodded and Unc drove me to the church.

The pastor was a warm, gracious man and a caring listener. He sat silently as I poured out my heartache about Mom's accusations, confiding things I'd never told anyone else. He assured me of his belief in me, and of God's love for me, and encouraged me to return to college. He told me he'd support me no matter what I chose. His loving acceptance clinched my decision to return to Miami. When Unc picked me up, I told him what I'd decided. He gave me some money for travel expenses and food, and put me on a bus to the campus that afternoon.

I arrived at my dorm room, unpacked, and had a lengthy conversation with my roommate about my absence from classes and football practice. A fellow lineman, he seemed to understand. Next, I made a dreaded phone call to the head coach. His secretary gave me an appointment to meet with him the next afternoon. I agonized: *Would he verbally shred me for missing camp? Would he take away my scholarship?*

The hands of my watch crawled in slow motion. No way did I want to face the music. Finally, the secretary ushered me into his office. "Glad you're here, Jim. Tell me what happened."

I explained the work I'd done with teenagers in New York and about Mom's leaving Dad and blaming me. He listened without interrupting, then said, "Jim, don't worry about your scholarship, it's still yours. No one will take it away from you. I still want you to play for us. You'll have a lot of catching up to do, but I believe you can contribute to the team. Do you want to start back this late in the season, or wait till spring and start then?"

I was deeply moved by his sensitivity and generosity. "Thanks, Coach. You'll never know what this means to me. I don't want to let you and the team down, but patching things up with my family will take awhile. I'd rather start working out for the varsity wrestling team later this fall, then come back in top shape for spring football practice."

"No problem. You have my full backing. Let me know if I can be of any help with your parents." I almost danced with relief as I left his office.

That fall, I started for the varsity wrestling team in the 191-pound class. My first match took place in a multi-team tournament at Ohio State University. Unfortunately, I injured my other knee a week later. After another surgery, it took long hours to rehabilitate that knee for spring football. Then, in spring practice, I re-injured the same knee. A third surgery. After my third day in the hospital, the orthopedic surgeon warned, "Jim, if you go back to either football or wrestling, you'll probably never run or walk right again." Those words broke my heart and ended my college athletic career.

During my recuperation, I began attending Inter-Varsity Christian Fellowship meetings at a local Presbyterian church. The Inter-Varsity faculty leader and the Presbyterian pastor spent hours listening to my complaints about being unable to play football or wrestle because of my injuries. They answered my theological questions and taught me how to apply biblical principles to my circumstances.

In the spring of my junior year, I started several small Bible discussion groups with athletes, fraternity and sorority members, and other students. I also recruited fellow athletes to start an FCA group. For our kickoff meeting, I invited three football players from Ohio State to speak. Twenty-five athletes showed up. The response of my teammates and others was better than I'd expected. Gradually, it dawned on me that I thoroughly enjoyed talking with people about their problems and explaining how a personal relationship with God could help them.

Later that year, Grandpa Stevenson died. Mom called me with the news, saying she wanted me to come to Pittsburgh for the funeral. She sent me money for the trip. When I arrived at the funeral home, I saw Grandpa in his casket. Gram was standing next to it, greeting people. I braced myself for her harsh words. As I walked up to hug her, she was true to form and froze like an ice sculpture. A weak smile tried in vain to cross her obviously angry face. "Jimmy, how nice of you to be here. You were Grandpa's favorite grandchild. I hope you know that your leaving Miami and not letting him or your mother or me know where you were for two months absolutely devastated him. You should be ashamed of yourself for treating us that way. No doubt about it, your selfish actions caused Grandpa's death. I hope you'll never do something like that again." Mom barely spoke to me. Finally, after the funeral service, she and Gram warmed up somewhat, but the message was clear: "Don't ever cross us again."

Though Gram had been a positive spiritual influence on me all along, ironically, when I began applying my faith, she tried to block my attempts at spiritual growth and helping others. She strongly opposed my participation in FCA and my summers spent

working with gangs in New York. She vented her opposition to my involvement with Inter-Varsity, the fifth-grade Afro-American Sunday school class I taught, and the numerous small Bible study groups I organized throughout my college career.

After nearly three years of pre-med studies and participating in a variety of Christian activities, I could no longer stay focused on science studies. The initial thrill of surgery had long since worn off, and I concluded that my abilities in chemistry and physics were too lacking for medical school. I began considering other careers: coaching, teaching, and social work. Even entering the ministry crossed my mind, though I quickly dismissed it, thinking I wasn't "holy" enough. Also, because of my limited experience, the thought of working in a church intimidated me. Besides, I believed that churches were outdated, ineffective vehicles for reaching people, especially the younger generation. I preferred the challenges and the intellectual give-and-take of a college ministry in a secular setting.

In my last year at Miami of Ohio, I continued seeking God's guidance for my future. I had no clear "leading" other than a deepening compulsion to tell people about Christ and help them with their problems. As I reasoned through my career options, the next logical step seemed to be enrolling in a theological seminary, so I could learn more about the Bible and how to help people. In the winter of 1965, I applied to and was accepted by both Princeton Theological Seminary, a Presbyterian school in New Jersey, and Gordon-Conwell Theological Seminary, an interdenominational institution in South Hamilton, Massachusetts.

Gram protested my attending a non-Presbyterian seminary. She marshaled her "clergy SWAT team" to persuade me that Princeton was the only way to go. After visiting both campuses and having lengthy discussions with many people, I chose Gordon-Conwell. Strangely, Unc, who was not much of a churchgoer, generously helped me with a lot of my expenses.

The autumn of my senior year at Miami, a fraternity brother set me up with a blind date, Leah Hayden. She was absolutely

stunning! Although attracted to her beauty, I was immediately drawn to her personality, her intellect, her spiritual hunger, and her practical, down-to-earth qualities. It felt like I'd known her all my life. We dated steadily for the next two and a half years.

Several months prior to graduation from Miami, the campus chaplains offered me the job of associate campus chaplain, working with students. I accepted, continued leading the Bible studies I'd already begun, and started new ones. The greatest thing that came out of that half year, however, was the thrill of meeting Leah!

In September 1965 I entered Gordon-Conwell Seminary. Bob Long and I roomed together as resident advisors in one of the Gordon College dorms. We bought motorcycles and tore through the multicolored New England countryside together. We body-boxed several times a week; my thumbs were continually sprained from glancing off his elbows.

Fear of rejection and betrayal continued plaguing me. It wasn't until Gordon-Conwell days that I risked becoming vulnerable, sharing some of my family background, guilt, fears, and resentments. For the first time in my life there was someone I could trust. Bob affirmed my skills and accomplishments. Above all, he helped me believe in myself. I reciprocated in similar ways, often joking him out of his anxieties over Greek and Hebrew. Sometimes, for hours at a time, he and I talked about our hopes, struggles, challenges, doubts, and failures.

We played tricks on unwitting victims, cracked jokes and laughed hilariously like little boys. We played racquetball, watched boxing and wrestling matches. We also ran two triathlons, a half-marathon and a practice marathon together. Some of our classmates thought we were just two happy-go-lucky, dumb ex-jocks, not spiritual enough to make decent ministers. In the years ahead, our families vacationed together in North Carolina during our children's youth.

My binge-and-purge addiction continued throughout the seminary years. It provided a workable way to maintain my college weight, and allowed me to eat anything I wanted, in any amount. I little suspected its harmful, potentially lethal, consequences. I

kept saying, "This is the last time I'll do this." But it wasn't.

Seminary experience involved far more than academic courses. Besides formal studies, I served as an intern with college students at Tremont Temple, a large Baptist church in downtown Boston. Our group included students from Harvard, MIT, Boston University, and other area colleges.

That May, Mom phoned, wanting me to accompany her to Bob's graduation from Farragut. He'd become the highest-ranking cadet officer and received numerous awards for leadership. I was immensely proud of him. Throughout our two-day drive to Florida, I couldn't get rid of a creepy feeling traveling with Mom. We needed to spend the night in a motel en route to Florida. As we entered the motel's driveway, my skin crawled.

As we unpacked, she undressed and put on a faded tan nightgown. She never said anything suggestive, just lit one cigarette after another and swigged down soft drinks. Fortunately, there were two beds. I was vigilant all evening and hardly slept that night.

Though Mom and Dad never divorced, they had a turbulent relationship for over thirty-five years, with a dozen separations by the time I graduated. From seminary days on, every time I visited them, my emotions shut down instantly. After being with Dad, it took me weeks to process my sadness and frustration. Following visits to Mom, it took even longer to overcome anger, depression, and the sense of culpability. Yet, I always hoped they'd somehow find a way to get back together.

The first two summers at Gordon, I dug ditches for a road construction company, sweated on a septic tank truck crew, interned at two churches, and sold kitchen knives. During my second year, I participated in several other ministries in addition to my course work. One was an internship at West Congregational Church. It was a varied learning experience that involved starting a Bible study with a dozen men, visiting sick members, teaching an adult Sunday school class, assisting in the pulpit, and helping with other pastoral duties. Also, I organized a high school youth group in Danvers, a town about six miles from the seminary.

As part of the Gordon education, I took a half-year clinical pastoral education course, which consisted of lectures on counseling methods and participation in small group sessions. An integral part of the course was work as a student chaplain to the men's violent ward at Danvers State Mental Hospital.

Though I'd taken counseling courses and done extensive reading in psychology, mental illness remained only an abstract condition to me. I knew little about schizophrenia, and had never heard of bipolar disorder or manic depression. I realized that some people became depressed and suicidal, but I was ignorant of clinical depression and its symptoms.

During Christmas vacation of my second year at Gordon, Leah and I became engaged. To earn enough money to get married the next summer, I took time off to work in a leather factory and with a linoleum contractor. Leah and I married in Cleveland, Ohio on June 24, 1967.

A dark cloud hovered over the excitement of our wedding. Mom (who was again separated from Dad) and Gram obstinately refused to let us know if they would attend. Just before the rehearsal, they showed up unannounced. Both acted civil, but were equally cold, wearing forced smiles to mask their indignation at Dad. I'm sure Gram had convinced Mom to overcome her animosity and attend the wedding. I overheard her saying to Mom, "Alice, for the sake of your children, you've got to be here. Just be polite." I was relieved they'd come, but Leah and I were continually on guard lest they do something to trouble the festivities. Except for stressing over Mom and Gram, our wedding was a storybook experience.

Unquestionably, Mom was severely mentally ill. One of the places to which she'd exiled herself was Buford, South Carolina, where she taught school and lived in a small mobile home that reeked of dog urine and cigarette smoke. Even though she lived hundreds of miles away, I still feared she would try to control my life.

Part Three

Job Happiness, Stresses and Horrors

By the sweat of your brow you will eat your food.
— Genesis 3:19

Chapter 11

Church Opportunities and Issues

AFTER GRADUATION FROM GORDON-CONWELL in June 1969, I accepted the position of assistant pastor at the Key Biscayne Presbyterian Church in Key Biscayne, Florida. I remember excitedly phoning Mom with the news. A long silence followed. No "Atta boy!" Then, terror struck. "Well, since you're moving to Florida, I'm going to move to Miami so I can be near you two."

"I'm glad you want to be near us, Mom, but frankly, we need to make it on our own here. We can't have our parents so close. If you insist on moving to Miami, we'll go somewhere else."

"OK, have it your way. I know when I'm not wanted. Your father and brother and sister don't care about me either. You hardly ever call or write. I guess you're all alike. I'll just stay here with my dogs. Since none of you care about your mother, you'll never know if I get sick or need help." She hung up.

The Key Biscayne church was a dynamic congregation of about 300 members, located in a small town that was a tropical, palm-tree-lined paradise. Everyone knew everyone. Many affluent homes lined the streets. Wild parties and drugs were plentiful. While I specialized in youth ministry, my responsibilities also included hospital and home visitation, teaching, Christian education, and some preaching. It was an enchanting, jam-packed half-decade, and Leah and I loved our time there. We met some special people who became lifelong friends, and we still treasure those relationships.

Mom visited us two or three times a year, or we visited her in Buford. I'm sure her self-pity, anger, and loneliness broke her heart and spirit and, eventually, her body. It became increasingly hard to communicate with her. She withdrew into herself, like an

injured dog huddling in a corner. Trying to converse with her was exhausting. Each question Leah or I asked was met with a one- or two-word answer. Beyond "How do you like the church?" and "How do you like the weather?" Mom made little effort to ask about us or about our work in Florida.

In January 1974, I accepted the call to become senior pastor of the First Presbyterian Church of North Palm Beach, Florida. The 325-member congregation was a loving, progressive, fast-growing church. When we arrived, Leah was five months pregnant. I have fond memories of carrying our pillows to the Lamaze classes at the Palm Beach Gardens Hospital in preparation for our soon-to-be-born child. We didn't know if it would be a boy or girl, but on April 8, 1974, Jim, Jr. was born!

I worked with a talented staff and a group of leaders at First Presbyterian. They were supportive, and shared a strong vision for both internal and outreach programs for youth and adults. Because of them, our congregation grew and thrived.

Gram had moved into an assisted-care nursing home in St. Petersburg. She wrote me nearly every week until the last six months of her life. For the most part, her letters were warm, newsy, and encouraging. Though Gram had exercised some destructive influences on me, I'm grateful for her many positive contributions to my life and ministry. She and Grandpa introduced me to their extensive network of friends. This mixing with people provided eye-opening opportunities to meet a broad spectrum of individuals and hear a variety of views. I doubt I would otherwise have been exposed to these because of Mom and Dad's limited socializing.

As a new father, I knew little about child sexual abuse other than what I'd personally suffered. I avoided doing much diapering and bathing of Jimmy, fearful I might have inherited some kind of sexual abuse gene from Mom and Gram and could be accused of touching him inappropriately. I didn't want to do to my precious son what had been done to me! My fears would have been allayed had I known that more than 70 percent of abused children do not become abusive parents.

In my second year in North Palm Beach, I began a Doctor of Ministries program at Fuller Theological Seminary, in Pasadena, California. For the next five years, I read assigned books and wrote lengthy term papers prior to my annual two-week intensive coursework at the seminary campus. Several church members graciously paid for part of my studies.

I was working seventy hours a week. My philosophy was, "Above all, give quality time to your family. But work-wise, go for broke. Better to wear out than rust out."

When Mom stayed with us for Thanksgiving, observing her broke my heart. One painful situation occurred at the church worship service. While everyone else was singing a hymn, Mom never opened her mouth. She just held her hymnbook and stared straight ahead. Gram's judgmental attitude certainly had inoculated her and Unc against institutional Christianity.

Mom had become pathetic. She'd gained far more weight, yet was a shell of her former self, as if someone or something had snuffed out her emotions. It felt like talking with a flesh-covered robot that looked like Mom. Gone were the spark of earlier years, the wide smile, and the twinkle I used to see in her eyes from time to time. Now she merely stared at me blankly. Instead of fearing Mom as I had in the past, I pitied her.

While I was in North Palm Beach, Mom and Dad reunited in a friendly truce the last three years of her life. They lived in a mobile home a couple of hours north of us near Daytona Beach. In 1978, a few days before Christmas, Dad called, "Jimmy, I'm sorry to tell you, your mother passed away this evening."

My mind and body numbed. I wanted to cry, but tears wouldn't come. I remember staring at Mom in her casket at the funeral home. She looked so sad, even in death. *What a tragedy: such a cultured, educated person, driven to a self-imposed exile of self-pity, resentment, and slow suicide by overeating and excessive smoking.* I felt terrible for having a sense of relief that she was gone.

I wanted to ache for what might have been — a warm, caring mother-son relationship — but couldn't. The only time I broke down

and wept was when Bob Long entered the mortuary to greet our family before officiating the service. I haven't missed Mom or wept for her once since then. Hopefully, someday I will.

The whole time I felt like I'd stepped outside my body and was an impartial observer of the visitation times, funeral service, and burial. Mom's own mother had beaten her down in every way. Like a brainwashed prisoner, I believe Mom had acted out patterns imposed on her by her parents. In turn, she mistreated her husband and children similarly. I think some of her emotionally and sexually abusive behavior toward me was probably unconscious.

e:In spring 1979, Leah discovered she was pregnant with our second child. What anticipation we shared for Jimmy's little sibling to be! We had our Lamaze procedure down pat. I wondered whether I'd experience the same excitement for this second baby as I did at Jimmy's birth.

Again, I was at Leah's side through her delivery, excitedly snapping rolls of photos. When the doctor announced, "It's a boy!" and held him up for us to see, he looked like Jimmy's twin brother. Now we had two sons who resembled their dad. I wanted to call him Jim, Jr., too, but we had picked out the name John months before. How proud Leah and I were to bring him to his new home and older brother!

I determined to break the pathological pattern passed from generation to generation in my family, resolving to do anything possible to forever stop those destructive, pain-inducing judgmental behaviors so they couldn't injure my sons. Every chance I got, I told Jimmy and John, "I love you. You're special." Since Jimmy's birth, I'd read book after book on parenting; I continued to educate myself in fathering in the years to come.

Starting when they were two years old, I took each boy on a "date" every week or so; my way of getting to know them better and trying to encourage them. I loved being with them. Also, it was a chance to vicariously relive a lot of the fun I missed growing up. We ate at McDonald's, slurped ice-cream cones, played on park swings and jungle gyms, fished, wrestled, camped overnight, waded

or sometimes swam lake and ocean shallows to islands, exploring "where pirates might have visited."

The three greatest experiences of my life have been marrying Leah and the births of each of our sons. I could not ask for more. After more than thirty-four years of marriage and raising Jim and John, they're still the most important part of my life.

I thoroughly enjoyed most of my time at North Palm Beach, but, after seven years, I began wondering whether the church had gone as far as it could under my leadership.

Chapter 12

Alarming Problems Facing Today's Clergy and Their Families

IT'S OFTEN SAID THAT A MINISTER can make or break a congregation. I believe that a church can have the same effects on a minister. Three of the five churches I've served inspired me to become a better man and pastor; the other two nearly broke me! From personal experience and from the horror stories I'd heard over the years, I was well aware of the incredible stresses that clergy were under. Most people wouldn't believe the pressures affecting most ministers.

Recent surveys of pastors by the Fuller Institute of Church Growth, Focus on the Family, and other organizations reveal that spiritual leaders of all denominations are facing an epidemic of personal and professional problems.[13] More than three-fourths of pastors and spouses struggle with serious depression and over forty percent suffer from schedule overload, exhaustion, and other stresses.[14]

Nearly a fourth of all clergy have been forced out at least once

in their careers.[15] Sadly, seventy-five percent of American clergy would move immediately if given the chance.[16] Little did I know that *I* was about to walk into a new church situation that would threaten my career, health, and even my life!

When interviewing with churches, I was candid about my theology, strengths, and weaknesses. I never flew the flag of my beliefs at half-mast. I wanted pulpit committees and leadership boards to be well versed in my theology, preaching style, leadership methods, ministry goals, and personal background information before accepting a position.

In 1981, I was contacted by a number of churches within a six-month period. It seemed that God was preparing us for a move. One of the churches I interviewed with was St. Andrew's Presbyterian Church in Beaumont, Texas. It was a well-to-do, educated church of about 1,800 members. They offered me the senior pastor position.

It was evident that some of its leadership were fiercely loyal Presbyterians and of a much more liberal theological persuasion than I was. From the start, I attempted to dissuade their pulpit committee. "You don't want me, I'm an evangelical. I try to hold a solid balance between evangelistic outreach and social action that meets physical, emotional, and social needs. My theology's too conservative for this church." But they kept coming back. "Jim, you're just what our church needs. We need a spiritual renewal. Our people will love you. We'll support you." I reasoned this might be a wonderful chance to use my strengths as a spiritual obstetrician/ pediatrician, introducing people to Christ and jump-starting them in the Christian lifestyle.

The church had many warm, loving members, but a behind-the-scenes civil war broke out, ignited by a handful of individuals. Unknown to me, a few had been scheming to derail my ministry before I arrived, and increased their efforts after I started there. They wrote vicious letters to the church leadership board accusing me of being a "disloyal Presbyterian," "too fundamentalist," and "an incompetent, uncaring pastor." When I preached a sermon on

the Twenty-third Psalm, the dissidents stirred up controversy over its content, accusing me of demeaning humans by comparing them with sheep.

I was forced to take a weekend retreat with the church's two leadership boards and a conflict management specialist selected by a committee of the Presbytery (a district of about 130 churches). On a number of Sundays, a small, angry group stood in the narthex, handing out petitions requesting the Presbytery to dissolve my pastoral relationship with the church. Needless to say, preaching on Sundays was tense!

Time and again, I agonized. *Why is this happening, Lord? I thought You brought me here to have a successful ministry. I've tried to be faithful in my preaching, and I work hard in my pastoral duties. Why have You led me into this buzz saw of mean-spirited criticism and hate? There's absolutely nothing I can do to please this little group. Maybe I deserve this — maybe it's Your way of punishing me.*

Apart from that small, vocal band, the congregation was caring and gracious. Despite the storm raging around me, Leah and I developed some wonderful relationships. I enjoyed terrific hunting trips with Jimmy, attended professional sporting events, and had the satisfaction of running a half-marathon in Houston with Bob Long.

Upon returning from summer vacation at the end of that first year, I received a number of threats against our family. "We're fed up with your ministry. If you don't get yourself and your family out of town, something permanent will happen to you, your wife, and your boys. We mean business." My insides churned with rage and fear. *These folks play hardball here.* I never told Leah or anyone else about those death threats until years later. There were other terrifying incidents, too.

As a result of the strain, I started having chest and intestinal pains. Leah started suffering physical symptoms, too. When we took nightly walks, I was so stunned I could barely move my legs. Thankfully, I was able to share my fears with a few friends in the church, Bob Long, and several confidants around the country. I

even phoned Dad. To my amazement, he raged at our treatment. For the first time in my life, I felt Dad really heard my pain and wanted to stand up for me. He even flew to Beaumont to be with us for several days. He urged me to get an attorney to sue the troublemakers.

It was a year and a half of conflict. Daily, I grew more concerned about the stress-induced physical, emotional, and spiritual damage that could result if we remained there. I certainly didn't want to risk harm to Leah and the boys from the out-of-control people who'd made such frightening threats.

Finally, after discussing my options with friends, I resigned. I had no idea where we would go or how I'd support my family. Pastors aren't eligible for unemployment compensation, and I faced the possibility of receiving no severance. Fortunately, the majority of the church prevailed over my dozen-or-so opponents, and the congregation voted to continue my salary for up to six months.

In 1982, a month after my resignation, a pulpit committee from the Covenant Presbyterian Church in Sharon, Pennsylvania, contacted me about becoming their senior pastor. The church was nestled in a beautiful valley forty miles northwest of Pittsburgh. The town's scenic location offered an outstanding place for a family, featuring a lake, park, free golf course, hunting, and fishing. It was also appealing because Bob Long and other friends were in the area, and Dad lived only four hours away.

Covenant Church looked like an ideal opportunity to heal my massive inner wounds. It was an old, theologically conservative church in the downtown section of Sharon. The majority of the congregation's 1,700 members had been Christians for a long time. My forte had always been working with non-believers and new Christians, not with mature Christians who'd long ago solidified their beliefs. This would be a challenge.

Again, I met opposition from the start. I didn't know that it was a church fighting with itself. Following my upbeat installation service, a lay leader informed me, "Dr. Stout, you're a fool for coming to this church. It's a can of worms, nothing but

a suspicious, judgmental, in-fighting bunch of fossilized Bible bigots. You'll be sorry you came here."

The steel industry was plummeting, and mills all over western Pennsylvania were cutting back or shutting down. The Sharon area wasn't immune. People were being laid off in steel mills and other businesses. Christian caring deteriorated into easily inflamed antagonism, jaundiced pessimism, and cancerous cynicism. Such was the emotional and spiritual climate of Covenant Church. Understandably, this tainted the reasonableness and love among many in the congregation, and carried over into the official business of the two boards that were a mix of white-collar management and blue-collar workers.

Suspicion and anger abounded at meetings. Only a few trusted each other. Often, when one church officer made a recommendation, another was quick to find fault with it. Few of the lay leaders could get their motions passed without lengthy debate. I yearned for a spirit of unity, tolerance, and love. As moderator, I was trapped in the crossfire like a labor-management arbitrator. I walked away from meetings feeling battered and exhausted, as if I'd just slugged it out in a ten-round street fight, depressed, angry, confused, and drained of hope that conditions would improve.

Surviving the faultfinding in the Sharon and Beaumont churches was all too similar to growing up at home. It seemed there was nothing I could do without drawing denouncements. I knew that even the best leaders, secular or religious, incurred opposition from time to time, but I felt I'd received more than my fair share.

The accumulated criticism, broken financial promises, and other church pressures began affecting my health. I started having diarrhea and abdominal pain. *No church is worth serving if it results in physical, emotional, and spiritual trauma! Something's got to give. Before long, Leah or I will collapse under the strain.*

By September 1984, I realized that bulimia was a serious eating disorder that could endanger my health, even threaten my life. Amazingly, without even reading anything about it, I simply decided to quit compulsive bingeing and purging, even if I bloated

up to 400 pounds. Since 1985, it's been an ongoing battle to "stay sober," avoiding solace in food. Though I still struggle with compulsive overeating, I've rarely binged and purged since then.

I grew more concerned about the toll the Sharon pastorate was having on Leah and me. I took a half-dozen burnout and depression tests from professional counseling books. Each showed I was in a very risky place, emotionally and physically. I was clearly manifesting most of the symptoms of clinical depression. All scores indicated I had "a severe need for professional help."

Paradoxically, over the past twelve years, I had taught classes and counseled people about stress, burnout, and depression. Illogically, I believed that while others had caved in from similar stress and depression, I could, with determination, stay on top of the strains. But it was only a matter of time before I discovered that I couldn't. I should have taken to heart the Bible's teaching, "So, if you think you are standing firm, be careful that you don't fall!"[17] Instead, the words fell on deaf ears.

I found myself frequently brooding, *Lord, you directed me into the ministry. Why have you given me all these problems? What have I done that's been so bad as to bring on this kind of mistreatment? Maybe I should have wised up after going through what I did in Beaumont. Why continue this uphill battle? Perhaps I should have left the ministry years ago.*

In addition to being treated venomously by small factions in the churches, I estimate that Leah and I lost thousands of dollars in broken financial agreements. It's difficult for a pastor to defend himself: he can't strike out at his critics or sue his church without harming his ministry. After minimal attempts to defend myself and stand up for my rights, I absorbed most of the negativity silently. Many who've been burned by church members, pastors, or denominational leaders leave the institutional church permanently. I don't blame them. Many clergy I know would've left the professional ministry after enduring only *one* major church trauma.

Sometimes an overmatched, injured prizefighter continues fighting bravely, but in vain. Smart boxers avoid serious, even permanent,

damage. If they're taking a bad beating, they drop to a knee and are counted out, or they let their corner men throw in the towel. Wisely, they "live to fight another day." However, like some fighters, I stayed in the ring too long, foolishly refusing to go down. I simply took too many punches, and some life-threatening damages were soon to come.

A large number of Covenant Church members had dug their heels in, resisting any kind of change. I protested to God, *I was emotionally raw before coming here, Lord. I thought this would be a place of healing. Instead, I've received more wounds, and gotten more burnt out and depressed. What can I do to expand this church's vision? Despite the opposition, I know I've won my spurs here, but I'm a builder, and this church wants a caretaker. What do You want me to do?*

Pondering the future, I took lengthy career tests, all of which reconfirmed my vocation and pointed to the professional ministry. In the midst of my darkest days, I never questioned my call to reach people for Christ and build them up in their faith. I did, however, ruminate over what would be the best vehicle for doing it, given my recent psychological injuries. Bob Long and others advised me against accepting another senior pastor opportunity. They knew of my precarious emotional condition, and feared I might take a few "hits" and have a serious fall.

Several weeks later, I called a ministerial colleague in Washington, D.C. "Could you meet with me to discuss my career options? I'll be there at a conference in two weeks." He agreed to get together. We met for breakfast and he gave me some valuable advice: "Jim, very few men in America can relate to both secular and Christian men like you can. You've taken a beating in a couple of your churches. I think it would be foolish for you to take a job as a senior pastor right now. That kind of position incurs too much criticism. Almost anyone can become a senior pastor, but rare are the men who can reach other men, especially leaders. Why not play to your strengths and do something only a handful of leaders around the country can do? How about taking a position as an associate pastor specializing in working with men? It will be a

far greater use of your gifts. And you'll have much less stress."

His counsel made sense. I updated my résumé. In the following months I was contacted by several ministries, a chaplaincy to Pittsburgh's downtown business community, the directorship of a clergy rehabilitation center, and several senior pastor positions. It seemed like God was again readying us for a change.

During these spiritual vacillations I received a phone call from my friend, Dr. John Huffman, senior pastor of St. Andrew's Presbyterian Church in Newport Beach, California. He offered me the position of Minister of Evangelism and Family Life, working with men and families, along with evangelistic outreach and membership activation. It was a broad job description, but I could spend half my time working with men and at evangelism, so the possibilities appealed to me, especially since I'd been urged to focus on men's ministry, operating from a local church base. It seemed like God was directing us to California, so I accepted the invitation and, in August 1986, we traveled to our new place of service.

The 4,500-member congregation was a caring, generous church with a wide outreach. Its cutting-edge approach to ministry was liberating. Each day brought a fresh opportunity; every program I started seemed to be appreciated. What an exciting change from my previous two pastorates!

That September, Jimmy entered seventh grade and John started second. It was a rough year of transition, especially for the boys: new schools, new classmates, and a new church. Making new friends and breaking into the pecking order was tough. Realizing that Jimmy and John were having difficulty adjusting to their new circumstances, I took off work many afternoons that first year to be with them. Some days I dropped in at the Boys Club where John spent time after school. We spent a week making a sleek wooden skateboard that he painted silver. Some evenings we went shopping for baseball cards to add to his collection, or visited local batting cages to sharpen his batting skills.

Leah and I worked at frenetic speed, juggling dozens of responsibilities. In addition to teaching elementary school, she undertook

all the tasks of settling into a new home and community, as well as doing house chores, shopping, cooking, and chauffeuring the boys to school, sports practices, and games. I put in long hours at pastoral tasks and launching new programs.

Because it was hard for Jimmy to break into the cliques at junior high school and the church youth group, I made special efforts to encourage him. He wanted to take up skim boarding, a type of surfing along the ocean's edge. After school and on weekends, we checked coastal surf shops from Huntington Beach to San Clemente, looking for the best deal on skim boards. Finally, he found a beauty. Several afternoons a week, I drove him to different beaches to ride the waves. Special times with each boy! By the end of our first year in California, our family had survived the move; we loved our location and treasured our new friends.

Several evenings each week I had committee meetings or counseling sessions. I returned home exhausted and fell into bed, but often, sleep wouldn't come and I spent an hour or two tossing and turning. I couldn't shut off my thoughts: my mind whirled with plans, appointments, and phone calls for the coming week. How could I get everything done? I doubt that anyone at work ever noticed the inner desperation behind my outer accomplishments.

Part Four

Depressions, Near-Suicides, and Hospitalizations

Save me, O God, for the waters have come up to my neck.
I sink in the miry depths, where there is no foothold.
I have come into the deep waters; the floods engulf me.
I am worn out from calling for help...

— *Psalm 69:1–3*

Chapter 13

Events That Trigger a Life-threatening Depression

RARELY DOES A SERIOUS DEPRESSION come suddenly, unexpectedly. There are almost always clear stressors that point to an approaching clinical depression. Like tiny fissures in giant rocks, depression's "cracks" in the body and personality can be detected by the sensitive eye. Physical, psychological, or spiritual symptoms can be warning signs of an oncoming melancholia. I'd been manifesting obvious signs for the past six years.

Near the end of the first year at St. Andrew's, I grew irritable, angry, and short-fused — an emotional time bomb. When I could fall asleep, I didn't sleep well. Fatigue blunted my energies. A persistent sadness plagued me, even in good times. I could laugh, but it felt hollow. I couldn't enjoy anything: sports, movies, TV, family outings, hobbies, or sex. I still relished eating, but stuffed myself just out of anxiety. My memory and concentration were unreliable. Time and again, Leah gave me lists of things to pick up at the store, but even with a written note I'd forget half the items. On troubling nights, I took long drives, listening to talk-show babble.

More and more I felt like a failure as a husband, father, pastor, and Christian. I grew suspicious of people's words, actions, and motives. Normally friendly and outgoing, I now avoided people whenever possible. When the phone rang at home, I frequently refused to answer it.

I sensed a vague, ominous gloom about life. My pessimistic outlook worsened to hopelessness, then to despair. It seemed as if God had withdrawn His presence and was judging me for all my wrongdoing. I felt cursed. Although I knew verse after verse

about God's forgiveness, no amount of prayer or Bible reading comforted me. I felt alone in the universe, cut off from family, friends, and God.

On a day off in early September 1987, I drove to a nearby suburban mall, looking forward to the escape a movie would bring. En route, I mentally replayed past negative events and reviewed my schedule for the weeks ahead. I was exhausted, angry, and extremely down. As I climbed out of the car, my legs could barely move.

Suddenly, a deep sadness swept over me. Despite how well things were going, everything seemed hopeless. I was depressed to the core, and saw no possibility of ever catching up with my ever-lengthening to-do list.

Thoughts of ending my life swirled in my brain, but I had no specific plans. The theater was only a few hundred feet away. It was all I could do to shuffle toward the box office. Halfway there I gave up and, stooped over like an old man, inched back to the car. It hit me that I couldn't take any more of life's punches. I was ready to break. When I arrived home, I phoned a therapist friend for a referral to a psychologist.

I knew I needed help; no one had to convince me of the life-changing benefits of counseling. I'd seen hundreds of people gain healthier, happier, more spiritually effective lives as a result of being counseled. But I'd also observed how denial, pride, and false confidence prevented others from getting help. It was obvious that attempting to handle my problems alone would get me in deep trouble. Not reaching out would be a sure set-up for disaster.

On September 10, 1987, I had my first psychotherapy session with Dr. Phil Sutherland, a clinical psychologist. After the session, Phil referred me to a psychiatrist who put me on an antidepressant. Unfortunately, serious side effects erupted almost immediately. He prescribed another; it too engendered bad reactions. Frustrated by the medicines, I stopped seeing him and had my family doctor prescribe other antidepressants. Initially, they were less disruptive.

At the time, I was unaware that family doctors and internists pre-

scribe a much higher volume of psychiatric medications than psychiatrists do. Yet, statistically, psychiatrists treat mental disorders much more effectively than any other type of physician. So, from September 1987 to May 1988, I gritted my teeth and endured the side effects of antidepressants and anti-stress drugs, and met with Phil weekly, all while working full-time. Talking with Phil gave me an immense sense of relief. It felt safe being with him. At last, someone who really listened and took my struggles seriously, who offered no lectures or trite solutions.

While I recognized the psychological value of delving into my childhood, I was hesitant to disclose my difficulties, or be perceived by Phil as whining or complaining. *Will he find out something about me and no longer like or respect me? Will he, like Mom and Gram, violate my confidentiality and gossip about me? Will talking about my parents' flaws break God's commandment, "Honor your father and mother?"*

Despite working with people all my adult life, I'd always felt alone. Maybe this was why Phil so often said, "You've been depressed all your life, Jim." By May 1988, having completed six months of psychotherapy and medication, the clouds lifted and I began to feel good again. My doctor let me stop taking the pills. "We don't need to keep meeting, do we?" I asked Phil. "I've been feeling much better. I haven't had a down time in months. I think I've got this depression licked."

He smiled. "I don't think we ought to stop, Jim. You still have a way to go." I was shocked. Reluctantly, I agreed to keep meeting with him. Directly and indirectly, Phil would save my life on dozens of occasions in the coming years.

I thought, *It sure looks like my meds and Phil's counseling have worked. Little incidents don't bother me as easily. I'm sleeping more, and getting some excellent insights into my childhood and church problems. If I keep this counseling up, any time now I'll discover some key revelations about how I tick and what I can do to heal my wounds. All I need to do is wait for these psychological "revelations," and then apply whatever I learn.*

I stayed busy at work, hoping the therapy sessions would soon hit pay dirt. I kept waiting, looking for a solution to "fix" me and solve my problems quickly, permanently. But the once-and-for-all "answer" never came. I've since learned that counseling doesn't provide a spectacular discovery about yourself that solves your problems instantly, dramatically, painlessly. Counseling and reading would afford me plenty of insights over the next few years, but I couldn't put many into action, so they simply remained academic concepts.

Despite unending exhaustion and lack of sleep, I took turns with Leah driving the boys to their team practices. I cheered at John's Little League baseball and soccer games and Jimmy's wrestling matches. How proud I was of our sons!

Then came the second, nearly fatal, crash! September and October of 1988 were hectic months. A flurry of activity was going on at the church, and I was working long hours. I never imagined that in only a few months I would be planning to take my life! I'd been on fast-forward a long time, working sixty or more hours a week for twenty years. Sooner or later, that pace grinds a person down. I'd seen many top-flight professionals bite the dust working those kinds of hours; I was no exception. Having been in California more than a year and a half, and experiencing wonderful successes in my ministry, I still was all too aware of my depressed, beaten-up condition. But I believed all along that I was on top of the melancholy: counseling with Phil and just a few more accomplishments at work would heal my wounds. After all, everyone seemed to love me, and all my programs were going well. Unfortunately, my life was rapidly accelerating out of control.

Like other addictions, workaholism takes an ever-increasing dose to dull one's feelings. For too long, I'd been so busy taking care of others' needs to attend to my own. I was giving more and more of myself away to people. There was little time left for me to relax, play, or just rest. I worked harder and harder developing church programs, counseling, organizing meetings and teaching, and kept busy attending school and sports activities with the boys.

Work was gradually overwhelming me. I couldn't catch up and couldn't stop over-committing myself. Much as I tried, slowing down appeared to be impossible. I backed off from friends and social outings. Sleep, when it came, was anxious, fitful. My concentration and memory progressively deteriorated; list making became obsessive. Even the most mundane responsibility required immense effort. I had to force myself to go to work. Every morning I awoke utterly fatigued, drowning in futility. *I'm burned out. Nothing's ever going to change. I dread working one more week at this speed. I can't tolerate another confrontation or criticism. I'm afraid I'll snap at someone. I don't care how successful my ministry is — life isn't worth living like this.*

I felt like I was going crazy. *As much as I know about time management, why can't I get off this treadmill? Are my accomplishments just a means of raising my self-esteem? Is success a way of proving to others and myself that I'm really OK and not the 'bad boy' I was branded growing up? Is hard work an unconscious way of seeking the approval I never got as a child? Is my workload overly burdensome because I don't like myself enough to take care of me?*

I suppose my accomplishments, though spiritually motivated, were also a way to earn people's respect. A fast pace and long hours numbed the haunting loneliness and residual pain of the past. By keeping busy, I had no time to think about personal issues, much less deal with them. But my achievements weren't a sufficient remedy for my unhealed wounds. The chronic stress and accumulated losses, combined with the verbal punches I'd taken over the years, were taking their toll at last.

Depression, like cancer, begins with a small, unnoticeable lump that grows silently. Then, one day, you have a lethal, four-pound tumor. In the fall of 1988, the second year at St. Andrew's, my well-organized life began falling apart. The sleep difficulties worsened. I grew more and more pessimistic. My emotional fuse shortened, leaving me impatient and edgy. I had little patience for others or myself. Constantly agitated over something, my well-hidden temper lurked just beneath the surface, ready to explode.

I became curt with Leah and the boys, sometimes losing my temper with them. Although being counseled by Phil, I noticed that little incidents made me raise my voice, yell, curse, or slam my fist on a table. This wasn't the normal me, but I couldn't control myself. After every four-to-six-week burst of increased productivity, I had severe letdowns. At the time, I didn't identify them as depressions, yet they immobilized me for days. Then they began lasting longer, and gradually grew more severe.

Daily my surroundings took on a strange sense of unreality, as if I was an actor in a play and at the same time, a spectator watching myself perform. Sadness shrouded me like rain clouds blotting out the sun. I hurt all over inside, and couldn't shake a dread about everything. The physical symptoms I'd experienced in Beaumont and Sharon returned: rapid heartbeat, gastrointestinal disturbances, chest pains, and diarrhea.

My mind played continuous re-runs of past church-related hurts and recent slights. Recalling past joys seemed almost impossible. *Nothing's enjoyable anymore. What's wrong with me? My church programs are going well. I've got a great wife and two fine sons. Why can't I dwell on the good things that are happening?*

My feelings were easily hurt. I was so thin-skinned that any negative comment came across like an ice pick stabbed in my chest. If someone said or did something I perceived as hurtful, I obsessed over it, unable to forgive, forget. Silently, I blamed others and myself without mercy. I tried to elude negative thinking by reading, taking long drives in the car, and going to movies, but my brain wouldn't shut off. One painful experience or resentment after another raced through my mind. I muted the whirling thoughts with a ravenous appetite for food. Momentarily, at least, eating comforted me.

I was turning into a different person. In spite of my well-received programs at church, I hated myself for incessant negative thinking. Past failures, bad choices, and sins overwhelmed me, burying me in self-recrimination. I felt like Shakespeare's Lady Macbeth, repeatedly washing her hands, unable to rid herself of the stain of

her wrongdoing, and I condemned myself in the court of my own mind. My mind was filled with endless self-deprecating self-talk: *You're a miserable excuse for a man, a phony Christian, a rotten hypocrite. You're a failure as a father, and a lousy husband. You're a poor leader. You've failed yourself, others, and God. Worse yet, God is hunting you down, ready to punish you.*

Without jeopardizing my work, I secluded myself, avoiding people whenever possible. Leah or the boys answered the phone; I couldn't muster the energy to talk. My memory became erratic, and I found it hard to concentrate on anything. When I felt up to reading the newspaper, I'd merely glance at the headlines, and could barely read the sports pages.

I thought I'd healed from my earlier depressive episode, but more and more, I felt my life was spinning out of control. I was too busy, too sad, and too afraid. I ached with all-pervasive emotional agony — far worse than any physical pain I'd ever experienced — and I couldn't escape it. As a result, all of life looked flat. In public, I wore a smiling mask that hid my private pain.

I started feeling better when summer came and my schedule slowed down. We had a splendid family vacation in July 1988 at Mammoth, a ski resort in northern California. It was probably the most restful time I'd ever had. All we did for three weeks was eat, sleep, fish, read, and hike. It was cleansing and inspiring. I returned to work thoroughly refreshed, but I was exhausted again just two months later.

When major depression sets in, your thinking becomes warped by intense inner pain. Your mind gets confused and illogical. Fear, despair, and suicidal thoughts I never imagined myself having blackened my thoughts. I assigned negative motives to nearly everyone. As hard as I tried to talk myself out of worrying about an upcoming event or potential confrontation, anxiety and self-blame kept me from coming up with a positive way to deal with the situation. I built mountains out of molehills, visualizing only worst-case scenarios. This self-destructive focus repeated itself with a vengeance. I began making specific plans to kill myself.

At this point, all my previously strong faith and biblical knowledge were useless.

For more than twenty years, I'd counseled severely depressed, oftentimes suicidal men; now I couldn't avoid obsessing about taking my own life. The wise choice would have been to go for professional help at once. I knew how ominous my thinking was getting, yet I rationalized it away, believing I could control my pessimistic attitude and thoughts of self-destruction. But I couldn't. A serious crash lurked on the horizon!

Then, three minor incidents converged within a short period, sending me into a suicidal tailspin that nearly cost my life. Eighteen talented Orange County laymen and I had been organizing a "Gathering of Men Outreach Breakfast" as an ecumenical effort, independent from any official Presbyterian program. Its purpose was to reach "up-and-outers," the un-churched business and professional men of Orange County. Details were falling nicely into place. The first disruptive situation arose a few months *before* the October breakfast. Some denominational men's ministry representatives told me to stop promoting the Gathering of Men Breakfast, since it wasn't a Presbyterian program. I refused, and resigned from their committee, incensed at their narrow vision.

Despite their opposition, I continued preparing for the event, which was an awesome success. The speaker gave an outstanding message to the 850 men jammed into the Irvine Hilton Hotel grand ballroom. We turned away several hundred men because no more could be squeezed in. Dozens committed their lives to Jesus Christ for the first time. Feedback on the event was overwhelmingly enthusiastic. A first try, it had some rough edges to be smoothed out for the next one, but it was nonetheless a spiritual high for my leaders and me.

The second event that contributed to my forthcoming fall occurred the week *after* the breakfast. I met with several Presbyterian pastors to discuss it. A couple made stinging remarks about its purpose, methods, and effectiveness. I doubt that they realized how deeply their words cut; for me, they were a replay of childhood

criticism, rejection, and humiliation. Days after that meeting, I mentally rehashed their critiques, outraged and wounded, my distress growing acute.

Even though I'd recently taken two "broadsides," the third nerve-shattering jolt happened when Dad visited us for a week at the end of October. Certain things about him upset me. I'm sure those personality quirks had existed for years, yet somehow I hadn't noticed them. Perhaps now I was so sensitive that they registered immediately on my emotional "Richter scale."

Dad and I spoke, but didn't really communicate. Whenever I tried to share about the recent success of the men's breakfast, he slid off the topic, delivering a long monologue about something barely related to what I'd just mentioned. It became painfully clear that each time I brought up some success I'd had, Dad not only wouldn't affirm it, but also wouldn't discuss it, changing the subject instead. For the first time, his seemingly innocuous words cut me deeply.

We conversed like two trains traveling along parallel tracks, never once connecting. It felt as though I didn't even exist. Dad's method of communicating wasn't new; it just startled me how utterly insensitive he was to my needs or, for that matter, anyone's. Years later, I came to better understand that he was simply incapable of relating with most people on a meaningful level.

Even in the midst of my professional success, those three hurts piled on top of the ones from previous churches to leave me staggering. I'd done my best, and had fought hard, but I'd taken too many shots. I wasn't sure where, when, or whom the next one might come from. I was too tired, too beaten up, to keep trying.

My normally sanguine nature faded daily into isolating hopelessness. I had a terrible sinking feeling, like being swept down in a whirlpool of despair. I believed I was, despite all my efforts, powerless to control my job, my family responsibilities, and my emotions.

Thoughts of suicide invaded all my thinking. I couldn't outrun them. It panicked me to dwell on what the future might bring.

When will the next criticism come? I'm exhausted; there aren't any workable options. Why try anymore? Reading the Bible is no help; I can't focus. The words are hollow. No amount of positive mental gymnastics improved my morose thinking. I began planning ways to end my life. That night I drove recklessly, searching for concrete walls or highway barriers to smash the mini-van into. Providentially, I couldn't find any.

The pain was unbearable. I no longer cared about what happened to me. There was no reason to live. *They'd be better off with no husband and father than one who's angry, bitchy, and unreliable.*

Many people misunderstand suicide, labeling it a coward's way out. Those who've never suffered serious depression have no idea of the excruciating pain involved. Is a prisoner of war a coward for finally breaking under excessive torture? For some, suicide is a cry for attention. I couldn't have cared less what others thought. I felt I'd been attacked, abandoned, and betrayed too many times, and I just couldn't take the hurt anymore.

Suicide is a philosophical and emotional problem for most people, including dedicated Christians. In fact, many Bible heroes have contemplated taking their lives due to debilitating depression. At one point in his life, the Apostle Paul mourned, "I have great sorrow and unceasing anguish in my heart.[18] Another time he shared candidly, "We were under great pressure, far beyond our ability to endure, so that we despaired even of life. Indeed, in our hearts we felt the sentence of death."[19]

Chapter 14

Life in a Psychiatric Unit:
Sometimes Awful, Sometimes Fun—

The Difficulty of Making an Accurate Diagnosis
of Bipolar Disorder (Manic-depressive Illness)

THE MORNING OF NOVEMBER 5, 1988, not long after Dad's visit, I began having chest pains, and checked into Hoag Hospital's emergency room. After several tests, the doctors released me, saying I was experiencing severe stress and needed to take time off work immediately or I was headed for a heart attack. I couldn't have gone to work then, anyway. The following days my insides churned. On November 10, I was so miserable that I stayed up most of the night, driving haphazardly, listening to talk shows, and stopping at all-night restaurants. In the morning, a frightening suicidal depression swept over me again. I started planning to kill myself. Willpower, positive thinking, praying, and Bible reading were useless.

I called Phil. "I didn't go to work yesterday — chest pains. Hospital said I wasn't having a heart attack, though. Drove around most of the night. Can't go back to work. Don't know what's happening, but something in me has shut down. I don't want to go on. Can I see you today?"

"Come as soon as you can."

I drove to his office and told him what was happening. "Jim, you can't go back to work. The best thing for you is to rest in a hospital for a few days." I'd cried very few times in my life, but tears flowed now. I'll never forget Phil's gentle words to the nurse at the Minirth-Meier Psychiatric Unit of the Community Hospital

of Gardena: "I've got a young man here who needs to come for a few days' rest. Will you make the arrangements?"

My mind tormented me with cruel thoughts. Though I knew hundreds of Bible promises, they were just words that seemed to mock me. *You should've been a better Christian. Now you're going to get what's coming to you. Everything your relatives predicted is about to come true. Your career's over. You're finished. So quit.*

That day, November 11, 1988, life had finally crushed my will to fight, even to survive. I'd crossed an invisible line and had given up on life, on God, on people, on myself. I would go back and forth across that life-or-death line again and again in the coming years. I drove to the psychiatric clinic in a mental fog. Thinking I would only be there over the weekend, I stopped to buy a paperback crime novel to read during my brief stay. Little did I know that it would be five long months before I would leave!

Totally drained, I could barely walk or hold the pen to fill out the insurance forms. My fragile spirit couldn't have suffered another rejection, real or imagined. At my intake interview, I was angry, exhausted, and prepared to run outside, jump in my van, and either crash into a concrete post or buy a gun to kill myself. When asked questions, I barely summoned the strength to respond in a hoarse, almost inaudible murmur.

A nurse gave me the booklet, *Handbook of Rights for Mental Health Patients.* It dealt with all the rights mental hospital patients are entitled to under the law. How reassuring it was, since I knew about the history of deplorable conditions and inhumane treatment that patients endured in many mental hospitals. Also, I'd observed firsthand the conditions at the Danvers State Mental Hospital while working there in seminary days.

A nurse in civilian clothes went through my belongings, taking out any sharp instruments and glass items: shaving lotion bottles, knives, scissors, and tweezers. "We'll keep these in the nursing station till you're discharged." Next, she led me to the unit. Still in a daze, I shuffled along with her. The loneliness I had felt all my life, and especially during the past weeks, was

magnified a thousand times. No one was with me to face this cryptic world they called "psychiatric hospital." I was now cut off from everything and everyone that had given me meaning, enjoyment, and support.

Terror of this place threatened to overpower me. I was ready to bolt, but exhaustion and an overburdened mind overcame fear. Somehow, I plodded along doing what I was asked. There were about a dozen patients on the unit, which could hold twenty or more. The nurse showed me to a simple, clean room with two beds, two dressers, and a bathroom. I told her, "I don't want anyone to know I'm here. I won't take any phone calls, either." Within days, my world shrank to this small, sterile cubicle.

The Community Hospital of Gardena was located a few miles south of Los Angeles. The clinic had a TV room where we had most of our lectures, group therapy, and psychodramas. We spent free time there lounging on sofas, watching TV. Down the hall was a small dining room where we gathered to eat. We could grab snacks from the refrigerator if we got hungry between meals. Outside was a patio where we could go for exercise.

I hardly slept the first four nights. During the entire stay, I probably averaged only five or six hours of sleep a night — a byproduct of depression, even with medication. One of depression's common symptoms is self-loathing and the conviction that God is rejecting you. When people suffer a tragedy, they often ask, "Why is this happening to me? What have I done to deserve it?" My warped thinking went a step further: *I deserve this hospitalization. It's God's punishment for my being such a bad person.*

My sense of being completely abandoned was like that of the psalmist who lamented, centuries ago, "... no one is concerned for me. I have no refuge ... my soul is full of trouble ... I am like a man without strength ... cut off from your care." [20]

The Bible speaks of the God, whom I believed in, saying, "Never will I leave you; never will I forsake you." [21] God said in the Bible, "... call upon me in the day of trouble; I will deliver you ..." [22] Now, more than ever, He seemed to be playing some cruel game of

hide-and-seek with me. I was too upset to pray; I opened my Bible, usually a source of strength, but found no comfort there.

I felt like the prophet Jeremiah, who, while going through a parallel trial, lamented, "I have been deprived of peace ... My splendor is gone and all that I had hoped from the Lord ... He has driven me away and made me walk in darkness rather than light; indeed, he has turned his hand against me again and again ... He has besieged me and surrounded me with bitterness and hardship ... He has made me dwell in darkness ... He has walled me in so I cannot escape ... Even when I call our or cry for help, he shuts out my prayer." [23]

Strange as it might seem, in the midst of my fearfulness, the hospital became a refuge. I certainly didn't consider it an enjoyable place, but it was a safe harbor where, at last, I could find shelter from the battering gales.

Normally, a patient could sign out to visit the hospital lobby or walk around the building for a change of scenery from that inside the unit. During a five-month hospital stay, however, I had no exercise other than a few twenty-minute walks.

During those long months I contemplated suicide almost daily. I was utterly pessimistic about life. Leaving its unremitting problems seemed like the only escape. Secondly, self-annihilation seemed the only relief from the all-consuming inner agony. No other kind of pain is so brutal, the unbearable torture extending day after day, night after night.

Numerous times before, during and after my hospitalization, I grew so despondent that I made pro and con lists for staying alive versus ending my life. Even on days when I was feeling better, I went through the tally matter of factly, without emotion. Only once, in dozens of those lists, did reasons to live outnumber those to die: just before leaving the hospital, when I felt flickers of hope, the pros outnumbered the cons by a slim margin.

Now I kept telling myself the distorted rationale I'd heard hundreds of times from others whom I'd counseled: *My family will be better off without me. Besides, my insurance will pay for counseling to help them adjust to my death and go on.*

When a patient was considered suicidal, he was put under one-on-one care. A nurse or tech was assigned to be with him twenty-four hours a day, staying nearby at meals, meetings, or in the TV room. They sat next to the bed when he slept; even when the patient went to the bathroom or took a shower, a staff member stayed right outside. I had many such one-on-ones, including a period when someone was with me day and night for eight days. Even after several months in the hospital, I was gripped by unrelenting despondency. For a long time it wasn't a question of whether I'd take my life, but when. Except for a few brief periods, neither medication nor counseling could stop my downward plunge.

What prevented me from taking the final exit? I wish I could say it was my faith. It wasn't. It was my family — Leah, Jimmy, and John — that kept me hanging on. I feared how my death might affect them. It became unbearable to consider that if things got too tough for of them, they might take their own lives as their father had. For their sakes I wanted to make it.

I couldn't shake the awareness that my death might devastate Leah and the boys permanently, even if they got expert counseling. I'd consoled dozens of families of suicide victims, and I knew that those left behind bore the brunt of their loved ones' self-annihilation. They were left to cope with awful confusion over the unexplainable act: the guilt, the hurt, and the anger. Even after they'd processed their shock and anger, many still blamed themselves.

The other roadblock to taking my life was false information. Several people told me, "Jim, if you leave here without having been properly discharged by the doctors, your insurance company won't pay your bills. Your family will have to pay." I believed them. Not wanting to leave Leah and the boys facing that burden slowed my plans. But in the worst moments, not even thoughts of my family, and leaving behind huge medical bills, were sufficient to deter me from planning to leave the hospital and kill myself. The pain was so all-consuming that I just wanted out.

I jokingly renamed our hospital "The Gardena Club." Each day,

patients in the unit participated in a variety of activities intended to promote group support, education, and encouragement. Our daily schedule changed from time to time, but always included a lecture on psychological issues, occupational therapy, psychodrama with role playing, personal counseling with a psychologist, and free time to sleep, watch TV, or socialize. In the occupational therapy room, patients could paint, make leather items, and do other handicraft projects. In a five-month stay, however, I never made a thing in that room: it symbolized the rebuilding of life, and I didn't want to heal, let alone rebuild! Also, one evening a week we had an optional family discussion session when patients and adult family members met in a large group with a psychologist to discuss issues we faced. Every Saturday or Sunday Leah brought Jimmy, John, and our lovable, rust-colored, 110-pound golden retriever, Dyno, to see me.

In addition to my regular sessions with a hospital psychologist, Phil drove from Fullerton to meet with me one hour a week. As a result of the teaching, group therapy sessions, and counseling, I gained new insights into my home background and myself.

The first three days in the hospital, I sobbed into my pillow often. For the next two months I was gravely disappointed in God, believing He'd abandoned me to fight my enemies alone most of my life. *Why so many betrayals? Why didn't You come to my aid when I was growing up? Where were You when I faced such terrifying opposition in some of my churches?*

I identified with the misery of Job, who moaned, "I despise my life … my days have no meaning … Terrors overwhelm me … days of suffering grip me … my gnawing pains never rest … I cry out to you, O God, but you do not answer … Have I not wept for those in trouble? … Yet when I hoped for good, evil came; when I looked for light, then came darkness. The churning inside me never stops…"[24]

I truly believed God was punishing me for past shortcomings. Knowing I was marinating in self-pity, I didn't care. I was mad at God, angry at life's unfairness, livid with certain people, and full of self-condemnation. I was sick of life. *Why keep punching? It's a*

thousand-round fight with no rest between rounds. I'd thrown in the towel. Living wasn't worth the anguish of disappointments and constant struggle. I no longer cared about anything or anyone. I didn't want to live, and certainly didn't want to try starting over.

I couldn't pray or read the Bible during the first sixty days at the hospital. While I never once doubted God's existence, all sense of His presence had vanished. By the third month, I was able to talk with Him. While still unable to read the Bible for my own comfort, I could show passages to other patients to console them. Amazingly, before being discharged, I led four informal Bible studies for fellow patients. Appearances, however, could be deceiving — during some moments of "normalcy" and fun, I remained suicidal.

None of the antidepressants and other medications eased my relentless depression. Once, I ordered suicide literature to be mailed to me at the hospital. It explained how to use various medications to achieve a quick, painless death. To my surprise, the head nurse intercepted it. I later ordered new materials mailed home, thinking Leah knew nothing about their contents and would bring them along with my other mail. She did realize the material and destroyed it, but I found other ways of getting the information.

For the most part, our unit was a laughterless place — until I embarked on my practical jokes. Occasionally, when I was "up," I took great pleasure in playing tricks on nurses, doctors, patients, and visitors. Everyone was fair game! There's something therapeutic about joviality. It helps you take life less seriously. Laughing at yourself and others can give you fresh perspective. It detaches you from your problems. I persuaded Leah to bring some of my practical jokes from home. Then I recruited two patients to join me, so I could teach them the fine art of "practical jokesmanship."

One of my favorite tricks was a soft rubber artificial dog poop. That imitation excrement had numerous fun-filled uses. We accomplices plopped it onto the floor in the women's shower, on top of patients' lunch trays, on the nursing station counter, on the TV room couch, and other unexpected places. It was hilarious to hear the shrieks. We tricksters shook with laughter!

After three months in the hospital, I risked letting some friends from St. Andrew's know my whereabouts. After that, five of them phoned or visited me periodically, a great source of encouragement. Their optimistic words and belief in me held out a hope on which to base trying to live again.

On one hand, the hospital afforded relief from the hurry and volume of my pastoral schedule. Not having to face deadlines or conflicts was a welcome rest. I never wore my watch in the hospital — how unbelievably refreshing it was to not have to check it all the time!

On the other hand, being hospitalized didn't insulate me from every conflict. Clashes with my denomination's insurance company constantly upset me. Every week or two, a member of my medical team would tell me, "Jim, the Presbyterian insurance authorities just called. They've refused to pay expenses beyond the next few days, even though we've told them that discharging you now will put you at high risk for taking your life. What more can we do? We're sorry, you'll have to pack your bag and prepare to leave." I knew I was brittle and in no shape to go home; if I left the hospital, I'd be dead within days.

I read a copy of my health insurance policy. Believing I had a huge amount of lifetime coverage for medical/psychiatric hospitalization, I questioned, *If I've got this much coverage and the medical staff is recommending further stay, why's the insurance company trying to force me to leave? I'd expect a secular insurance firm to act uncaring, but this is a Christian organization! They certainly ought to honor their commitments and put people ahead of dollars. It's tough enough struggling to stay alive in this place; having to fight my denomination's insurance on top of everything else is just too much. This is just another contract broken by people I thought were trustworthy. Why try to get better? It's not worth it.*

Worrying about coverage and hasty discharge caused me to slide deeper into depression; many times it made me ready to commit suicide right there in the hospital, or flee and do it on the outside. To everyone's surprise, one insurance crisis after another was averted

as the insurance representatives changed their minds, allowing me to stay another week. I lived week to week for five long months, uncertain whether I'd be forced to leave the hospital regardless of strong opposition by the medical staff. All that contention impeded my recovery, and nearly cost my life many times in the years ahead.

By day, I shuffled the halls with the blank glaze of one in a drugged stupor. Nights were the toughest times. I dreaded them because usually I couldn't fall asleep until 3 A.M., even heavily dosed with sleeping pills. The psalmist must have experienced similar insomnia: "When I was in distress, I sought the Lord; at night I stretched out untiring hands and my soul refused to be comforted. I remembered you, O God, and I groaned; I mused, and my spirit grew faint. You kept my eyes from closing; I was too troubled to speak." [25]

The benefits of listening to music are numerous: it boosts the immune system's ability to fight illness and speed healing, reduces muscle tension, stress, and pain. Many nights, I slipped into the TV room to listen to music and write. I preferred sad-sounding classical music, like the Mozart requiem, which echoed my inner hurts.

I spent many late-night hours writing down thoughts and feelings to share with Phil and the hospital therapists. Although not "feeling" deep emotions when I wrote, the mere exercise of putting reflections on paper provided a fresh perspective on my problems.

One afternoon, a female patient showed me a book about sexual abuse. "Would you like to borrow it?"

"Yeah, sure. Thanks."

Each chapter ended with a list of questions for readers to determine whether they'd experienced similar symptoms. Incredulous, I answered about eighty percent in the affirmative. *Maybe there was more to what Mom and Gram did than I remember.*

Patients' families were invited to a festive dinner at Thanksgiving, Christmas, and Easter. The occupational therapy room was decorated, as was our dining room. Leah and the boys came for those special

days. I always took the boys to the dining room and got them Dixie cups of ice cream from the refrigerator. Having my family visit kept me in touch with the reality of the outside world. Their presence strengthened my love for them. Most importantly, our weekends and holiday get-togethers slowed my plans for suicide.

Leah's weekly sacrifice, driving the forty-minute trip each way to see me in the hospital, demonstrated her tremendous courage, sensitivity, and inner strength. While we butted heads over some longstanding issues that surfaced during my hospitalization, her efforts testified to her persevering love for me. I'm grateful for our more than thirty-four years of companionship, and for the incredible way she stuck with me through my mental ordeals.

In the hospital, I went from depression to depression, with few manic symptoms. Nothing seemed to alleviate the misery — not medications, doctors, or psychologists. I felt like Humpty-Dumpty: I'd had a great fall and no one could put me together again. I'd all but given up. Bob Long flew from Pennsylvania to visit for four days when I'd sunk into a particularly deep despair. His unconditional love and his acceptance of my helpless situation were tremendously healing. His visits and the afternoon outings that the staff let us take pumped hope into me.

As expert as the doctors were, I think they were confused about my diagnosis. Only in the last month did they prescribe lithium. Sadly, misdiagnosis of manic-depressives happens time and again. A National Depressive and Manic-Depressive Association survey of people living with manic-depressive illness (funded by Eli Lilly and Company, and conducted in 2000 by Wirthlin Worldwide) confirmed that 69 percent of bipolars were misdiagnosed an average of three and a half times by four physicians before receiving an accurate diagnosis.[26] The study further found that for those who were misdiagnosed, the time from the onset of their illness until they received a correct diagnosis was more than *twelve years!* (Patients endured almost six years of symptoms without going for assistance and another six and a half years of actively seeking professional help, but going from one wrong diagnosis to another.)[27]

Little was known then about the negative effect of most antidepressants on bipolars. Research has attested to the fact that the effectiveness of antidepressants is far less than portrayed to consumers. [28] Research now corroborates that treating depression in bipolar patients is much more complicated than treating "regular" clinical depression alone, because prescribing the wrong antidepressant, or one without a mood stabilizer, can often trigger mania, extreme agitation, or suicide attempts. [29] I didn't realize it, but nothing would ever be the same for me again.

The insurance company urged the hospital staff to let me leave about a month early. I agreed, understanding I'd receive five outpatient sessions a week with Phil, and a weekly group therapy session through the rest of the year.

Chapter 15

Serious Insurance Conflicts and a Near Disaster

ON APRIL 4, 1989, I WAS DISCHARGED to what I thought would be the start of fuller healing. Instead, I learned two weeks later that the insurance agreement that I thought I had — early discharge in return for outpatient care — didn't exist! In disbelief, I was left out in the cold, feeling totally abandoned by fellow Presbyterians.

Enraged, I grabbed my belongings, jumped into the van, and drove for hours. For nearly two months, I lived out of the van and cheap motels. No one knew where I was. Everyone was looking for me, including the police. I was so infuriated that I stopped taking all medications. Clearly, I was in what psychiatrists call a

"mixed state," a combination of mania and depression: energetic agitation with profound despair. This condition is considered the most dangerous stage of manic-depressive illness, because it's extremely difficult to treat and can lead to suicide or violence toward others. [30] Evidence concludes that severe irritability accompanies up to 80 percent of manic and depressive episodes, and almost always occurs in mixed states. [31]

My insurance problems weren't unique. There are thousands of similar horror stories of people wrestling with their insurers over coverage. But those with mental illness often fight tougher battles. While manic depression definitely has a medical basis, as of this writing, a host of American insurance companies discriminate against it. Tragically, due to poor insurance aid, an enormous number of manic depressives find it difficult, if not impossible, to get the kind of psychiatric care and medications that can help them get better.

At the time, I thought I was experiencing only acute clinical suffering and burnout. I never imagined I was dealing with a fragile mood disorder called manic depression. It seemed logical that, with a few more months of counseling and a concerted effort to change my response to negative treatment by others, I'd be able to return to work. I wasn't aware that there is no known cure for manic depression — a recurrent condition that requires medication as its *primary* treatment. I had no idea that going off medication exacerbated my mixed condition and endangered my life.

Not taking my pills was rolling the dice, risking severe damage to my internal organs, plus a diminished effectiveness when I resumed taking the meds. Medical facts verify that without proper medication, the symptoms of the illness will most likely return within two years.[32] The consequences of *not* taking meds for the disease will exacerbate the episodes: they will grow more intense, occur more often, and be less helped by medication.[33]

Some experts believe there is a *50 percent* chance of recurrence after a *single* experience of major depression. [34] The danger of depression, of course, is suicide. Self-inflicted death is a very

real threat to seriously depressed persons. American women are at least twice as apt to try killing themselves as are men. Yet U.S. men are four times more successful at actually committing suicide.[35] Case histories indicate that people recovering from depression soon after their discharge from a mental hospital have one of the highest incidences of suicide.[36] Numerous studies over the past sixty years have reported that the life span of severely mentally ill people is much lower that the general population. Among the investigations was a 1991-93 Massachusetts research project that revealed a startling pattern: people with serious mind disorders died almost *nineteen* years earlier; the largest single cause of early death was suicide, which was almost *fifteen* times higher than in the general population.[37]

I thought constantly about ending my life. Sometimes I drove to cemeteries and sat in my car watching funerals or I walked around looking at grave markers. One time, late at night I sat on the bed of an Anaheim motel room, debating whether to use a .357 magnum pistol or a combination of rum and medications to kill myself. As I was deciding, someone knocked on the door. I stashed the "items" and cracked open the door. "Hi! Want some company sweetheart?" Apparently, two prostitutes were procuring business. "No thanks, try someone else." Then, I double-locked the door. But that strange, brief interruption thwarted my attempt.

Two afternoons later, I'd poured a drink, again arguing with myself over lethal pills and alcohol versus a handgun. In the midst of counting pills, the phone rang. "Sir, I apologize for calling, but I am trying to clarify our records. We don't want to over-bill you. Could you please come down to the motel office and help us out? It'll only take a minute."

"Sure, I'll be right there."

For a second time, an exit plan was halted. Another "suicide malfunction" occurred on an abortive trip to Pasadena. I'd contacted someone to buy pills, planning to mix a fatal "cocktail." Arriving, I reached in my pocket only to I discover I'd left my wallet in my motel room in Cerritos some fifty minutes away. Thankfully,

my terminal plans were miraculously interrupted those times and in a number of future ones.

Finally, in a phone call with Leah, I was persuaded to end my lengthy retreat. Driving home, I circled our block several times, not knowing what to expect, checking to see if police were waiting to re-hospitalize me. My heart pounded; fears ricocheted across my mind: *What will the neighbors think when I drive in? What'll it be like to eat meals every day with the family again? Will church members and friends stop by to see me? What can I say? If I sink into a worse depression, how can I hide it from Leah and the boys so I won't upset them?*

Everything seemed strange at first. My seven-month absence had taken a toll on her and the boys. I thought, *Maybe within a month or so things will return to normal.* Not so. You simply don't pick up where you left off after being gone so long, especially when your family has been aware of your life-and-death struggle.

Chapter 16

More Important Facts about Bipolar Disorder

A FEW WEEKS LATER, IN JUNE 1989, I heard some enticing news from two St. Andrew's members who also suffered from bipolar debilitation. They recommended a psychiatrist who used cutting-edge medicines to treat his patients. Leah encouraged me to make an appointment at his office in Pasadena. After my first two-hour session he diagnosed me as having bipolar disorder, a mental illness that involves extreme mood swings between energetic elation and life-threatening despondency.

In its milder stages, bipolar disorder produces a highly motivated, self-confident person who's astonishingly creative, has great social skills, and can work harder than many. In its worst manifestations, the disorder can lead to uncontrolled anger, violence, psychotic detachment from reality, or suicide.

"Jim, I can treat you weekly in my office for about three months, or I can admit you to the Las Encinas Hospital here in Pasadena. If you go the hospital route, we can complete all the testing and medicine trials in less than four weeks. What do you want to do?"

I entered Las Encinas a few days later. The staff put me through an extensive battery of tests to determine whether any sports injuries or tumors were causing my problem. Everything confirmed the diagnosis of manic-depressive illness. My brain disease resulted in driven workaholism and periodic anger outbursts, combined with cyclical depressions. For years I'd plowed my manic episodes into athletic aggressiveness and long, high-energy workweeks. I'd reasoned that my melancholies were merely energy slumps to recuperate from periods of hard work.

While I'd heard the terms "manic depression" and "bipolar disorder" before, I had no idea the terms were used interchangeably. I began reading some hospital literature on mental illness in general and my newly diagnosed condition in particular. My education in manic-depressive illness and depression began.

Statistically, one out of five Americans will undergo a serious mental or emotional crisis each year, and will be hospitalized more than those having cancer, diabetes, heart diseases, and arthritis.[38] More specifically, it is reported that the number-one reason for Americans being hospitalized is mental illness. At any time, individuals with psychiatric disorders occupy 21 to 24 percent of hospital beds.[39] In fact, depression and manic depression are considered to be the most common mental health problem in the United States.[40] According to the National Institute of Mental Health, over ten million Americans experience depression each year.[41] Also, bipolar disorder affects about three million people in the United States.[42] Together, they affect approximately one out of eleven people in

the U.S. at some period in their lives.[43]

Studies reveal that at least one person in five with clinical depression will try to take his life, and almost *50 percent* of those with bipolar disorder will attempt to end their lives at least once.[44] Research shows that for some manic-depressives suicide is an impulsive act. For others, it's a well thought-out plan based on accumulated despair or life traumas. However, previous suicide attempts are probably the most important predictor of coming self-destruction.[45] Other strong forecasters of suicide are repeated stress, relationship problems, deeply felt apprehension, or angry turmoil.

Bipolar disorder strikes indiscriminately at all ages, races, creeds, and classes, affecting men and women equally. There is disagreement among mental health professionals regarding its origin. Some experts consider manic depression to be caused only by environmental factors, like viruses, a dysfunctional home background, life trauma, or even personal sin. However, the preponderance of evidence indicates that this brain malfunction runs in families.[46] Legions of scientists believe the illness is indisputably an inherited brain disease, resulting *only* from genetic flaws that produce chemical imbalance in the brain. Many conclude that because of its hereditary and physical components the brain defect is not caused by poor parenting or an individual's weak will.[47]

Another huge group of mental health professionals asserts that the disease comes from a combination of being genetically vulnerable to the illness *and* undergoing enough stress to activate its symptoms.[48]

Cutting edge psychiatric and psychological professionals advocate the treating of bipolar affliction with both medications *and* psychotherapy. They warn that psychotherapy alone is not enough to stabilize manic-depressives. In fact, the popular medical school textbook, *Manic-Depressive Illness*, strongly advocates for psychotherapy *along with* medication in treating manic-depressives, but sternly warns against counseling without also using meds.[49]

I've certainly found the need for both meds *and* counseling in my experience. In battling manic-depressive illness for over thirteen

years, I've found that *25 percent* of the bipolar battle is *medications*. Pills are an absolute necessity; without them, getting better is next to impossible. But *75 percent* of the struggle is *learning how to handle or avoid stresses.*

With manic-depressive illness, mood changes can come as frequently as hours, days or weeks apart, and as long as months or years between episodes. Medicines, when they "fit" the patient, stabilize the manic highs and depressive lows to the point where the swings are less dramatic, less dangerous.

My reading in the years ahead proved to be eye opening. It startled me to see how research into manic depression validated a number of facts that I'd personally experienced:

- Stress, both good *and* bad, can worsen symptoms of mania or depression.[50]

- In 60 percent of the cases, the first occurrence of major depression or mania is precipitated by a significant stressor.[51]

- Negative life events *increase* the number of mood relapses and *lengthen* the time it takes to recuperate from a bout of mania or depression.[52]

- If no major negative stressor precedes the relapse, it takes an average of *four months* to recover.[53]

- If a significant negative incident occurs before a setback, it takes an average of *eleven months* to get better.[54]

- The more mood changes one has, the more vulnerability to future setbacks *increases* and the effectiveness of certain medications *decreases*.[55]

- While recovering from an experience of depression or mania, there is an *increased* susceptibility to suicide.[56]

A number of my relatives have struggled with serious depression. I'm sure my mother had some kind of mental illness, perhaps manic depression, borderline personality disorder, or schizophrenia.

Scientists estimate that if one parent has manic depression and the other parent does not, their child has a 28 percent chance of getting either depressive or manic-depressive illness.[57] Knowing this sobering statistic, I watched Jimmy and John closely, constantly concerned about any signs of impending disorder.

After spending hour after hour researching the causes, I decided that it didn't matter what or who caused my disorder; I had to cope with it and overcome it. The practical reality was that something was causing me to have extreme mood swings. It didn't matter what they called it or what caused it, unless the name and origin would help me deal with the "monster." The big question for me was: "Now that I have this mind disease, what am I going to *do* about it?"

More than half of bipolars lose touch with reality at times. Fortunately, I never had visual or auditory hallucinations or delusions of grandeur, or went on sprees, spending thousands of dollars on unneeded items. But I faced my own tunnel of horrors, and more would come in the years ahead.

Like diabetes and some other diseases, manic depression isn't something you cure; it's something you *manage*. While some authorities believe that it's entirely a medical illness and should be treated *primarily* with drugs, a growing number don't share that view. The line between the biological and emotional influences on the disease is blurry. More and more bipolar experts agree that there's a complex interplay between genetic-biological predisposition *and* psychological-environmental vulnerability to the disorder.[58] *Stress* plays a key role in the timing, frequency, intensity, and duration of manic or depressive episodes.[59]

My psychiatrist maintained that my toiling sixty-plus hours a week for twenty years wasn't caused primarily by poor time-management skills or lack of willpower. Instead, he believed my chronic workaholism originated primarily from manic, driven energy, and secondarily from my home background and other traumas. Other therapists differed, thinking my upbringing exerted the principal influence on my work habits.

Patients react to the uncertainties of their illness in a variety of ways: many cope by denying its severity, or the possibility of recurrence, even its very existence. They refuse medications, counseling, and peer support. Others rage against their illness by doing everything in their power to heal. I chose to take charge of my recovery, and fought in different ways in the years ahead to beat my inner "beast." Dylan Thomas' poem, "Do Not Go Gentle Into That Good Night", motivated me to stand up for myself with the medical, pharmaceutical, and insurance establishments, and to fight with all my might to get well.

During my stay at Las Encinas, I received many cards, letters, and visits from a few friends. How encouraging these expressions of concern were, especially when my moods swung from the depths of despair to childish giddiness. Finally, almost four weeks after entering Las Encinas, my psychiatrist decided I'd improved enough to be discharged. He thought my medication "cocktail," — a number of different meds taken at different times of the day — had stabilized me.

I benefited from both hospitals. At the Minirth-Meier Clinic, I received biblical and psychological teaching integrated with caring psychotherapy. Together they helped me come to grips with some of the pain from past abuses. Las Encinas Hospital provided a thorough physical and chemical analysis of my brain and body. Today, after years of studying, I believe my manic-depressive illness was caused by the combination of an inherited chemical imbalance in my brain, deep hurts in childhood, and church injuries in adulthood. Its episodes, I'm convinced, must be controlled by both medication and stress-reduction.

Part Five

Treading Water to Survive

Fearing we would be dashed against the rocks, they
dropped anchor from the stern and prayed for daylight
                                                    — Acts 27:29

Chapter 17

Facing Losses

ON JULY 11, 1989, AFTER MORE THAN SIX MONTHS of psychiatric hospitalization and two months of life-on-the run horrors, Leah and John picked me up from Las Encinas. I'd been away from my family for a total of eight months! Having had virtually no exercise during that time, I'd put on fifty-five pounds, and had become a prime example of how drugs, mood changes, and inactivity can increase weight.

My second homecoming was as disorienting as the first. Pulling into our driveway, the house seemed only vaguely familiar. Walking in, I felt like a stranger who didn't belong. Even the furniture and pictures on the walls seemed odd.

"Honey," Leah said, "I'm so glad you're home. The boys and I need you. We know you're going to get better. The people at church love you and are behind you. We're all in your corner and we'll work with you to beat this illness."

I didn't feel nearly as optimistic about my future as she and others did. They didn't see the scary bleakness I saw ahead, but I mustered, "Thanks. I know I can beat it too. It'll just take a little time."

It was a difficult adjustment period for all of us. In fact, emotionally and financially, the next six years would be a roller-coaster existence. Much of the turbulence would be stirred up by my mood swings — from depressive isolation, to fast, loud, nonstop talking, to short-fused agitation, to angry explosions.

My first year at home, I couldn't stop feeling paranoid about meeting people — particularly those whom I knew. The thought of having to talk about my situation petrified me. It terrified me to leave the house, even to walk around the block or take a short drive. Each venture out the front door required enormous courage.

For those six years I lived in denial of my medical condition, thinking the psychiatrists were incorrect in their diagnosis of bipolar sickness. I believed that chronic stress, coupled with major depression and a history of exhausting overwork, had finally broken me, but surely not a biological disease in my brain!

Few days went by without panic and a sense of impending catastrophe. Suicidal impulses shadowed me everywhere. In an odd way, those thoughts helped me cope. They were comforting, because they promised a way of escape if the torment became unbearable. No matter how bad things got, I always had a way out.

I'd experienced no readily identifiable mania — only nonstop depression mixed with agitation — so I didn't believe I had manic-depressive illness. Looking back, I see that in fact some symptoms of mania, such as extreme irritability, had surfaced from time to time. Never in life had I sworn as much and as often. My conscience constantly twinged. *Why can't I stop swearing so much? I ought to be able to control my tongue better. Maybe this is proof that I'm innately bad and God has really left me.*

Some friends generously gave us a Jacuzzi. It became a welcome relief to soak in it every day, thinking and meditating. Likewise, at home I lounged in my La-Z-Boy chair by the hour, listening to tapes of Mozart, Bach, and Handel. Yet, in the midst of my calm solitude, I continued to feel guarded, anxious.

My temper often boiled just beneath the surface. Sometimes underneath my friendly smiles I was really mulling over a suicide plan. I was often so edgy that I tensed every time the phone rang, and literally shook when hearing loud noises. I asked the family to tell people, "Dad can't come to the phone right now. Can he call you back later?"

Many people with handicaps have visible evidence of disability: a wheelchair, a walker, a seeing-eye dog, or a cane. Like most people with a mind disorder, I displayed no outward signs. I didn't fit the image many had of the mentally ill: I didn't twitch, have a wild-eyed look, or huddle catatonically in a corner. I looked and talked "normal." No wonder mental illness is confusing to many observers.

Because my manic depression symptoms weren't obvious most of the time, I worried what others thought of me. *Do they think I'm faking an invisible illness or that I'm lazy 'cause I'm not working? I hate pretending everything's all right when it isn't. What should I say if someone criticizes me for taking pills, or for seeing a therapist, or taking so long to get better?*

The first several months home I kept thinking, *Things aren't really that bad. In a few weeks I'll feel like my old self and this hopelessness will have dissipated. I'll go back to work and start setting goals for the years ahead. I won't need the medications much longer. Reading about emotional issues, and a few more months of psychotherapy sessions, will settle old issues and I can get on with my life.*

Month after month dragged painfully on. Still no freedom from depression's cruel pain. After a few months back home, I began facing the hard facts: I'd spent eight months in hell. What had happened to me was real, and scarier than my worst nightmare. Healing and returning to my old life wasn't going to happen overnight or even in months. Now I had to survive outside a sheltered hospital environment, and begin a lengthy recuperation.

The first two years after being hospitalized were one long battle for survival. The first was the worst. I struggled with one crisis after another, fighting to stay alive on a day-to-day basis. Depression never lifted for long; a few days or a week, then it would return. I ached with indescribable inner pain and experienced loneliness on top of loneliness. I barely hung on. The slightest negative comment sometimes put me down for weeks. A single rejection or negative event could trigger a depressive episode lasting up to six months, in which suicide was an ever-present option.

I went days at a time without shaving. I slept until noon or later, then couldn't sleep at night. With little energy, house chores were next to impossible. Jimmy, John, and Leah got angry, thinking I was lazy, seeing me lounge around the house in my bathrobe, watching TV, asking them to run errands for me.

On "good" days, I worked at reinventing myself, daydreaming and planning for the second half of my life. I struggled to let go of

my former career, refusing to give up hope of working again as an active pastor, yet knowing I couldn't handle the long hours and inevitable conflicts that came with the job. This process of mourning losses and redrafting the future would repeat itself dozens of times in the years to come. It wasn't until almost a decade later that I was able to resolve the career issue.

My psychiatrists frequently experimented with medications: over the next thirteen years I would be prescribed at least thirty-seven different ones! The meds were so strong that they caused severely burdensome side effects. I experienced ongoing blurred vision and dizziness; my balance got so tipsy I had to sit down to put on my pants.

Leah, John, and Jimmy weren't eager to go places when I was driving. John finally admitted, "Dad, you drive too dangerously. You almost hit a bridge rail last week when I was with you. Another time, you swerved and almost hit a car in our lane. I'm scared to ride with you. Please be more careful." Jimmy and Leah nodded in agreement. No amount of rationalization about "southern California traffic" could excuse my unsteady driving.

They forced me to face the fact that my manias, depressions, and medications were making me drive dangerously. My pills distorted depth perception and lengthened reaction time. Without a doubt, I was endangering others and myself — I had to stop driving immediately.

Leah was so shaken up over my driving that, for the next few months, she insisted I have friends chauffeur me to see Phil, and my psychiatrist, and any other places I needed to go. I recruited two friends from the church and paid them to drive me to appointments and on errands. It was costly, but it probably saved my life and others'.

Talking with people at any kind of social, sports, or church event was enormously taxing, and wiped me out for a day afterward. For this reason, I shied away from most socializing. Though I relished watching the boys' school and sports events, it took courage to overcome the fear of having to talk with people, especially those

who knew of my "situation."

It terrified me to explain my hospitalization, so I had to break the ice in small increments, pushing myself to meet with friends — one at a time — for breakfast, lunch, or coffee. To help overcome my anxiety about being with people, Leah gently encouraged me to go out to dinner periodically with her and one other couple. Every few weeks, I'd write or call Bob Long in Pittsburgh. Sometimes we'd talk and laugh for an hour.

I tried exercising, but with moods, sleep deprivation, and drug-related fatigue, it was an uphill battle. I couldn't jog or walk more than a few miles because of knee pain, and I couldn't ride a bicycle, because the meds made me too dizzy. One August evening I went to the nearby YMCA to go swimming. I put my foot in the water, looked around, saw a dozen people, and panicked. I headed back to the locker room and called Leah to come pick me up.

By September, I'd recovered enough to drive again. Every week for the next few years, I drove forty minutes each way to meet a fellow alumnus from the Gardena Club for lunch near our old hospital. He and I swapped jokes and shared the problems and challenges we faced — a tremendous uplift!

In each church I've served, I started men's Bible studies, breakfast meetings, and small support groups. The men's groups in the North Palm Beach church and St. Andrew's were the most dynamic of all. During my illness, I received dozens of cards, letters, and phone calls from them. Their encouragement helped me keep going.

As in the hospital, sometimes, during my darkest moments in the years to come, I wrote down my thoughts and feelings — nearly every day a page or more of thoughts about feelings, relationships, and insights into my illness. Writing provided no catharsis, only a sense of clarification of what was going on.

It became increasingly clear that I couldn't beat the illness alone, so I worked hard to develop a support system. I stayed in touch with friends by phone, even though mood changes often forced me to cancel. Four friends from St. Andrew's invited me to join them in a weekly support group. While some people had been

"hope killers," these men were "hope builders." None knew much about mental illness, but all were helpful in countless ways. When frustrated or defeated, I heard again and again, "Hang in there, Jim. We're praying for you. You'll make it. Be easy on yourself. Remember, 'All you can do is all you can do.'" They became a key part in my healing process by listening, connecting me with daily life, and focusing my attention on taking baby steps toward becoming sociable again. They were indeed a safe harbor.

Ed and Sue Egloff, dear friends from St. Andrew's, sent cards and wrote me throughout my hospital stays. They became our family's adopted grandparents, and sent flowers, cards, letters, and assorted gifts to each of us. Ed called every week or so and took me out for lunch. To me they were Christian love personified.

Early that fall, and in the years ahead, when feeling okay, I took each boy on "dad and lad" adventures to amusement parks, college and professional sporting events, and on camping, fishing, and hunting trips. Watching them have fun was wondrously satisfying.

Christmas 1989 arrived. Having been home from the hospital only six months, the weeks before and after that first Christmas were acutely sad for me. The incongruity of festive decorations all around, and my inner misery, made the season almost unbearable. Every store was decorated, and many played carols. Homes in our neighborhood sported colored lights; their lawns displayed Christmas scenes. But I wasn't swept into the holiday spirit. I dreaded it, and cringed just looking at our family's tree and trimmings. I wanted to attend the St. Andrew's Christmas Eve service with the family, but was frightened of people's stares and comments. Strong tranquilizers fortified my courage and numbed me into blissfulness, but afterward, I couldn't remember a thing about the service.

In the first eight months after my hospitalization, I saw Phil five times a week. By 1990, we had cut back to three. I continued seeing the psychiatrist every few weeks. Each time, I reported how the pills were working and any side effects. Initially, he prescribed frequent blood tests to monitor the lithium's therapeutic

level and to check for potential organ damage. He had to change my medications and dosages often to avoid the risky side effects I experienced. However, too often the meds had little effect on my moods. *These pills aren't working. How can I make it? Maybe the next depression will take me down for good.*

Chapter 18

Problems Adjusting to Work

IN JANUARY 1990 I RETURNED TO WORK at St. Andrew's. The leadership board graciously allowed me to start slowly, working only a few hours a day, until I was able to resume full speed. I was eager to get my life back on track, but apprehensive that the pressure, pace, and conflicts that came with pastoring might be too much.

I handled the first month reasonably well, visiting hospitals, counseling a few church members, and reading the mail, but fear of having to talk with people hadn't gone away as I'd hoped. I dreaded committee and staff meetings. In fact, I stayed in my office more and more, doing paperwork and making phone calls. Due to low energy and mood changes, I canceled nearly half my appointments.

One medication side effect was hand tremors. My handwriting was so small and jerky that my secretary and others could hardly read it. I had short-term memory loss, so recalling dates, events, names, and conversations became embarrassing. Sometimes I couldn't hear well, and had to keep asking what had been said. These were, of course, side effects of my meds, but they affected my self-confidence and ability to function at work. It was exceedingly aggravating.

Throughout my hospitalization, and during this period, the church had been paying my full salary — generosity beyond all expectations. Few businesses and even fewer churches would have been so supportive. Knowing my productivity wasn't up to its previous level, I resolved to double my efforts. I determined to conquer my illegible handwriting, memory difficulties, fear of people, and constant exhaustion. No one was prodding me to accomplish more; I was my own worst taskmaster. Yet after three months, I still couldn't put in the quality of work and number of hours I believed my responsibilities required.

Bob Long flew out to encourage me that spring. For most of the four days, we stayed at a friend's beach house. We took long walks and drives, sharing experiences, joking, and just loafing. Even though we'd shared personal troubles and triumphs over the years, I'd never shed tears. This time, I wept uncontrollably as I described my childhood, church struggles, and other conflicts. It was the first time I'd cried in his presence. Those tears were profoundly therapeutic.

How comforting it was to have someone listen, accept, and believe in me. This had happened only a few times in my life and was overwhelming. In a boxing match, it's critical to have someone in your corner, patching your cuts, encouraging you, correcting you, and sending you back into the fray with a confident strategy. Before I met Bob, I'd had few corner men in life.

In the years ahead, I'd need his help even more, but in different ways. I'm grateful too for Phil Sutherland and others who acted as powerful corner men through the coming turbulent times. Of them, I can echo the thankful words of the Apostle Paul, who said of a friend, "...he often refreshed me and was not ashamed of my chains."[60]

However, for all the benefits of Bob's visit, it didn't take long to see that I was fighting a losing battle at St. Andrew's. Medication side effects were becoming unbearable and I slid further into depression. By May, I saw the painful reality that I wasn't going to make it there. The ministry responsibilities needed much more than I was able to give. I resigned effective June 15, 1990. In keeping with their magnanimity, the church gave me a generous severance.

But I felt I'd let down everyone: church members, friends, and family. I was ashamed to attend services. It was heartrending to be on the church campus and reminded of my losses, what I used to be and do.

The memory of cleaning out my office is still vivid. I gave away some six hundred books to seminarians and friends. It took hours to pack the remaining hundreds of books and cabinets of files, and make dozens of sweaty trips, hauling them home in our minivan to store in the garage. After the last box was loaded, I walked upstairs for one final look at my former office. Nothing left but an empty desk, a sofa, three chairs, and a dozen filing cabinets. Bare wooden bookshelves lined the walls. That once-warm, well-furnished room was suddenly empty, sterile. *My ministerial career is over. No more counseling, or preparing sermons, or officiating at weddings, baptisms, and funerals. I've given it my best shot, but just couldn't make it. This ghoulish illness has ruined my career. I hate what it's done to me and my life.*

In a matter of minutes, I ceased to be a minister with an established reputation. I embarked on an uncharted path, with a young family and the limited economic security of a disability income. Everything seemed beyond my control. I had nothing to look forward to other than an uncertain journey. "Mr. Type-A Goal Setter" had no goals, plans, schedule, or structure. In this newly evolving life, I'd stepped into a foreign land with no roadmap. Having no plans was terribly unsettling. I panicked. *My whole life's been thrown off course. Will I ever be able to control these moods? I still feel called to preach and pastor. Can I ever work again? How will our family survive financially?*

I kept thinking this was all a bad dream that was happening to someone else. But the facts were, in a year and a half I'd gone from effective leader, mentor of men, and pastor of many, to unemployed and hopeless. I was now a "has-been" with no official identity: just, "Jim Stout," no more, no less. My St. Andrew's business cards were useless now. I had no title, no office, no secretary — everything that had defined me as a man was gone.

Chapter 19

Finding Understanding Friends

*M*anic-depressive illness, a ruthless thief, has stolen my dreams and plans. An aching sense of loss swept over me. Up to this point, I'd been in and out of denial about my disorder, career, and future. I'd believed all along that rebuilding would be fairly easy, but living with a mental illness isn't that simple. It takes courage and persistence just to survive, let alone do the hard work of recovering enough to achieve a degree of stabilization.

Fortunately, I'd started receiving disability benefits about six months after leaving the second hospital. But we'd incurred huge medical bills. Each month Leah and I were falling further behind, paying on a bank line of credit and maxing out our credit cards. Thankfully, some friends from St. Andrew's helped us refinance our home, or we could have been in danger of losing it.

Like many mentally ill people, I was caught up in the exasperation of navigating through a bureaucratic system. I wrote letters and made endless phone calls to denominational leaders and insurance company representatives, seeking solutions to our coverage issues. Rarely did I get a satisfactory answer. The insurance strife continued intermittently in the years ahead.

One of the many things I learned from the lectures at Minirth-Meier Hospital was the importance of *supportive relationships*. Time and again, the psychologists stressed how critical positive relationships were to our healing. In my experience, I've found it's crucial to develop caring friendships. Sometimes you'll find a person who's sustaining; other times you'll be disappointed by toxic ones (often, family members or relatives). Stay away from these if you can. Not only will they let you down or criticize you, they might even turn on you. Occasionally, even your relatives and

close friends will be unavailable to meet your needs. Maybe they'll be busy with work responsibilities or in a bad place emotionally. When one relationship isn't working for you, find another. In fact, always try to have several people you can go to. Likewise, I've seen how important it is to *keep cultivating friendships.* Again, some individuals will be helpful, others draining. The key to recovering is to bond with caring individuals. Knowing this, I kept reaching out to friends, calling and meeting with a few every week.

Regardless of my efforts, I frequently isolated. It was humbling to apologize to so many people for not returning their calls or for breaking appointments. To some, I gave lame excuses: "I'm sorry for being late to call you back. My schedule's been crazy. Please forgive me." To others, "I'm really sorry for not returning your call for three weeks. I haven't been well. I've gotten your messages, but was too depressed to answer. Don't take it personally; it has nothing to do with our friendship. When I'm depressed, I withdraw, and simply can't talk to anyone. Please try to understand, and keep calling, even when I don't respond for a while. When you leave messages, I know you're reaching out, and it means a lot to me. I'll phone you when the depression lifts. Thanks for your calls and for your patience."

Some stopped phoning, and I never heard from them again. A few persevered. Fortunately, my closest friends understood the many times I bailed on lunches or didn't return their calls. I'm exceedingly thankful for their loyalty, care, and untiring efforts on my behalf.

Twice, I visited a support group for manic-depressives, but it was so disorganized that I never returned. Someone suggested I try an incest survivors' support group. I phoned eight, always getting a similar response: "Hey mister, our group is for women. Men abused us, and we want nothing to do with them. Don't call again."

Although Leah and I had our share of spats, she was tremendously sensitive when it came to going places where I'd have to be with people. She'd say, "Honey, there's a special concert at the church next Friday night. If you want to go, I'd love to go with

you. But if you're not up to it, or change your mind at the last minute, it's OK. I don't want you to feel obliged either way. I'll understand." Her low-key approach really took the pressure off.

She continually encouraged my efforts to be disciplined in taking meds, going for counseling, learning about the illness, and meeting with friends regularly. She was quick to compliment signs of improvement: not withdrawing as much, helping with house chores, and not staying up so late at night.

I lived perennially off balance, enduring terrible side effects from meds, and relapsing into frequent episodes of despair or agitation. In those nightmarish stretches, I could see only problems. Dwelling on setbacks became a fixation. In the midst of this, Leah affirmed me often, giving the encouragement I desperately needed: "Honey, I can't imagine how tough it is for you. But I want you to know how much it means to the boys and me that you're doing all you can to get well. You've got tremendous courage. In spite of how bad you feel, you still made it to both your doctors' appointments this week. You're taking your medications every day. You cleaned up the family room and washed the dishes, too. Thanks for trying so hard." Realizing my memory was poor, she said, "You've complained about having trouble remembering things. Would it help for me to remind you once in a while to take your pills, or when you have an appointment with your doctors? I promise not to nag you."

Still disbelieving the bipolar diagnosis, I thought my "depressive breakdown" was a sign of weakness, an inability to cope with job difficulties. I resolved to wade through any future tough times, grow thick-skinned toward rejection, and work harder at changing my attitude toward discouragement. I firmly believed my efforts would soon eradicate the depression. Despite my sincere intentions, will power wasn't enough. My life was already in the process of changing forever.

Chapter 20

Stigma's Distressing Effects

I GREW EXTREMELY ANXIOUS ABOUT going anyplace where I was known, embarrassed that they knew about my illness. Many "normal" people have false ideas about mental malfunction. It hurt my pride that others might pity or reject me because of what they perceived as a character defect, a weakened ability to handle life's pressures, that caused me to "flip" and have a "nervous breakdown." Conversations drained me; anxiety over what others could be thinking or saying about me, or what they might say to me, left me constantly guarded.

Word about my brain disorder and my tangles with the denomination's insurance company had spread quickly. The term "fair-weather friend" took on new meaning as my circle of friends and professional colleagues began to shrink dramatically. I experienced firsthand the lonely, hurtful sting of stigma for my neurological condition. Many relationships suffered or ended over the next decade, especially those with clergy. It was like being a modern-day leper, an untouchable. Only a couple of pastor colleagues ever phoned me, most never returned my calls or letters. I took the silence of the rest of my ministry peers as total abandonment.

I learned what it must be like to buck the system of a large organization, company, or religious denomination. Several ministers courageously confided in me that they were afraid to confront our Presbyterian insurance company regarding their own medically related issues. They were afraid to invite me to speak at their churches, and being seen socializing with someone known as a "disloyal denominational troublemaker." They believed it could cost them their careers. Agonizingly, I received fewer and fewer calls from fellow clergy to speak, teach or meet with them. *Have I become*

persona non grata *because of my mental illness? Are my peers afraid to associate with me due to my confrontations with the Presbyterian insurance system?* I felt like a man without a country, abandoned by my clergy equals, and many friends and acquaintances.

Dyno was my daily companion. It was reassuring to have his big brown eyes looking at me, his tail wagging with enthusiasm. At least *he* was loyal! He loved being petted, and soaked up as much attention as he could get. I took him with me wherever I could.

I pushed myself onto the offense, trying to reestablish previous connections with peers and develop new ones. *This must be what retirement is like. You're out of the loop with former job-related relationships. Most of those contacts fall by the wayside. Retirees, cancer patients, and divorced people experience similar losses. They too must develop new links, or shrivel up in loneliness or resentment. I guess a psychiatric disability doesn't make me unique after all!*

Finally overriding my anxiety, I joined the YMCA. Then, I joined a water aerobics class that was predominantly female. Our teacher exemplified dedication and caring. She and the "girls" welcomed me warmly, laughed at my jokes, listened patiently to my manic chatter, and never ostracized me for illness-induced absences. All too often, I was so drugged with assorted pills that I fell in the locker room while dressing or undressing. The exercise group benefited me physically and gave structure to my schedule-less life. Although many nights I was so low that I had to drag myself to the pool, the swim class gave me a great emotional lift and a feeling of accomplishment.

Chapter 21

Family Struggles with Pain and Loss Due to Mental Illness

ONE OF THE MOST TRYING THINGS about bipolar illness is its un-predictability, which keeps the patient and his loved ones and friends confused and off balance. Throughout my prolonged healing, Leah was, for the most part, gentle with me. Occasionally, though, her pent-up anger came out, due to incurring so many significant losses: her husband's health and career, her ministry as a pastor's wife, our finances, and more. In addition, she had to assume sole responsibility for our insurance, taxes, and bills. Besides being unreliable due to my moods, I simply couldn't concentrate on financial details.

Afraid to trigger my depression, mania, or anger, Leah and the boys often withdrew from me. They were aggravated by my memory lapses, silent isolation, not doing my fair share of chores, sleeping all day, refusing to answer the phone, temper flashes, and numerous other irritations. I grieved over the time I'd lost with them due to my condition, and ached for what Jimmy and John had lost: their father had been away from them for so long, and was unable to respond to their needs.

It's depressing to be around a depressed person; it's scary to be with someone who's in an argumentative mania. Leah, Jimmy, and John often asked themselves, "When will all this end? How long will it take for him to pull himself out of his angry agitation? Will he ever get over his relentless dourness, withdrawals and frequent flare-ups?" Like many family members of depressives or bipolars, they thought, "If I could just say or do the right thing, he'd get well and stay well."

It's hard for family members and friends to see manic depression as an *illness*, rather than just willful displays of withdrawal, argumentative clashes, or charming, outgoing warmth. They often feel their loved one's mental disease is somehow their fault, that something *they* said or did caused it. Families often try to hide the illness from friends because of social prejudice against "crazy people." Jimmy and John didn't want me talking about anything to do with mental illness in the presence of their friends. Afraid I'd be in one of my "moods," they avoided bringing classmates home.

When I intuited that the boys were blaming themselves for my erratic behavior, I pulled them aside and explained, "Guys, Dad's got manic-depressive illness. It's a medical disease, like diabetes or high blood pressure. *You* didn't cause it and *you* can't cure it. Sometimes I'm just not myself. It's a sickness that leaves me cranky, or angry, sad or depressed. Sometimes it makes me not feel like talking to anyone on the phone or being around people. When I get impatient with you, or blow up at something, it's not *your* fault. It's my illness.

"I'm doing my best to beat it. I see Phil every week to talk about what I can do to get better. I visit my psychiatrist regularly. He gives me pills to help control my sadness and anger, but they don't always work. I love you very much. I'm going to keep fighting and I'm going to get well. Our family's been through a lot together; God will help us through this, too.

"Remind yourself that if I'm overly quiet, it's because my disease has made me sad; it's *not* because of you. Remember how sometimes I talk too much, too loud, too fast? That means I'm getting manic. When you see me doing that, no matter where, please give me the "time-out" sign. It'll alert me to shut up.

"I really appreciate the ways you've helped me. You've done my chores when I didn't feel well. You've answered the phone for me. You've worked hard in school and on your sports teams in spite of how tough it's been. When you tell me you love me and say encouraging things, it means so much to me."

Initially, Jimmy and John showed no observable effects of being without their father for eight months, but off and on, their pent-up frustrations over my illness surfaced. Like their mother, they had suffered the loss of companionship with their fun-loving father. As a group, we had to live with the stigma of a mentally ill family member.

By now both boys were becoming noticeably ill at ease talking with me, and pulled away from me, their anger evident. Neither wanted to go to sports events, movies, or even out to get hamburgers with me. It was tough to be shut out by others, but being snubbed by my sons was devastating. I missed doing things with them terribly.

Their attitudes troubled me. *Are Jimmy and John avoiding me because they're going through normal youthful emotional changes, or because they think I deserted them for over half a year? Are they angry because they think I'm too lazy to work or do house chores? Are they afraid I'll lecture them with hours of manic talk, or embarrass them in front of their friends? Are they anxious they'll say or do something that'll send me into a fit of anger or a depression?*

Even though I knew that some of their moodiness resulted from academic stress, peer pressure, and self-image struggles, it was difficult to avoid blaming myself for our strained relationship. I was convinced that *I* was the cause of their distancing themselves, and I suffered unending remorse for the injury my long absence and mood swings had done them.

All I could do was accept, as best I could, my sons' frustration, hurt, anger, and sadness. *Can they ever forgive me for the pain I've caused them? What if they can't get over it and we never can have a close relationship again? Will they ever process their losses and figure out how to relate to their unstable father in new ways?*

Frequently, I had to bite my tongue so I wouldn't raise my voice at the boys. After what I perceived as a slight from them, I'd sink into self-pity that lasted weeks. Had I not received input from Leah, Phil, and a few friends, I'd have continued wallowing in self-condemnation. Time and again, they counseled, "The boys

are going through normal moodiness for kids their age. Give them space. Be patient. They'll come around. Stop blaming yourself." Yet their aloofness continued, off and on, for the next several years. Even though there were strained moments between the boys and me, I tried my best to rebuild our relationship.

The members of St. Andrew's were overwhelmingly supportive of our whole family, both while I was hospitalized and as I recuperated. In addition to scores of letters, cards, and phone calls, many brought food and bouquets of flowers. Some took the boys to sports events, movies, skiing, and other activities. One family planted flowers in our front and side yards. A few gave us checks to use for clothes, food, or a night out. Once, we were given an anonymous thousand-dollar check. We felt truly cared for by that loving church family!

I fought nonstop depression, with only a few plateau days. Things people said or did triggered three-fourths of the depressions; medicinal side effects caused the other one-fourth. Fortunately, I persevered, waiting for the misery to abate.

Most of the time, my daily uniform was a pair of dark-blue sweat pants, golf shirt, and jogging shoes. My routine differed little from day to day. I slept until noon, then watched TV and lounged in my La-Z-Boy chair, reading newspapers, magazines, and books. My reading focused on true crime, child abuse, dysfunctional families, suicide, manic depression, and incest. Sometimes I drove to a movie. Often, a soak in the Jacuzzi brought welcome relief to my back and knees.

One benefit of my illness was spending more time with our family. Leah and I tried to go out one morning or evening a week. We saw movies, ate at inexpensive restaurants, and took walks. I attended most of the boys' athletic events: crew races, Little League baseball games, wrestling matches, and track meets. Though it was formidable conversing with people, those were special times.

Christmas 1990, my second year home, was slightly more "up" than the first. I had several positive days, and was able to absorb some of the holiday spirit. During the good days, I read the Bible

and prayed regularly, but on bad ones, everything fell apart. I worried what the new year might bring.

Chapter 22

More Stigma: Toxic Church Members and Clergy

BIPOLAR DISORDER OR ANY MENTAL ILLNESS can be very isolating. Few understand what you're going through. You alone endure the ups and downs; you alone experience the awful side effects of medication. When you withdraw from people to lick your wounds in silence, they don't know how to reach out to you, or are afraid of you or embarrassed to be seen with you. Thus, the mentally ill all too often suffer in solitude, outcasts, misunderstood and feared by society. A recent U. S. Department of Health and Human Services report notes,

> In a time of vastly increased medical sophistication, which virtually guarantees greater numbers of restored mental patients, discrimination against them continues ... for example, research studies have found that most Americans think that the two worst things which can happen to a person are leprosy and insanity. In American society, ex-convicts stand higher on the ladder of acceptance than former mental patients. Asked to rate 21 categories of disability, from the least offensive to the most, respondents placed mental illness on the bottom of the list.[61]

Sadly, such bias surfaces in public attitudes, personal remarks, job opportunities, lack of fair insurance coverage, and elsewhere. Worse than the illness itself is *how* people treat you. When they

know you have a mental disorder, they tend to avoid you, or walk on eggshells around you, not knowing what to say. Interestingly, people who *don't* know that you're mentally ill treat you "normally."

Myths and stereotypes about mental illness have long persisted. Those labeled mentally ill are considered as having "gone off the deep end," "gone bonkers," or "gone crazy." They're referred to as psychopaths, serial killers, loonies, schizos, wackos, maniacs, fruitcakes, lunatics, and other derogatory names.

Many think that mentally disabled people are dangerous, but usually the opposite is true. Most mentally ill individuals tend to be passive and withdrawn. Those in treatment are more often the *victims* of crime rather than instigators of it. A close inspection of the details reveals that mentally ill people commit only about 5 percent of the violent acts in America.[62] However, while mind-damaged people tend to be inert, bipolars can have fierce outbursts of aggression. Almost half of all manic episodes involve one or more physically violent actions. Anxiety that they might ignite this heightened irritability can weigh on family and friends, who worry that what they say or do could set off their bipolar loved one.[63]

Sadly, for both spiritual and secular people, mental illness is misunderstood as a sign of inability to cope with life. Over 40 percent of the respondents in a new study by the National Institute of Mental Health felt that depression was caused by personal weakness.[64] Sympathy and understanding are readily offered to people with cancer, heart disease, and other serious ailments, yet, for the most part, people afflicted with mind ailments elicit no such response. Instead, they're blamed for being weak in character and told, "It's all in your head." Those unfamiliar with biochemical imbalances don't understand that willpower alone can't fix a broken brain.

When it comes to psychiatric disorders, too many Christians cling to superstitious fears, distorted thinking, and flawed biblical interpretation. Some believe that the mentally ill are faithless sinners who should be shunned until they repent. Depression and manic depression definitely have spiritual and emotional components, but

they're not *just* religious and psychological problems. They are, in fact, also *physical* diseases. Our hearts, liver, kidneys, and lungs get diseased. Why not the brain also?

I suppose my condition embarrassed, puzzled, frightened, or frustrated many. Oh, how I identified with the psalmist's words, "My friends and companions avoid me because of my wounds; my neighbors stay far away." [65] How abhorrent it is that spiritual people, who ought to be helpful and caring of the mentally ill, snub them and pile on maltreatment, instead. Ostracism in varying forms came from some friends, and especially church people.

Time and again, I observed the shallowness of relationships that masqueraded as "Christian love." Having endured what I had, my stomach tensed at hearing clergy and laypersons make statements like, "You can do all things through God," "*Real* Christians *always* have an inner joy and peace," "If you pray, claim God's promises, and believe enough, you'll be healed." I grew paranoid about church members and fellow pastors avoiding me or saying hurtful things. Attending church and Presbytery functions was terrifying.

Since my college years, Christians had been a major influence in my life, either in helping or injuring me. On one hand, my family and I wouldn't have made it without the love, encouragement, and support of people of faith. On the other hand, some people who claimed strong beliefs wounded me deeply.

Unfortunately, many manic-depressives lose all motivation to improve, because their health professionals tell them, "There's no cure for your illness. You'll just have to learn to live with it." Contrary to common opinion, statistics reveal that a high percentage of depressives and bipolars are not only functional but also live successfully and productively. Less than 15 percent are repeatedly unresponsive to any method of healing.[66]

While most St. Andrew's people were inspirational, a handful occasionally dragged me down into inconsolable slumps. My knee-jerk reaction around church members was to tighten up inside, thinking, *I know they can see the negative effects of my pills: I stutter and walk with a slow, uncertain gait. I have a facial twitch and*

can't remember names. I'm ashamed to be known as a "mental case." *I feel I've let them down as their pastor-leader.* One key lay leader told me, "Jim you'll never be able to go back into the professional ministry. The nature of your illness will make you unacceptable. You'll have to settle for *any* job to support your family now. You've got a lot to offer to others, but remember, you've got an incurable mental disease; you've got to be realistic about what and how much you can do." His words crushed my hopes of starting over. I left his office stunned, angry, hurt. By evening, I'd sunk into a dejection that lasted three months.

Some individuals scolded, "Jim, I'm sorry you've had a 'nervous breakdown,' but you need to slow down. Organize your workload better. Don't push so hard." Their words implied that I was at fault for my hospitalizations: I worked too hard; I couldn't handle pressures on my job; I was too weak to say no to people's demands. Others avoided me, but told their friends, "Poor Stout. What a shame he's mentally ill. Be careful what you say, it might set him off."

Most of my "comforters" were impatient, not understanding why I couldn't pull myself together and get moving. Surprisingly, the harshest remarks came from clergy and church people: "How can a *pastor* possibly be experiencing what you're going through?" "Good Christians should never be depressed. God's provided everything you need. Why can't you simply trust Him better, Jim?" "There must be a sin in your life that's causing all your problems. Confess it, so God can forgive you, and you'll be free from this depression and mania stuff." "He sure must be trying to teach you something." "Why do you need pills and psychologists, anyway? Isn't God powerful enough to help you with your problems? Where's your faith?"

I attended fewer than four Presbytery meetings in future years. Like worship services and church activities, they simply stirred up too much pain. Most clergy and lay leaders were obviously ill at ease with me and made obvious attempts to avoid eye contact. Others offered comments like, "Stout, aren't you ready to return to work yet? You're just feeling sorry for yourself, milking this

mental illness stuff for all it's worth. Are you *still* taking medicines? Are you *still* seeing a therapist? If you'd just pray more and trust in the Bible's promises, you could move on with your life. You certainly aren't trusting in God, or you'd be better by now. Have you ever considered that you're probably possessed by demons? Come to our prayer meeting next week — we'll exorcise those demons."

It was hard enough trying to maintain a positive outlook without having to endure guilt-inducing, self-esteem-destroying, spiritually harmful words from well-meaning but insensitive or judgmental Christians. Such "advice" only heaped new pain on my already tender spirit. I understood why the Apostle Paul admonished a group of Christians, "…your meetings do more harm than good."[67] Ninety-nine percent of the time, the comments were well meant but made in ignorance of what it's like to live with a mental illness. One percent were cruel jabs, deliberately intended to shame me.

Increasingly, I became an untouchable in my career field. My psychiatric hospitalization, I'm sure, caused my clergy peers to question my professional abilities. It seemed as though I'd lost my reputation as a strong, capable Christian leader overnight. Based on comments from various church members and fellow clergy, my credibility, competence, and spiritual dedication were questioned. Except for a few friends, most people seemed to distance themselves from me as though I had leprosy. Ministers no longer returned my calls; invitations to speak or preach all but evaporated. The psalmist must have endured such rejection when he wrote, "…I am the utter contempt of my neighbors; I am a dread to my friends — those who see me on the street flee from me.[68]

It still took courage to attend Jimmy's and John's church, athletic, and school events. I tightened up whenever anyone asked, "How are you doing, Jim?" Often, the week had been a battle with hopelessness. I hated saying, "Oh, just great. It's been a good week. I think I'm improving every day." It took immense energy to carry on a conversation. At worship services, I was surrounded by people eager to greet me. While I appreciated their affection, I

invariably went away drained. Strangely, being in large crowds where no one knew me was easier — it was a relief to be anonymous and not have to be on guard or have to speak.

Although I knew that everyone heals differently, it made me jealous when I heard about former hospital alumni having returned to work. *Why's it taking me so long to get better? What's wrong with me? Why aren't my medications working? I'd love to do any kind of work, but I wouldn't last long. Things would go fine for three weeks, and then I'd get depressed or manic, and couldn't handle the pressures, and I'd be fired.*

In the United States, clergy outnumber psychiatrists almost ten to one.[69] Also, for more than twenty years, studies have consistently shown that nearly 40 percent of the people seeking help with an emotional problem turn *first* to religious professionals, a much higher number than those who turn to psychiatrists, psychologists, and family physicians.[70]

Regrettably, *nearly half* of the mentally ill and their families who turn to people of the cloth for help are badly disappointed. One recent survey done by the California Alliance for the Mentally Ill acknowledges that 40 percent of its families questioned had sought the help of clergy. But when confronted with a mental illness "situation," the religious leaders were found to be *last* in helpfulness.[71]

Spiritual shepherds tend to be generalists, not specialists; their knowledge of psychiatric disorders is limited at best. Many are noticeably uncomfortable with mentally disturbed individuals. Their schedules are crammed with ministerial duties, leaving little time for those who are mind-damaged and can't be actively involved in parish activities.

Trying to learn how Christian clergy viewed mental illness, a nationwide survey of pastors, mostly from mainline denominations, reveals that *more than 50 percent* of religious leaders believe that demons and/or sin is the major cause of mental illness. No wonder there is such a ignorance of mind dysfunction in churches today![72]

One of the challenges to spiritual communities is not just tolerating others, healthy or ill, but accepting, including, valuing, loving, and equipping them to help others. I was starved for a kind word. I needed someone who'd listen to me patiently, without interrupting or giving unwanted advice. Fortunately, friends called or sent notes nearly every week. But would their support be enough to see me through the hard times?

Chapter 23

Recurring Depression and the "Treatment-resistant" Patient

IT'S HARD TO MAINTAIN A JOYFUL ATTITUDE when your mind is rebelling and your body's writhing with the side effects of medicines. I tried to appear normal, and became adept at masking my mood changes. Almost no one saw me at my worst, because during those times I withdrew from everyone. Even Leah and the boys were often unaware of my mental state. As a youth, I'd discovered that people get very uncomfortable talking about pain. So now, to all but a few close friends, the façade went up: "I'm doing much better every day, thank you." But it strained me to continually pretend to be happy when I felt dreadful.

The devastating consequences of my illness were starting to sink in. I no longer had the same resiliency. I couldn't handle life's common frustrations and stresses as I had before, and I was miserable. Often, I echoed the exasperated cry of the prophet Jeremiah, "Why is my pain unending and my wound grievous and incurable? [73] Weary of emotional upheavals, I stopped taking my medications twice that year, for a week or more each time. *Why put up with all*

these horrible side effects? The pills aren't working, anyway.

Some days I could accomplish twenty tasks, other days perhaps three, often none. For someone who'd always been a stickler for being on time for appointments, my 1990 consistency was discouraging. *Why plan? Odds are I'll end up canceling most of these meetings. People will give up on me for breaking so many appointments.*

Reading became a trusted coping mechanism, a comforter, and an escape. On good days, analyzing came easy; I retained masses of information. On bad ones, I couldn't read more than a few paragraphs without losing concentration.

I wasn't aware that I'd been bucking the odds of recurring bouts of depression and mania. Depression is a chronic illness. Medical and psychological data bring to light that up to 80 percent of depressives suffer recurrences.[74] Also, there's an almost guaranteed *cyclical* nature with bipolar disorder. Evidence demonstrates that this recurrent condition virtually always repeats itself.[75] Findings show that only a tiny percentage of patients have just one episode in their lifetime. The question for most bipolars is not *if* but *when.*[76]

Bipolars and other people living with psychiatric brain disease are frequently faulted for "non-compliance" (refusing to take their medications). True, some are in denial about their illness and need for medication. Others, particularly those in a manic state, feel "normal" and believe they no longer need medications. But a large number forgo their pills because of the awful side effects.

Starting with my first psychiatric medication in 1987, I never had a philosophical problem with taking medications. I didn't like having to swallow pills, but I realized that taking meds for manic depression was no different than if I had a heart condition, high blood pressure, or diabetes.

Lithium and other pharmaceuticals pulled me out of *some* downward spirals, but not all of them, and not without cost. Even on high doses, I still had severe, even suicidal depressions, and I suffered numerous negative side effects. My sleep was continually interrupted by having to urinate twelve to fifteen times a night. I fought memory loss, diarrhea, and nausea, and always felt exhausted. On

days when I dared venture out of the house, I frequently had trouble connecting people's names and faces. I couldn't follow the simple printed directions for filling out the drugstore form for developing film. Adding columns of figures was impossible. I had to ask the bank teller to help me fill out a deposit slip.

Doing anything was an event: showering, feeding Dyno, or walking twenty feet to the mailbox. During my first year home, I had barely enough energy to vacuum the living room. Gradually, I tried to accomplish one or two easy tasks a day, however small: sweep the kitchen, write a note, wash the dinner dishes, or some other simple chore. It gave me a feeling of accomplishment that I was at least doing something to contribute to the family.

It worried me that Jimmy or John might also get the bipolar ailment, so I continued sharing with them and Leah what I was learning about it. I wanted to alert the boys to the symptoms in case they manifested some, so they could spot the illness early and go for help. Also, knowing the facts about it would help Leah and them feel less guilty and less stressed about my behavior and their reactions to it.

By the end of 1990, I discovered I was not totally helpless against my mental disease. I could exercise *some* influence over it. Sometimes I could will myself through difficult periods. That didn't stop all the mood swings, but doing something positive or even preventative focused me enough to endure … and occasionally avoid them. I *chose* to get up rather than sleep all day, *made* myself work on ministry tasks, *compelled* myself to make phone calls, *forced* myself to go out with friends, and even *pushed* myself to attend some social activities.

Until now, Leah and the boys thought I'd soon be on track, and life would return to normal. It had taken over two years, but they now realized that I had a serious long-term illness. In coming to grips with this fact, they, like me, experienced again a deep sense of loss: their dreams of the husband, father, and family life they'd always counted on. Things would never be the same again for any of us.

We put high hopes in mental health professionals. "After all," we thought, "who knows more about manic depression than psychiatrists and psychologists? They're the experts, trained in dealing with cases like this. They'll fix things with the right medication, the right counseling method. We just need to be patient and give it time." Meanwhile, all of us lived continually off balance. Despite receiving fine professional counseling and taking medications religiously, I wasn't improving. I tried one med after another, enduring their disruptive side effects, only to find that none worked for long.

Some medical practitioners called me a "treatment-resistant" patient. Others accused me of not taking my pills. With the combination of negative side effects, the limited performance of psychiatric medications, and hassles with insurance coverage, it's amazing that *more* patients don't discontinue their meds out of frustration. I noticed that family members too got exasperated seeing their loved ones suffer inadequate, if not harmful, results from medications. Increasingly, I watched families become disillusioned with the medical establishment, and burn out or drop out.

Chapter 24

Searching for the "Whys" of Mental Illness

WHENEVER I FOUND MYSELF SLIPPING into self-pity, I tried to remind myself of the inspiring people who'd weathered similar trials and still used their skills to impact others. Handel, one of my favorite composers, struggled with severe mood disruptions most of his life. Some say that in one of his torrents of creativity, he wrote *The Messiah* in only twenty-three days.

It strengthened my desire to persevere knowing that so many successful individuals had coped with extreme mood swings. Winston Churchill, Michelangelo, Twain, Pound, O'Neill, Poe, van Gogh, Hemingway, Lord Byron, William Blake, Coleridge, Melville, Shelley, Tennyson, Lowell, Goethe, Schumann, Rossini, Tschaikovsky, Mahler, Rachmaninoff, Anne Sexton, Virginia Woolf, F. Scott Fitzgerald, Joshua Logan and others had fought depression, loneliness, despair, resentment, rage, and self-pity. It was reassuring to know that I wasn't alone, that many had dealt with the same obstacles and, despite their problems, made major contributions to the world. I found inspiration realizing that Bible heroes, Moses, Elijah, David, Jeremiah, Jonah, Paul, and even Jesus, in his humanness, manifested symptoms of depression, and yet overcame its tenacious grip to accomplish great things.

As 1990 came to a close, I found that as helpful as will power was in controlling some of my fragile emotional reactions, it could not win the big battles without a life game plan and specific strategies. Trying to survive one day at a time, I'd been in too much pain up to this point to deal with the larger issues of my life. When you're going through a traumatic experience, almost any "reason" for your suffering sounds like a trite theological slogan or cold philosophical argument. Now it was a struggle to begin reassembling the pieces

of my life and attempt to build some kind of future. I tried hard to make sense of what had already happened and what was currently happening to me.

Answers that used to satisfy me were no longer meaningful. I'd lost confidence in myself, in others, and in my relationship with God. I desperately wanted to "fight the good fight," to finish my race, but I would need more help with the battles.

Faith never came easily to me. I've always been a skeptic who demands proof. I'd often reflected on why God would cause or allow my mental problem, but I understood that more was at stake than merely satisfying intellectual curiosity. Indeed, I realized the need to discover a purpose for my disorder if I was to survive, let alone reclaim my life. This meant asking hard questions about God, life, and myself.

On one hand, I knew that *faith* was essential to balanced living. The writer of Proverbs underscores its primacy: "Trust in the Lord with all your heart and lean not on your own understanding..." [77]

On the other hand, faith must be balanced with *critical thinking*. After all, God urges, "Come now, let us reason together..." [78] Jesus taught that the most important commandment is, "Love the Lord your God with all your heart and with all your soul and with all your mind..." [79] I'd always taken "reason" and "mind" seriously. To me, this was a directive to use my *mind* in understanding God's ways while at the same time *trusting* in His character and purposes.

For years I had taught with conviction about God's loving, sovereign, all-knowing nature. Now, those easy, black-and-white "theological answers" no longer anchored my ship when storms raged. To make it, I needed to understand God's dealings with me in more meaningful, practical ways.

There seemed no acceptable explanation for why He would permit a debilitating mental illness to ruin an effective pastor's usefulness. I had to reason through the "why" if I was to get to, "Now that I've got this bipolar illness, what am I going to do about it?"

Nietsche said that a person can endure life's worst crises if he

knows the *why*. The book, *Man's Search for Meaning,* and other writings of psychotherapist Dr. Viktor Frankl, a Jewish survivor of four Nazi death camps had long intrigued me. He observed that prisoners who found a *purpose* in the midst of their suffering could bear the deprivation and tortures better than their peers could.

In my private search for the meaning of my suffering, I started with the basics: "Is there really a God? If so, what's He like? What's His purpose in letting some people go through such nightmarish experiences?" I examined the options of how to view the One whom people call "Higher Power," "Life Force," "First Cause," "Spirit of the Universe," "Allah," "Divine Mind," "God," and myriad other names.

Some believe that God exists only in people's minds as a wish-projection. I considered the possibility, but couldn't accept that explanation. If the world made no sense, as Sartre and others postulated, I saw no alternative to absolute despair, or suicide, or to turning Epicurean and trying to derive the most possible fun from a meaningless existence. But I had confidence that there was purpose behind the universe. For me, life and suffering were more than chance. Mental, like physical illness, had to be more than just bad luck.

I examined the possibility that God is helpless or doesn't care about influencing His world. Deists believe that God created the universe and then withdrew, letting it and its inhabitants fare for themselves without any intervention on His part. This belief, I reasoned, would rob me of any source of meaning, peace, and joy in tough times. I decided that to hold this view, I'd need to become a bitter cynic, hating God and my circumstances, or become a fatalistic stoic, blindly accepting whatever bad cards were dealt me.

I looked at another option: that God was angry at his disobedient creatures, had cut us off from his love and cursed us. My experiences in youth certainly predisposed me toward this kind of cruel, vengeful God. I had to honestly consider that God might be similar to some of the harsh authority figures of my childhood. I'd learned that people often project their experiences with

their primary caregivers onto God. Since I'd gotten so much criticism from Mom and her side of the family, common sense dictated that I'd be at least somewhat influenced by them. But if I were to believe in a remote, unkind God who was similar to Dad and "the Big Three," it would mean turning angry, cynical, or fatalistic.

After considerable reading and thinking, I concluded my deliberations by returning full circle to my core beliefs, enlarging my concept of God, and to a desire to find *how* to exercise my faith in a way that could sustain me through future ordeals. I renewed my belief in a power greater than myself, One who could restore me to balanced living and prepare a place for me in heaven after I died. This personal power I called "God." I reaffirmed that this invisible, loving, caring God had visited earth two thousand years ago in human form, the person of Jesus Christ. This elementary faith was helpful, but merely believing in God didn't answer my questions about my suffering.

If God cares so much for me, why has He allowed such terrible things to happen to me? Is it because of my sins and wrong choices? The Bible states that God "…does not willingly bring affliction or grief…"[80] I knew the God of the Bible never inflicted judgement on people without having first warned them many times. While I obviously wasn't sinless, I thought my psychiatric disorder was a far more severe punishment than my sins deserved.

Perhaps God hasn't stepped in to help me because He wants to use this hardship to strengthen my character. But if His main purpose is 'schooling' me, no thanks! No amount of learning will ever come close to making up for what I've been through and what I've lost!

I concluded, *God wants to use the troubles I've faced to advance His work. He doesn't want to waste anyone's successes, failures, sins, and sufferings, including mine. Hopefully, when others observe how God helps me, they'll be drawn to Him for support too. I know that He is using my hurts to equip me to pass on to others the help He's given me. Some way, perhaps not even through the professional ministry, I'm convinced God will use my life to help bring others to Him.*

Many of life's tragedies simply cannot be understood. I took comfort reading that Job, who endured one disaster after another, cried out to God at least sixteen times, "Why?" But God never answered his questions. Instead, Job suffered through one loss after another, as sometimes I would have to, without explanation.

Even though I'd stumbled through many dark times without feeling God's presence, I clung to the hope that eventually I'd experience His comfort with or without divine answers. Job's sufferings helped me to be patient and realize that sometimes there are no acceptable answers for suffering or injustice. With that outlook, I believed I'd never face a situation when I wouldn't know the reality of a loving Heavenly Father who'd say, "It's all right, Jim, I still love you."

It's often difficult to visualize any positive thing coming from some horrific situations. Even after the sincerest attempts to fathom why tragedy occurs, sometimes all you can do is accept that only God knows why bad things happen. However helpful explanations for suffering might be, no amount of "good reasons" can adequately explain or offer comfort for tragedies like the death of a young child, a husband's desertion of his family, a young mother dying of cancer, or a happy college student developing a serious mental illness.

In the absence of satisfactory explanations for my mental sufferings, I rejected the concept of a meaningless universe and opted to believe in one created and controlled by a *personal* God who had my best interests at heart. This meant relying solely on the personality of God, expressed fully in Jesus Christ. I simply trusted that somehow God had a benevolent purpose for my suffering. In times of darkness and questioning, I held on to what He said in the Bible: "... my thoughts are not your thoughts, neither are your ways my ways ... in all things God works for the good of those who love him ..." [81]

As I worked through basic faith issues, even the best attempt to account for my suffering provided only a skeletal framework for interpreting what had befallen me, what was currently happening,

and what might happen in the future. I recognized that I'd need more than intellectual beliefs to see me through.

Despite my biblical knowledge, negative events and hurtful words easily triggered destructive thinking: *Why can't my psychiatrist find a pill that works without unbearable side effects? Why haven't I been healed? I must not be worth restoring.* Too often, I let sour thoughts ferment, causing a crippling downturn. The main thing that kept me from falling into the pit was *talking* about my thoughts and feelings with Leah, Phil, and a couple of friends.

I realized from Scripture that even Jesus didn't heal everyone He met. The Apostle Paul was never healed of the ailment that plagued him. He wrote, "...there was given me a thorn in my flesh ...to torment me. Three times I pleaded with the Lord to take it away from me."[82] Yet God never took away Paul's problem. *Since everyone in the Bible wasn't healed, I'll need to trust God for if, when, or how much I'll be healed.*

Periodically I grumbled. *It's not fair that I've been hurt so many times and have to struggle so much to stay on top of my emotions. It just isn't right that I have to experiment with one medication after another and live with their terrible aftermath.*

I reminded myself that Jesus taught, "In this world you will have trouble...."[83] Suffering is woven into the fabric of life. Sooner or later everyone goes through tough times; it's only a question of when and to what degree. Our jobs, possessions, and financial security are tenuous. Mental health, like physical health, is fragile. Jesus also said that God "...causes his sun to rise on the evil and the good, and sends rain on the righteous and the unrighteous."[84] Sometimes bad guys prosper and good guys suffer. Some individuals have worse hardships than others. *This means my problems are not a sign that I'm under God's curse. They're just the result of living in a broken, fallen world. No one, including me, gets a free pass from suffering.*

The Christian scriptures declare that "...no one can say, "Jesus is Lord," except by the Holy Spirit."[85] When periodically accused of being demon-possessed, I listened cordially, then explained,

"You're entitled to your opinion. But I think you're dead wrong. The Bible teaches that Satan and his demons exercise their destructive influence in the world whenever possible. It explains that he can possess certain non-believers, and he can exert destructive influences on a follower of Christ, but he can *never* possess a Christian. I believe Jesus is my Lord. Therefore, while I can be harmed by Satan, I can't possibly be possessed by Him."

Chapter 25

The Value of Humor

L AUGHTER PROVIDED ONE OF THE KEY ingredients to surviving my hospital and post-hospitalization experiences. The Bible speaks of humor's benefits, "A cheerful heart is good medicine, but a crushed spirit dries up the bones." [86] Researchers have discovered that a hearty laugh is one of the most helpful and least expensive treatments for anxiety, fear, frustration, and depression.[87]

Writing of his concentration camp imprisonment, Viktor Frankl emphasized the role of humor in survival. He even trained a fellow prisoner to develop a laugh-filled attitude. Both traded funny stories daily. The therapeutic value of humor is widely accepted in medical and psychological circles. It's reported that numerous hospitals now have "laughing rooms" where they play comedy videotapes.

I don't understand the dynamics of humor, but I firmly believe a good laugh momentarily lightens the darkness. It takes the edge off anger and softens stress. A joke can temporarily replace the seriousness of life with a better-balanced perspective. Although I still experience bleak periods, I'm convinced that laughter has been a strong factor in my recovering.

Regardless of whether anyone else laughed, I loved telling jokes and pulling pranks on friends and strangers alike. Such light-heartedness was enormously satisfying and outrageous fun. Sometimes I used it to communicate that I wasn't the typical "crazy zombie" people imagined "mentals" like me to be.

Suffering, however, was a different story. For years, I'd observed how people reacted to it: their difficulties either brought them closer to God, or drove them away from Him, hardened and embittered. I knew if I didn't let go of the resentments for my unfair treatment, I'd end up a miserable cynic. Bedrock beliefs helped me understand at least partially why such bad things had happened to me. But to rebuild my life, I had to move *beyond* an intellectual grasp of biblical explanations for suffering.

My ongoing prayer was, "God, I sincerely want to be freed from this terrible illness. But if You choose not to heal me, please give me the grace to cope and to use my experiences and abilities to benefit others."

I resumed driving. Though improved, it was still risky, especially when I was upset. During those periods, I tended to slide through stop signs, take turns extra-wide, or drive too slow or fast. After three small fender-benders, numerous comments from the boys, and threats by Leah to reinstate my having to be chauffeured again, I drove less and paid closer attention.

I continued visiting libraries, and buying books, magazines, and audiotapes to learn about dysfunctional families, bipolar illness, depression, and sexual abuse. Also, at a local hospital, I attended several outpatient support group meetings for people living with manic depression. Disappointingly, they weren't helpful. I felt intimidated by the fifteen people who attended. A few monopolized the time, so most of us were unable to share for more than a few minutes.

Only Leah and a few close friends knew of my uneasiness about socializing. Paranoia based on past experiences continued to fuel my anxieties. Some social situations kicked off panic attacks over my dread of criticism. I feared even well-meaning comments like,

"Why haven't you been to worship more often, Jim?" As a result, I kept secluding myself as much as possible from church and social events.

I knew too well that isolation would chain me to my moods. It was like recovering from knee surgery: unless I went through physical therapy, exercising through the pain, my knee would never work right. Healing would come only from hard work. It began to sink in that this would be a long-haul fight to get better. I increased the number of get-togethers with friends to six a week. Still, I had to cancel half of them.

Chapter 26

Taking Responsibility for Recovering; the Role of Faith

THE JANUARY 5, 2000 ISSUE OF *The Los Angeles Times* had a fascinating article on the value of optimism. The piece mentioned the results of dozens of studies, and listed the benefits of an optimistic outlook. It described how in most endeavors, optimists excel more than pessimists do. They respond better to stress, depression, and physical ailments, and even live longer. Slowly, I shifted my attitude from complaining to asking myself, *What can I learn from my trials?*

If you've been habitually neglected, criticized, and humiliated, it's hard to imagine anyone genuinely caring for your welfare. *How can I place myself under God's care when I've rarely experienced healthy caring?* It became obvious that I'd need more than pills and counseling to get better. Part of the answer lay in a renewed relationship with God. I decided to step out in faith and

re-commit myself to God by turning my will and life over to His care as best I could. This meant increasingly surrendering my circumstances to God: "Lord, please help me accept or change whatever stresses come my way."

Regardless of how hard I tried to overcome it, chronic sadness persisted. Plus, I wasn't sure what to do about alternating high-energy spurts and their opposites, dangerously deep dejections. Too prone to self-pity and chronic resentment of others' words and actions, I had to let go of those feelings and move on, because if I didn't, those cancerous emotions would destroy me.

Some diseases become so advanced that the damage is irreversible. It wasn't easy dealing with the reality that I might never heal, or might only partially recover from the chemical imbalance in my brain and the accumulated emotional injuries I'd sustained. If so, I'd need a stronger faith to see me through the years ahead to survive, heal, and rebuild my life.

I found three truths especially helpful during turbulent times: First, the God of all comfort was always with me. I reminded myself constantly, "God is for me." [88] I hung on to that promise like a drowning man clings to a life preserver. Some of God's other statements became anchors in the midst of raging storms: "...Fear not, for I have redeemed you; I have summoned you by name; you are mine. When you pass through the waters, I will be with you; and when you pass through the rivers, they will not sweep over you. When you walk through the fire, you will not be burned ... Do not be afraid, for I am with you ... " [89] Yet, helpful as they were, God's soothing words didn't always console me. Second, heaven will eventually be my real home, where everything will be made right. Third, I had to *choose* whether to live or die. *Living will take courage; dying will be a quick and easy way out of what sometimes might be unbearable pain. Leah and the boys, and Phil and my friends believe in me; I don't want to let them down. I'll keep fighting. I'll choose to live, not just now but every day and sometimes every hour.*

I realized that if I didn't shed the attitude of powerlessness over my illness, I'd never make progress — and I could very easily die.

As long as I viewed life as having handed me the curse of an incurable mind malfunction, I'd continue to see myself totally victimized by its tossing me about like a helpless cork in the ocean.

I told a friend, "*I've* got to take responsibility for my *own* healing. I'm willing to use any pill, any counseling method, anything that works. Things won't get better if I just sit back passively and follow every recommendation that medical professionals make just because they say it. Obviously, they don't have all the answers. *I've* got to become the main manager of my recovery. In fact, I'll need to take charge of every aspect of my life. No one's going to wave a magic wand and make me better. *I'm* the one who's got to do it. *I'm* the one swallowing the pills. *I'm* the one who must get counseling. *I'm* the one who needs to learn about my illness and medications."

A fellow manic-depressive told me, "It wasn't until I realized it was up to *me* to get my moods under control, and that there was no magical cure, that I began to turn the corner on the road to wellness." His words motivated me to take charge of my treatment. Though I understood the seriousness of my brain disorder, I didn't surrender to it. Hope started to flicker: *If I try hard enough I can get on top of this.* I started accepting my illness, and moved slowly from a defensive survival mode to a proactive one.

The treatment I get must be tailored to my needs. I don't care if the doctors call me "uncooperative," or "treatment-resistant." I'll have to experiment with what works best for me. If it means trying new doctors and different medications, and changing dosages until I succeed, I'll keep trying. Whatever it takes, I'll do it!

Since seminary, I'd practiced goal setting, and had taught hundreds of others not only its value but also how to make specific plans. Following my hospitalization, I had no goals, no interest in what lay beyond the horizon other than keeping my head above water. My only focus was day-to-day treading water through one crisis after another.

In 1992 I started setting small goals: exercising at swim class at the "Y" on Monday, Wednesday and Friday evenings; walking Dyno two nights a week; and talking or meeting with three friends

a week. Then, knowing that my moods would probably interfere with these newly set objectives, I decided to give myself an "A" if I completed *half* of them. If I finished 40 percent, I gave myself a "B," and so on. This gentle grading system all but assured a feeling of accomplishment. Yet, there were weeks when I still flunked many or all of my tasks because of my mercurial mental states.

Time and again, I fell short of my expectations and had to revise my goals. Often I got so discouraged that I went weeks without attempting to make any plans. It was hard to *not* put myself down for my "failures." I had to force my mind to be gentle with positive self-talk: *Remember, Jim, you've had an extra-tough week. You grade out at 30 percent, despite losing four days to the "Big D"—an amazing feat. Next week you'll do even better.*

Chapter 27

The Benefits of Professional Counseling

LOOKING BACK, IT'S CLEAR THAT the mood cycles began back in my junior year at Farragut. I would work furiously for a month, then crash for about a week. I never attributed the productive energy bursts to anything other than my normal work style, nor did I see the "run-out-of-gas" times as depressions. Now I recognize those repeated periods as the beginnings of mild manic or depressive episodes.

With a growing knowledge of bipolar disorder and depression, I decided to chart my emotional shifts. *Maybe doing this will help me see whether medications, stress, or biological changes are causing my ups and downs.* My psychiatrist liked the idea. But as helpful

as it might have been, I couldn't keep the chart more than a week due to mood disruptions. So I quit trying to record my moods.

While medications are an absolute requirement for mood stabilization, "talk therapy" (counseling, psychotherapy) is *equally* necessary. A good therapist encourages medication management and teaches you how to manage the ups and downs of the disorder. Those who successfully live with the mind disease attest to the life-changing benefits of counseling. Most say that medication restrains their illness, but counseling enables them to live with it.

Friends help greatly, but a good therapist is essential for anyone living with bipolar disorder, especially for those who've also been seriously traumatized. I wouldn't have survived my illness, let alone recovered enough to rebuild, without professional counseling. Being listened to and receiving wise advise helps with fears, guilt, self-esteem, and relationship problems. It aids in recovering from relapses, and lowers stresses that can trigger manic or depressive recurrences.

While accentuating the vital importance of counseling in the recovery process, authorities emphasize that no one counseling approach works better than another. My interviews with dozens of therapists and hundreds of depressives and manic-depressives over the past thirteen years validate that finding. In fact, studies indicate that patients receiving *only* medications or those having *only* psychotherapy tend to be far more vulnerable to relapse than those undergoing *both* treatments.[90]

I couldn't trust my memory, so each time I met with Phil or my psychiatrist, I brought a list of items to discuss: bad side effects, mood changes since our last visit, present tensions, failures, successes, and questions. Most sessions with Phil were spent discussing immediate strains: home pressures, and hurts from a few church members and clergy. To minimize stress, Phil and I developed strategies for coping with people who shunned me and for handling criticisms and disappointments. Phil's counsel helped tremendously, but because I was so easily hurt, our best plans often couldn't prevent my downward slides. Much of the time it felt like I was going from one emergency to another.

It's hard to believe you're loved when you feel tainted to your core. Most of my life, I'd believed I was bad, and I couldn't imagine that someone who knew all about me could love me. Aside from Leah, Bob Long was the first person with whom I experienced this kind of unconditional acceptance. Phil was the second. When I didn't believe in myself and my future, they believed in me. Besides them, several other friends also served to prop up my sagging ego.

Without a doubt, I owe my life to Phil, Bob, and Leah. Were it not for their ceaseless encouragement, I never would've survived my hospital stays, much less the ordeals I was now going through. They prevented me from ending my life dozens of times, usually without knowing it. What was said of Job assuredly describes Leah, Phil, Bob and other dear friends: "Your words have supported those who stumbled; you have strengthened faltering knees." [91]

Phil always respected me despite my mental illness. I sensed from the start that he genuinely cared. Besides being a sensitive listener, he had an incredible balance of wisdom and common sense. Few people had ever taken time to ask me questions about myself and truly listen to me. Phil did. He validated me just by patiently hearing my words, my silences. His supportive, insight-oriented cognitive therapy helped me learn far more about myself than I'd ever imagined. His guidance gave me the courage to deal with relapses, and taught me how to adjust when things got rough. However, being counseled was far from painless, overnight enlightenment. It involved hard work, facing many thorny memories, and then developing coping skills to deal with the circumstances that had sewn the seeds of my seesawing disposition.

Unquestionably, meds and counseling had kept me alive, though I believe some drugs actually pushed me into anxieties, depressions, and manias. Most of the time, however, they acted as chemical buffers, moderating my acute ups and downs. Unfortunately, though numbing my variable emotions, they also dulled my ability to remember important information about implementing the plans Phil and I mapped out.

After four years of intensive sessions with Phil, I finally realized that psychotherapy wasn't going to yield some magical,
once-and-for-all insight that would dramatically heal me. Self-knowl-
edge alone doesn't have the power to change anyone's life. Plainly,
I needed more than pills and psychotherapy.

Almost by necessity, I began re-framing my view of God. Since
college days, I'd read plenty of books on the nature of God and
preached many sermons on it. Yet, for all my academic grasp of the
"truth" about God, I couldn't erase my emotionally twisted views,
both of Him and of myself as His child.

The brain and the viscera sometimes contradict each other. In
reality, I hadn't stopped letting childhood experiences influence
my understanding of God. Despite my knowledge of psychology
and theology, I had projected Mom, Dad, and Gram's personality
traits onto God. For the most part, they'd been unavailable, so God,
too, seemed distant. They were difficult to speak with; likewise,
praying to God was generally unsatisfying. I was told repeatedly
that I was a bad boy, a disappointment to my primary caregivers, so
I believed that God, too, was upset with me because of my badness.

Though I had "correct" theological beliefs about God, my inter-
nalizing of who He was and how I viewed myself were robbing me
of joy. I realized that to heal past wounds would require me to
stop visualizing God as an enlarged, invisible version of Mom,
Dad, Gram, and Unc.

Intellectually, I knew the God of the Bible was far bigger than
my clouded understanding, but I was stuck with a lot of emotional baggage that blurred my picture of Him and what He thought of
me. The strength to change my understanding of God, life's difficulties, and myself came from two sources: people and the Bible. I
continually received loving respect from Leah, Phil, Bob Long,
and others. In countless warm human ways, they embodied God's
love for me.

My ministerial passions had always been working with men
and clergy. I'd long ago noted that men in church leadership positions, and male ministers, were often the "walking wounded."

Historically, little has been done to reach, heal, and properly equip men for their personal, family, and professional tasks. I prayed for a part-time ministry that could use my gifts and flex with my illness. In 1991 I had lengthy talks with friends, including the Gathering of Men founder, Dr. John Tolson, and its president, Dr. Larry Kreider. Our conversations focused on my joining the Gathering's staff as part-time area director for south Orange County. Positive confirmation came from every side. And so a new career began.

During my previous three-year incapacitation, others had operated the yearly Orange County Gathering of Men Breakfasts, achieving great success without any paid professional leadership. I wanted to build on their dedicated work. Taking the first step, I recruited additional members for an executive board and started raising support for the new ministry. Despite my ups and downs, and only being able to work part-time, I raised enough funds to jump-start an Outreach Breakfast similar to the one I'd helped organize four years earlier. This time, the October Breakfast response was gratifying too.

By 1991, I'd been on more than a dozen medications. With each new one, I got my hopes up, but none relieved my turbulence for long. Sooner or later, each produced annoying, sometimes perilous, side effects. *Will* anything *work for me? How much longer must I endure nausea, diarrhea, memory loss, hand tremors, headaches, dizziness, and exhaustion? I certainly don't want to live like this for the rest of my life.*

Jimmy's senior year was busy with both the track team and rowing for the Newport Aquatic Club Crew Team. In June 1991, Dad flew out for Jimmy's graduation from Newport Harbor High School. I'd learned from counseling not to look forward to *any* changes in Dad. I didn't anticipate compliments, or questions about Leah and the boys, nor any substantive conversation. I prepared myself to accept him as he was, without trying to change him or hoping he would change. With realistic expectations, I didn't suffer as big a letdown. I was trying my best to trust God to help me lower my expectations and accept the things about Dad that I couldn't change. I'm sure this kept me from a major depression.

We were living on Leah's secretarial earnings and my limited disability income. In one instance after another, God stepped into our lives, using people to help meet our financial needs. One example of His faithfulness happened in August 1991, when Jimmy entered Brown University and rowed for their national championship crew team. He received considerable financial aid from the school and from several friends who knew of our plight.

Work, I discovered, is a key element in rehabilitation from mental illness. It raises self-esteem, gives purpose, and provides satisfaction. But for mind-damaged people, a full-time, part-time, or even volunteer job can be extremely trying, because discrimination pervades the workplace. A national study shows that as many as one-third of those with severe mental illness have been rejected for a job — despite being fully qualified — due to a mental disorder "label."[92] It's reported that more than one in five mentally ill individuals are turned away even when they *volunteer* their services.

Earlier in the summer, I'd spoken with Dr. Mark Roberts, the new senior pastor of the nearby Irvine Presbyterian Church, about the possibility of joining his staff as a volunteer to strengthen their men's ministry. He was enthusiastic. In September I started working up to five hours a week, meeting with the men's leadership core group to develop monthly breakfast outreaches, vitalize their yearly retreat, and expand small support groups. Occasionally, I assisted in worship, taught a few Bible studies, and preached. My first year there was especially satisfying.

That fall I made scores of phone calls and also set up meetings to organize the Gathering Breakfast. Again, it succeeded as an effective outreach. Coinciding with Jimmy's departure for college, I entered a manic phase of high productivity that lasted, except for a three-week low, until Christmas.

Chapter 28

The Rewards of Marriage Therapy

R ARE IS THE MARRIAGE THAT GOES UNSCATHED through emotional injuries such as Leah and I had endured. Suffering tests any relationship: dormant issues, unrecognized and unresolved, usually surface when tragedy strikes. Ours was no exception. Mental illness can destroy a marriage.

Following my hospitalization, marriage counseling became critical if we were to make it through the rocky road ahead. We needed help coping with the stress of my fluctuating moods and our economic uncertainties.

In 1984, while back in Sharon, our relationship had been strained by church-related traumas. We knew we couldn't repair our communication problems on our own. Rather than tough it out, hoping God would somehow magically fix our difficulties, we saw a therapist for a number of marriage counseling sessions. We continued therapy off and on after arriving in California, unaware that we'd face even bigger strains on our relationship in the coming years. Although hemorrhaging off and on from many unhealed wounds, I was ready to try moving beyond mere survival to recuperation, but I worried whether our marriage could beat the odds and make it.

Sometimes a marriage involves 98 percent giving by one partner. It certainly had been true many times with Leah and me during the seven years after my hospitalization. Much of the time, I couldn't contribute anything to her needs. She was the one who had to give, and she sacrificed by taking charge of the boys, working hard at her job, caring for the house, cooking, doing our finances, and trying to encourage me. Again and again, Leah rose above her pain to comfort and pray for me. I was truly fortunate to have

married a woman of incredible faith, courage, beauty, talent, and wisdom. Unquestionably, she suffered emotional deprivation during that period. How grateful I am for her steadfast support through those frustrating, painful years!

We'd weathered some rough storms; each of us was tempted a number of times to throw in the towel. Sometimes our feelings of love evaporated. I wondered if they'd ever come back. *I've lost everything. I'll never work again. My life's over. Leah's just staying till the boys leave home. Then she'll divorce me.* I credit her with the determination to stick it out when I wanted to give up. "We can do it," she'd say. "I don't care how much we've hurt each other or how little affection we feel right now. I'm committed to making our marriage work. I'm not going to quit." Likewise, I'm sure her pain, anger, and loss of hope squashed her love for me plenty of times.

I knew that we'd never make it if we tried to fix our marriage *by ourselves.* It would take third-party intervention to resolve old issues and rebuild a stronger relationship. As dismal as things occasionally got, we were committed to our marriage. We sought another series of counseling sessions with our marriage therapist. She guided us with added insights into each another and ourselves, and worked with us to develop better ways of communicating. The process got ugly at times, but we determined to overcome our mutually inflicted wounds, which were exacerbated by my illness.

Gradually, I built on our counselor's optimism and Leah's dedication to finding solutions to our issues. I constantly needed positives; their outlook gave me the hope I desperately needed. Those were enormously painful days, but step by step, our marriage counseling certainly paid off, making a big difference. Old ways of relating were changing. Our communication slowly improved.

Our twenty-fifth wedding anniversary, June 24, 1992, was nearing. It had been a convulsive year, with quarrels over recurring themes, but we were resolved to healing our differences. As a symbol of my devotion and gratitude for our twenty-five years together, I gave Leah a silver necklace holding a cross with a small diamond

in its center. We celebrated with a five-day trip back to our old Boston haunts with Bob and Marilyn Long.

In a strange way, our time reminiscing with the Longs, and visiting Gordon Seminary, Rockport, Boston, and other old stomping grounds, strengthened our relationship. It was a splendid vacation. Maybe it was getting away geographically from painful reminders of my hospitalization and illness, or perhaps it was the carefree laughter. Whatever else our anniversary trip did, it gave our strained marriage a fresh start.

With that momentum, Leah and I continued our sessions with our therapist, who acted as referee, mediator, hope giver, and teacher. We learned how and why we pushed each other's buttons, and how to avoid doing so. We learned ways of really listening to each other. In all, we developed healthier ways of relating.

What a difference a gifted marriage therapist makes! She enabled Leah and me to patch up our marriage and enter into a whole new dimension of togetherness. Healing and rebuilding our relationship took hard work, courage, patience, forgiveness, and compromise, but our friendship deepened and we became allies, rekindling our love in the process.

Chapter 29

Living Between the Worlds of Mania and Depression

UNFORTUNATELY, MEDICATIONS FOR bipolar-debilitated people are limited in their effectiveness. All available meds carry potentially life-threatening risks, and patients may become resistant to them as their illness goes on. Lithium, long considered the gold standard for treating bipolars, is not the cure-all that many think. Unfortunately, more and more evidence shows that this long-trusted drug doesn't work for 40 to 80 percent of those treated. [93] Moreover, credible data show that lithium is ineffective for rapid cyclers like me. [94]

Many mental health professionals believe that bipolar patients go off their medications because they don't want their creativity and euphoric high stifled. While this is true for many, the testimonies of countless patients reveal that the two most common reasons are weight gain and intolerable side effects.

Twice that year, I stopped taking my meds for two or three weeks, because I didn't think they were working, and because I was disgusted with their side effects and my increased weight. Frequently, I wondered whether my pills were actually *causing* the very depression or agitation they were supposed to stop.

In November I flew to Florida to speak at a friend's church in St. Petersburg. It was a wonderful experience, but I'd taken on too much. Returning utterly exhausted, I collapsed disconsolately for several weeks. Soon after that, I shot into an expansive mania. One evening before Jimmy returned to Brown, I asked him to sit down with me to discuss his finances and classes, and to share new information about my illness. Oblivious at the time, I spread a three-inch-thick pile of notes and papers in front of us. A month later, Jimmy said, "Dad, remember our discussion before I went

back to college? Were you aware how manic you were? Did you know you lectured me nonstop for over two hours? I never got a word in. It was awful, Dad."

"I'm so sorry, Jim. I didn't realize. Please forgive me."

The next time he came home, I brought up the previous, extra-talkative Dad situation over dinner: "I need your help, guys. You shouldn't be forced to listen to a loud, gabby lecturer. I don't want to embarrass you in front of your friends. When you sense I'm getting manic, give me the "time-out" sign that you use in sports. It'll signal me to reduce my verbal speed and volume, and alert me to listen more and let you talk."

Everyone smiled. Then we howled as Jimmy recounted my two-hour "lecture." That simple "time-out" sign worked! It helped me become sensitive to when I was moving into mania. From then on Leah, Jimmy, and John used it as their "secret signal." I shared it with friends, and asked them to use it with me too.

Rapid cycling is one of the most destructive forms of bipolar illness.[95] A rapid cycler is one who has four or more major mood changes in a year. Obviously, I qualified, since my mood shifts were occurring every several weeks, and sometimes as often as a dozen times a day. For this reason, my psychiatrist revised my diagnosis to "manic-depressive, rapid cycler."

Through research, I discovered a possible relationship between my childhood sexual abuse and my dangerous rapid cycling manias and depressions. Credible data demonstrate how early life experiences influence the development of bipolar disability.[96] Case studies show that patients who were sexually abused have a greater incidence of ultra-rapid-cycling and suicide.[97]

Knowing how quickly I could escalate into a mood change, I was constantly aware of my precarious situation. I learned not to take good days for granted. In fact, I grew extremely anxious whenever I felt overloaded or became impatient, irritable, sad, fidgety, overly energetic, or exhausted. Those warning signs indicated bad days ahead: another cycle of depression or mania was about to strike. I was never sure which.

Some of my depressions and most of my manias had crabby, near-violent sides; I could blow up any time over mundane comments or minor difficulties. The night of our 1992 Thanksgiving, heavy-heartedness struck unexpectedly. Afraid it had come for an indefinite stay, I wanted to see how badly depressed I was, so I tested myself with the Beck Depression Inventory, one of the most widely used scales for rating degree of depression. I was "off the chart," confirming that I was in serious trouble. I hung on, plagued by melancholy throughout the Christmas holidays, somehow enduring for Leah and the boys' sakes.

Eventually, the unhappiness abated, granting me a few mellow days before Christmas. Then, two days afterward, I sensed trouble brewing. My brief Christmastime sentimentality evaporated. Without warning, I encountered a full-blown mania and didn't sleep at all for the next four nights. All I remember about that hellish period was how utterly overwhelmed I felt as I stewed about catching up on the previous fall's work and having to tackle so many new projects early in January 1993. It was too much. I reacted furiously at anything and anyone. When people are manic, it's almost useless to try to convince them they've got a problem. In the worst stages of mania, I became aggressively argumentative. It hurts me to think of all the emotional pain I inflicted on Leah, the boys, and others, then and later. Suddenly, as quickly as it had come, the mania left, and I resumed a life instead of an existence — but not for long.

My ups and downs drained Leah's physical, emotional, and spiritual strength. She never knew when the next crisis would strike. To maintain her stability, she nourished her spirit with a remarkable devotional life and the close support of friends. For everyone's well-being, she had the courage to set boundaries with me. When I became agitated to the point of shouting or swearing, she said, "Jim, your behavior's getting out of control. If you don't stop, I'll take the boys, get in the car, and drive over to a friend's house." Her warnings nearly always jerked me out of my moods enough to respect her limits. Instead of blowing up at home, I took long drives or went to movies to dissipate the inner upheaval.

In the spring, I spent six days in Florida, combining business and pleasure. One of Bob Long's friends arranged for Bob and me to stay in his Ft. Lauderdale condominium. We spent four days cracking jokes, discussing our ministries, crying together over painful stresses, jogging along the beach, and seeing as many as four movies a day. Pure relaxation, it was a great mix of fun, sharing, and encouragement. It was so meaningful that we made it a priority to get together every year.

Later that week, I spoke to seventy men at the First Presbyterian Church of North Palm Beach men's breakfast, and later at their dinner meeting. Also, I held several Gathering of Men fundraising meetings. These were wonderful opportunities to share my "mental illness odyssey" and get reacquainted with dear friends to thank them for their love and prayers. It was an uplifting but exhausting time.

Returning to California, I immediately plunged into one of the longest doleful bouts I'd had since the hospitals. This one lasted months. Few were aware how close to suicide I was, because I carried out my day-to-day tasks with a smile. But I'd withdrawn from all but the most vital responsibilities.

This latest episode sobered me into realizing that manic-depressive disorder involved much more than just one's moods. It affected *every* area of my life: family, relationships, self-image, general health, and faith. I realized the battles ahead would require hard work, daring, and perseverance.

Following that close call with death, I committed myself to studying my bipolar "enemy" thoroughly. In boxing and other sports, it helps to learn all you can about your opponent. Then you map out strategies to win. I wanted to continue learning everything I could about the illness, my psychological issues, medications, and how to cope and recover. I made up my mind to learn from people who'd gotten well, stayed well, and reclaimed control over their lives.

In spring 1993, Dad flew out to spend five days with us. One afternoon, he met with Phil and me. I confronted him about my sexual abuse and other painful childhood memories. He said defensively,

"I don't remember that. It could have happened. But let's talk about something positive." Same old denial. I'd always held back my indignation at him because I felt sorry for him. As in times past, I felt horribly guilty for being angry with a naive harmless man who was simply incapable of dealing with emotions.

Chapter 30

Self-Education: More Than Half the Battle

MENTAL HEALTH PROFESSIONALS, as well as hundreds of successfully recovering patients with whom I've spoken, believe that self-education plays a key role in recovery.[98] I worked hard to educate myself on my illness and emotional injuries. My research had started in the first hospital. After my discharge, I'd scouted the self-help sections of bookstores and libraries for anything related to depression, bipolar disorder, medications, and sexual abuse. Sadly, there was little out there on manic depression or practical information on living successfully with mental illness.

In the years ahead, I sought all the information I could find. I read several hundred books, countless magazines, journals, newspapers, and newsletters, and attended numerous mental illness conferences, workshops, seminars, and lectures. I listened to dozens of audio and videotapes. I interviewed several hundred people living with depression and manic depression, as well as many psychiatrists, psychologists, and therapists.

I learned that I shared many traits with victims of emotional, sexual, and physical abuse: nightmares of people chasing me, difficulty getting to sleep, problems of trusting, fear or avoidance of the perpetrator, weight gain, negative self-image, not feeling

God's closeness or love, and other symptoms. Those characteristics confirmed the horrors of my childhood, banishing any lingering doubts that my sexual abuse had actually happened.

I renewed my commitment to controlling my illness. Educating myself improved my quality of life, and would literally save my life in the future.

Too often, my mental health providers were simply using educated guesses on how to best treat me. After more study, I was able to diagnose my symptoms enough to explain and even suggest medications and other approaches to my caregivers.

Manic-depressive illness is a very serious, often deadly, neurological condition. A summary of the facts reveals that 70 to 90 percent of all suicides are associated with depression or bipolar malady.[99] Alarmingly, the findings of thirty studies show that nearly one in five manic-depressives commit suicide.[100]

Usually, the spouse is the one who bears the brunt of manic episodes. That was certainly true for Leah. My sons also had a hard time sorting out "Normal Dad" from "Bipolar Dad." As I learned more about my affliction, I tried to "teach" them, but they resented many of my attempts because I often "preached" at them in a pushy way.

The hour-long drive to Pasadena to see my psychiatrist was wearing on me, so I reluctantly switched psychiatrists. I took Leah with me to meet the new one, because I realized that the nature of mood disorders tends to make patients' reports unreliable at times. Since Leah tended to observe my emotional fluctuations more clearly than I did, I felt it would help the doctor to hear her viewpoint.

The Gathering's only major push each year was the October Outreach Breakfast. Although it was a once-a-year event, it took months of preparation: recruiting, meetings with leaders, counseling, planning for follow-up with men who had made spiritual decisions, and other administrative details. Fighting intermittent anxieties hampered my labors. On good days, I accomplished the work of three men, driving myself at a hectic pace to get things done. I wondered, *Are these high-octane energy bursts results of*

my natural driven personality, or are they episodes of mania? While having some exceedingly productive days, I often lost days due to isolating from manic irritability, depressive meltdown, or lack of sleep.

Meanwhile, men and churches from other cities in southern California were contacting me about starting similar men's evangelistic ministries in their areas. Their enthusiasm was energizing, but the combination of fighting the unstable moods and the stresses of fundraising and putting on breakfasts wore on me. The thought of organizing additional ministries elsewhere felt overwhelming.

Such undertakings would have been easily done under normal circumstances. But wrestling with emotional turmoil constantly knocked me off my work rhythm, making me reactive rather than proactive. When a downturn occurred, I could hardly function. Everything, even opening mail, making a phone call, or writing a thank you note required extra effort. Due to lost work time, I continuously played catch-up. Worst of all, I condemned myself repeatedly for not accomplishing what I'd planned, which deepened my discouragement.

That fall, Jimmy entered his sophomore year at Brown. I missed him terribly. John started eighth grade. Two weeks after the Outreach Breakfast, John and I took a four-day trip to the Lake Tahoe area. We had a terrific father-son adventure, hunting, fishing, and horseback riding. Besides thoroughly enjoying the camaraderie with the boys, my times with them were like a second chance at childhood. I probably enjoyed each adventure as much or more than they did.

Since our arrival in California in 1986, Leah had taught elementary school and worked as a secretary. On October 16, 1993, she was offered the position of Minister of Visitation at St. Andrew's. Excitedly, she accepted and began her new twenty-hour-a-week ministry, which involved visiting hospitals and nursing homes, conducting funerals, and assisting in the pulpit. St. Andrew's also provided her with scholarship aid that covered four courses a year at Fuller Seminary. She loved her job and studies! Her wages at St.

Andrew's and my disability income made it possible for us to squeeze through the coming years.

After each incident of instability, I held simultaneous conversations in my head: one worried, *When will the next episode come? It's frightening to go from happiness to hopelessness in minutes.* The other pledged, *This will be my last bad mood change. I'll find the right pill. I'll put into practice what I've learned about managing stress.* However, even with the best intentions, the mood swings continued.

In November 1993, five years after my hospitalizations, it hit me: *This bipolar mind disease has forced me to put my whole life on hold for half a decade. I've been living in a time warp, merely existing, numb to the world, robbed of enjoying my family, friends, and career. I hate this illness!*

Even in the most enjoyable times, I felt like a stranger looking in on someone else's fun. But it was more pronounced now. Accompanying each joyous occasion, the committee in my head yelled, *You don't deserve to have fun. Besides, it won't last. You're a mean, selfish, bad person. You can fool others, you can smile on the outside, but we know you're a fake. Sooner or later, they'll find out what a dreadful person you really are and reject you in a flash.*

Later that month, I suffered two severe panic attacks that were accompanied by a racing pulse, chest pains, and difficulty breathing. I thought they might be heart attacks.

During the early stages of my manias, I felt good about everything and everyone. I acted pleasant, sought people out, became very creative, was driven with gusto, and needed very little sleep. In conversations, I became more persuasive, frequently jumping from one topic to another, seldom listening. As the mania accelerated, I got impatient, contentious. Leah and the boys felt that I was much harder to live with when manic than when depressed.

On January 9, 1994, the day after Jimmy headed back to college, I launched into another mania. Gone was the reclusive "Mr. Pessimism" of previous weeks; I became a blend of the energetic, all-wise "Mr. Optimism" and the talkative "Mr. Sociability." In *my* eyes, I had far more profound insight than others. These warning

signs of oncoming mania should have been easily recognizable, but everything felt normal. Then "Mr. Anxiety" took over. Beneath my restless productivity, agitation, and rage, suspicion of everyone and everything predominated. When at last I saw the danger signals, it was too late.

The mania lasted five months. Initially, I went four straight nights and days without sleep. I was so energized that I slept less than two hours a night during most of January and February.

Throughout March, April, and May, I was so wired that I subsisted on less than four hours' sleep a night. I worked at a panicked pace, yet was easily distracted. Sometimes I literally ran from room to room at home, throwing myself into one project after another. *Time's crucial; it can't be wasted.* I couldn't stop planning; my to-do list expanded by a dozen pages every day. In one month I wrote fifty sheets of detailed tasks to be undertaken. Hundreds of ideas sped through my mind. I couldn't slow them down or shut them off. Everything had to be done on a self-imposed deadline. Surprised by all the household chores I'd done, Leah had no idea what was going on. "My, how much you've accomplished, Jim. How'd you do all this?"

"Amazing what a little touch of mania will do, Honey." We howled together!

It was torture to overflow with plans and be unable to turn off the engine at night. I literally vibrated with so much energy that I couldn't sit still in restaurants, movies, or meetings. I read and wrote for hours, and made phone calls until my ears hurt from the pressure of the receiver.

Little things that normally wouldn't have mattered infuriated me. I told off bank tellers, gas station attendants, and others. I had to get away for fear of saying or doing hurtful things. To distract myself, I saw movies day and night. I spent hour after hour driving nowhere, listening to talk shows and news broadcasts, in hopes that they might slow me down and prevent conflicts with people. I went from one theater to another, unable to get comfortable. The edginess remained.

I craved sleep but couldn't relax. I *had* to keep going. More things had to be done. Like a hamster on a treadmill, I didn't know when or how to stop. Even when I sat in my La-Z-Boy, I juggled several things at once: watched TV, read the newspaper, ate a snack, and wrote notes.

It was horrendous to feel completely exhausted, crave sleep, and yet be unable to rest. I spent many nights at Norm's and other twenty-four-hour places, reading magazines, books, and every newspaper from the racks. Even aware of the risks of mixing alcohol and meds, I tried drinking wine to dull me. It worked sometimes, and I'd drive home, collapse into bed to enjoy a few merciful hours of sleep. Usually, it didn't.

After five nightmarish months, the mania went away as swiftly as it had come, and a low-level melancholia settled into its accustomed place in my mind and body. From then on, I was vigilant, waiting for the next steep drop or surly high.

Chapter 31

Life-saving Discoveries about Medications and Recovery

I RECONSIDERED THE POSSIBILITY that my mood swings might be caused by the *meds* alone, rather than by adverse circumstances. My studies have led me to some startling discoveries. All medications have risks, and *most* carry serious ones.[101] In fact, medical experts caution the use of *all* meds, due to the possible harm and even death that can be caused by side effects or interactions with other drugs.[102] Furthermore, results from clinical investigations stress the need to have meds adjusted to *individual* needs rather than

general dosages of "one size fits all."[103] Knowing this, I vowed always to be informed about every pill I took, whether prescribed, over the counter, or a seemingly harmless vitamin.

Medication is usually prescribed to treat an acute episode of mania or depression, or to prevent relapses. Contrary to what I'd believed, meds don't make you feel good all the time. At best, they ease suffering by helping you sleep or by lessening the anxiety, fidgetiness, anger, and pain, enabling you to deal with your problems. My medication track record was poor: all my meds had caused negative side effects, some minimal, others intolerable. I'd been overmedicated at times. At best, medication hadn't been effective.

Thinking that meds were the only solution, I endured unpleasant side effects, ever-changing moods, and loss of hope that things could get better. I broadened my research to include the latest information on recovery from psychiatric illness, physical disabilities, and addictions, thinking there had to be other answers.

During a session in July 1994, Phil remarked, "Jim, as long as I've known you, you've been fighting for survival. You haven't been able to work much on healing and rebuilding. Now you're ready." Phil played a critical role in my recovering. Time and again he demonstrated unconditional love for me, believing in me when I didn't believe in myself. "I know you're going to make it through this, Jim. We'll work on it together."

When I began moving from a five-year survival mode to a recovery mode, it was often two steps forward, one step back. At times I took ten steps back in order to move ahead just one.

While the goal of treatment for bipolar disorder is full remission of all mood disruptions, this rarely happens. Many people find that their episodes not only recur but often increase in frequency over time. One-half to two-thirds of mentally ill people recover significantly. Most aren't, as many believe, permanently incapacitated, infantile, helpless "crazies." It heartened me to realize that I could recover sufficiently to be happy and productive again. To rebuild I would need both medications *and* an active recovery program involving acceptance, self-education, counseling,

peer support, and service to others. Some ask, "Isn't it dishonest to speak of recovery when depressive or manic-depressive symptoms are likely to persist in some manner throughout one's lifetime? After all, no one is really cured of a mental illness." It's a valid question.

As I found, recovery is a concept that overrides debate on whether mental illness is caused by genetic or environmental factors. You can recover regardless of how you view the cause of your illness. The episodic nature of a severe mental illness doesn't prevent recovery. When you're recovering, it doesn't mean that your suffering will end, symptoms disappear, and you'll function exactly as before. After all, people with physical injuries like amputations can recover and live meaningful, fruitful lives, even though their physical problems never go away.

The most important part of recovery is *self-renewal,* which involves ongoing healing, physical, emotional and spiritual. It can't be rushed. Everyone's recovery is different. This means continually adjusting your perceptions, attitudes, values, feelings, roles, skills, and goals. As I'd already experienced, and was to rediscover, recuperation doesn't occur in a straight line.

Reading about recovery and meeting successfully recovering manic-depressives and depressives excited me about the future! I began to believe that I could recover, even if my mood changes never went away. I could move beyond bipolar symptoms and take charge of my life again.

I accepted my condition but refused to give in to it. Although I would probably never be able to do some of the things I'd done in the past, I doubled my efforts to re-enter some form of full-time professional ministry, knowing it would require restructuring the pace, hours, and type of work I'd do. I'd have to toughen my thin skin to take the confrontations, criticisms, and conflicts that would come with any leadership position. It excited me to dream of going forward and reshaping my life along these adjusted parameters.

Whatever it took, I wanted to be an active agent in my recovery. To begin with, I reaffirmed the critical need to monitor my

thinking, my moods, and anything that could potentially destabilize me. Knowledgeable of the symptoms of depression and mania, now I had to get into the habit of avoiding situations that could trigger serious incidents. I paid close attention to people, sleep patterns, self-defeating attitudes, and work habits that could cause relapses.

Past experience showed the importance of taking every warning sign of an approaching mood shift seriously. Because I could go up and down many times a day, once a depression or mania started, it could snowball quickly. I'd learned the hard way that the longer I delayed dealing with a mood swing, the harder it was to control. If one seemed to be coming, I needed to act quickly to interrupt it before things got too bad. I got in the habit of asking myself, *Am I showing any early warning signs in my thought patterns, attitudes, or emotions? What am I thinking about right now? How am I feeling at this moment? Sadness? Anger? Resentment? Self-pity? Am I talking too much, too fast, too loud? What can I learn from this? What strategy can I implement to avoid similar problems in the future? What action should I take right now to nip this in the bud?*

All I had was a vague hope that I could stabilize enough to heal and begin rebuilding my life. I lacked specific plans for combating stresses and mood changes. Even with my insights and commitment to take charge of my renewal, I often failed miserably. Sometimes rehabilitation meant taking a "mental health day" (or week) to recuperate from someone's hurtful comment, or pushing too hard to meet a deadline, or other aggravation. About half the time, I couldn't handle stress, so I canceled meetings, appointments with friends, and other engagements. But I felt more in control.

I picked up my medications at the drugstore one afternoon. After two days of taking them, I had severe chest pains. Thinking I was having a heart attack, I phoned my psychiatrist. It took enormous effort to mention my fears to him because I didn't want to come across as a hypochondriac. He assured me, "Jim, you're all right. Those are only temporary, minor side effects. You're on too

low a dosage for any heart attack. Keep taking them." I was embarrassed to have brought it up.

I continued taking the pills for the next five months. One day, while lunching with a fellow struggler, we were discussing our medications. His was the same type as mine, but I noticed his pills weren't the same color. I asked, "How come we've got different-colored pills if they're both made by the same company?" Then I read the dosage on my bottle; it was *double* what my doctor's prescription said they should be!

I asked the pharmacist to check my original prescription record. I explained the chest pains I'd been having for five months. I watched him read it. His eyes widened. Handing me the prescription slip, he said, "I'm so sorry. I don't know how this happened. Guess our computer's made a very serious error. You've been taking twice the dose written on your prescription. No wonder you've been suffering chest pains. It's a miracle you're not seriously ill or dead!" Immediately, anger reddened my face. I said nothing as I grabbed the prescription and stomped out. I never went back. That was my first lesson in never completely trusting pharmacists, psychiatrists, or doctors, and checking out *every* prescription.

The next day, I visited another drugstore belonging to a well-known national chain. The pharmacist bragged, "Oh, yes, all of our pharmacy records and supplies are computerized. This avoids human error, and it speeds up your service. Rest easy, no need to worry with us." I switched to his pharmacy and everything went fine — for a while. In the years ahead, I would have several more extremely serious reactions due to druggists' or psychiatrists' errors. Obviously, I hadn't learned my pharmacy lessons well enough.

From that close call and based on reading about medications, I could no longer afford to be a passive pill taker. Too many things could go wrong. I needed to protect myself by learning more about meds, and monitoring any unusual mental or physical changes in myself. This accelerated my ongoing study of psychiatric drugs.

The pharmaceutical industry has become one of the top moneymaking enterprises in the world. Yet, with the phenomenal progress

have come significant, sometimes life-endangering problems. Some medical authorities are gravely concerned that America is caught in an epidemic of medicine side effects, excessively high dosages, and harmful interactions with other drugs. In fact, medication re-actions are the *fourth* major cause of death in the U.S., topping deaths by car accident, alcohol and illegal drug use, AIDS, diabe-tes, contagious diseases, and murder.[104] It's estimated that at least 125,000 die every year because of prescription medication mis-takes, and another 140,000 die from side effects. This is more than *ten* times as many deaths as from illegal drugs![105]

Physicians, psychiatrists, and the Food and Drug Administra-tion (FDA) are major sources for drug information, but they're not the only ones, nor are they as reliable as many believe. A 1998 study financed by the NIMH (National Institute of Mental Health) found that *over 70 percent* of patients were given the wrong dose of psychiatric medicines.[106]

I'm concerned that fellow mentally ill people become educated, on-guard consumers who are knowledgeable of potentially adverse, drug-induced reactions. This is critical for five reasons:

1. The proliferation of new, powerful medications;

2. Doctors are over-worked and inundated in drug information;

3. Psychiatric knowledge has increased dramatically, but it has a long way to go to be an exact science;

4. Many pharmacists, rushed by expanding workloads, make hasty and sometimes inaccurate decisions; and

5. The FDA (Food and Drug Administration) is having an in-creasingly difficult time testing and monitoring medications for effectiveness and long-term safety. Since 1977, more med-ications have been shown to be harmful and removed from FDA endorsement than in previous years. Studies reveal that *51 percent* of approved drugs have toxic side effects not no-ticed before approval.[107] It's alarming to note that in the last

four years the FDA had to disqualify ten prescription medications, a vaccine, and an anesthetic from its list of ratified drugs.[108]

The FDA was established in 1906 to protect the public from harmful or ineffective drugs. But even with FDA approval, investigations reveal that the safety of long-term use of many new medications is unknown, since problems sometimes surface years after a drug becomes available.[109] According to a recognized study, only *1 percent* of dangerous drug reactions is reported to the FDA.[110]

Like many manic-depressives, I was on several medications. Because of suffering so many side effects, I often wondered whether there were any harmful interactions among them. After more research, it became obvious that mixing meds requires ongoing education, alertness, and the courage to question your doctors and pharmacists.

Everyone responds differently to medications, depending on weight, age, sensitivity to drugs, and how additional pills will mix with the ones they are already taking. There isn't a foolproof way to predict who will be helped and who harmed by a medication. At best, it's a calculated gamble that the pill you and I swallow will work as it's supposed to, hopefully without negative or possibly lethal side effects.

Most people believe their pharmacy is infallible. Wrong! In an extensive 1997 survey, pharmacists said that the pace and volume of their work resulted in almost 60 percent of their mistakes.[111] We patients usually count on pharmacists to catch doctors' mistakes. However, a major survey reveals more shocking news about American pharmacies: the computer systems used to catch prescription errors are not as dependable as many believe.[112]

How easy it would be if there were one med that helped every depressive and manic-depressive patient. Unfortunately, no single pill or dosage works for everyone. There's no ideal method of predicting which drugs will or won't be effective. For this and other reasons, physicians make educated guesses when prescribing more than one medication.

Personal experiences and reading about psychiatric medications taught me the necessity of checking prescription labels, potential side effects, possible interactions with other drugs, the need for more long-term studies, and the importance of blood tests for certain meds. This new approach to managing my medications would require persistent effort. I respected my psychiatrist's expertise, but I was also realistic enough to know that he and other doctors are overly busy. Often, as well meaning as they are, psychiatrists and other physicians don't ask enough questions about symptoms, negative reactions to meds, and stress.

That's why I took a list of discussion items to every psychiatric appointment: my mood status, any unusual physical or mental changes I'd recently experienced, and a list that included every psychiatric med I was taking, and all other medicines, like nonprescription drugs, vitamins, and herbs. This felt necessary because my psychiatrist too often asked, "Now what medications do I have you on, Jim?" After hearing that a few times, I made no apologies for asking questions.

One day, I went to the large chain pharmacy to pick up my prescription. Returning home, I pulled the vial out of the bag and put it on the shelf with others. After dinner, I grabbed the new bottle and its companions, and gulped down all but the newest pills with a glass of water. Then, just before taking the new ones, I glanced at the information on the bottle: wrong prescription, wrong dose, wrong patient! Steaming, I stuffed the bottle in my pocket, rushed to the pharmacy, and slammed the container on the counter. "What's going on here?" I demanded. The pharmacist picked up the bottle. She stammered, "I'm so sorry, Mr. Stout. I don't know what happened. You've obviously been given someone else's prescription. Have you taken any of these yet?"

"No."

"Somehow, one of our staff gave you another person's pills."

She pulled up my prescription records on her computer, and turned the pages of her medication reference book. "Mr. Stout, you're lucky you didn't take any of these. Their interaction with

the other medications you're taking could have made you violent-
ly ill or killed you. I apologize for our mistake." She filled another
bottle, typed some information on the front, and showed it to me.
"See, this is what you should have been given."

"Thanks," I mumbled. "Will you give me whatever printed information you have on each of my medications? I've gotten them
with most of my prescriptions, but have misplaced some and haven't
always read them carefully."

I vowed, *This will never happen to me again. I've got to be ultra-
careful* every *time I pick up meds at the pharmacy.* From then on,
whenever Leah or I picked up my meds and brought them home, I
went through a safety ritual, even on refills. I read each label to
make sure it was the right med, with *my* name, and the color,
shape, size, and dosage prescribed. I kept the pharmacy printout
on each med right next to the pill bottles, and monitored side
effects and any mental or physical changes constantly.

I browsed bookstores for the latest books on medications. My
favorite was *The PDR Pocket Guide to Prescription Drugs.* Its easy-
to-read information clarified the printouts the pharmacist provided.
That inexpensive book would save my life several times.

Even when visiting doctors or dentists for something unrelated to my mental disability, I was cautious. If he wanted to prescribe
a med, I first gave him a list of my prescribed psychiatric drugs
and over-the-counter medications. No way did I want to chance a
bad interaction. From time to time, my psychiatrist wanted me to
try a new medication. On each occasion I asked him about its
purpose, possible side effects, and potential negative interactions.
Then I'd say, "Thanks, Doc. Before I try it, though, I'll read up on
it. Then, could we can discuss its pros and cons?" or, "I realize
you're trying to do what's best for me, Doc, but no thanks. I've
read about the medication and it seems too risky at this time. After all, it's my body and I want to feel confident that what goes
into my mouth is safe." He never argued. When I did decide to
take a new one, I asked him for instructions on taking it, and
wrote down his answers.

As an athlete, I'd learned to listen to my body. Now that was necessary again, in addition to paying attention to psychological changes. Whenever my thinking, feelings, or bodily functions didn't seem quite right, I immediately checked the printouts and medication book. Once in a while, I found that a med was *causing* the depression or mania it was supposedly treating!

When experiencing a disturbing symptom, I quickly phoned my druggist or psychiatrist. Sometimes what was listed as a rare side effect and considered minor by my doctor was a major annoyance for *me*, and I'd ask him to change the med.

When taken over a long time, several of my drugs carried risks, like tardive dyskinesia, a condition causing uncontrollable muscle and facial movements. Since I'd suffered from hand tremors and facial twitches a few years earlier, I watched for signs of any problem.

Addiction to alcohol and other substances is a major problem for bipolars: nearly 70 percent of them abuse alcohol or drugs to alleviate mood-related distress.[113] Incorrect alcohol and substance use can worsen sleep, warp judgment, provoke mixed, agitated or depressed states, impair the effectiveness of medications, injure relationships, or hasten a suicide attempt.[114] Yet, despite knowing the dangers of mixing alcohol with meds, I still occasionally drank a glass of two of wine to dull my pain and get some sleep. Most of the time, it didn't help; all I got was a slight buzz and more troubled sleep.

My work at the Irvine church continued to go well, but it was becoming increasingly stressful. In August, I preached, and was so drained that I slept the next day and a half. Job-related anxieties rankled me until, rather than jeopardize my mental health, I resigned. But following my departure from the Irvine church, I headed south quickly. It was now critical to catch myself before becoming too immobilized to pull out.

The early warning signs of another depression on its way were clear, but I was powerless to prevent it. Nothing made me feel better. I considered checking into a hospital, but dismissed the thought, terrified that the insurance company might refuse treatment or

force me to leave prematurely. Gone was any desire to phone a friend for help, not even Bob Long. As a result, I slipped into another bout of despondency that lasted several months.

In spring 1994, Dad flew out to be with us for six days. Even in his eighties, each time I saw him he'd hug me and kiss me on the head, neck, and cheek. I cherished his affections, but still squirmed inside when he was so demonstrative. It also bothered me hearing Dad always say, "*We* love you, Jimmy." I don't remember him ever telling me, "*I* love you, Jimmy." His words brought back memories of years past, when he and Mom were separated and he always used the plural "we." Now, even after his second wife, Alice, had died, he continued to say, "*We* love you."

I had an active, talented, local Gathering of Men board. They were wonderfully supportive. I shared as best I could concerning my rocky journey with mental illness. Though the men didn't understand much about it, they respected my abilities. They wanted not only to be part of a growing ministry, but also to help me put my life back together.

Everything was burgeoning, so the board decided it best to rent an office. We found one in Newport Beach, just a mile from home. I recruited volunteers to help with filing, typing, copying, and mailings. The ministry couldn't have succeeded without their hard work. Several times a year, we mailed over 900 newsletters to friends, donors, and contacts around the country. Each issue included a family update, a ministry progress report, and information about my disorder and my efforts to cope with it.

Many people with manic-depressive illness don't perform well in pressured work environments. I found that handling deadline-oriented work overwhelmed me. It felt wimpish not being able to weather pressures and confrontations, but my stamina and resiliency just weren't the same as before. Details of organizing Outreach Breakfasts, fundraising, and other administrative aspects of running the Gathering ministry weighed on me.

The combination of self-imposed pressure and the opportunities to expand to other areas wore me down. I'd put in two or three

weeks of hard work, then hit a wall of insomnia, exhaustion, and isolation, during which I was almost useless. Most people had no clue about the severity of these ongoing emotional battles; they saw only the friendly, upbeat Jim Stout and his outer successes.

Being able to use my gifts to help others was and is a dominant factor in my recovery. I thoroughly enjoyed speaking, teaching, counseling, guiding, writing, organizing, and motivating. A phrase from the Bible became especially meaningful to me as I sought to use the pain I'd endured to mend others: " ... the God of all comfort, who comforts us in all our troubles, so that we can comfort those in any trouble with the comfort we ourselves have received from God." [115]

I looked forward to opportunities for sharing my emotional odyssey with manic depression. That year, and in years ahead, I was invited to tell my story to various groups: the patients and staffs of hospital psychiatric wards, mental illness conferences, seminars, support groups, churches, and Bible studies.

By this time, I'd gotten to know over a hundred individuals living with mental disabilities. Knowing firsthand how lonely it could be adapting to a mind malfunction, I yearned to reach out to others in similar straits. *There needs to be a place where these folks can go to be listened to, encouraged, and taught coping skills. Given what we patients have in common, there could be instant communication. Some things,* only *a person with a mental disorder understands.*

Chapter 32

A Support Group Makes
All the Difference

IN 1994 I DECIDED TO START a support group for men and women living with mental illness. Although Orange County had groups for family members, there were few for patients. I used my Newport Beach office to host the group. Soon, a woman therapist joined me to co-lead the group. Our meetings, held during weekday lunch hours, averaged nine or ten people, most referred by psychiatrists, psychologists, therapists, pastors, and family members. We had a fairly even mix of schizophrenics, manic depressives, and depressives, with diverse backgrounds and an average age of twenty-five. Some had dual diagnoses involving alcohol, drug, or other addictions. Some were Christians; many weren't.

The advantages of encouragement groups for physical diseases, addictions, and mental illnesses are well documented. Healing and recovery take place in *relationships*. Such groups provide a safe place to be valued. They also offer solace, companionship, affirmation, and guidance. As a leader-member of the group, I too benefited. It was very comforting to have in my corner others who really knew the inner and outer battles of mental illness.

Chapter 33

The Potential Risks of Work: Hours, Pace, and Deadlines

THE OFFICE VOLUNTEERS WERE INDISPENSABLE, but we needed more help, so I recruited some of the support group members to donate their time. Soon, our office team comprised both "normies" and mentally ill individuals. At first, many of those with brain disorders could work little more than a half-hour. Simple tasks like folding a few dozen fliers, stuffing thirty newsletters, or collating twenty articles exhausted them.

Gradually, their confidence, self-esteem and stamina grew. "I didn't know I could do this stuff. Two months ago I couldn't have left my house because I was so depressed. I'll bet I can help do the whole mailing next time. Maybe in a couple of months I can also try taking a class at one of the community colleges."

Their output multiplied as they gained confidence and saw their work as a way to serve others while equipping themselves for jobs in the workforce. Because of the excellent work some did, I referred them to employers for whom they later excelled.

Unfortunately, I found myself slipping into the old workaholic patterns again. Many times I'd start for the office, then panic. *I've got twenty calls to make, ten thank-you letters to write, a lunch meeting, two men coming for career counseling, and fifteen other things carried over from the past three days that must be done today. I can't get on top of this workload, and I can't face another day of pressure.* All too frequently, I'd turn the car around and head home to call and cancel my appointments.

To try to relax and disengage from work, I tried painting and photography, which had always intrigued me. I enrolled in a watercolor course at nearby Golden West College, but attended only

one class, and then sank into a three-month downer. However, several times that year I hauled out my paints and made some feeble yet enjoyable attempts at painting.

Driving John and his friends to surfing beaches was a way of forcing myself out of isolation and motivating myself to socialize. I savored the opportunities to watch him and his buddies enjoy themselves so much. Most of the afternoons, I dropped him and his buddies off, then hid out in a small pizza place, reading journals while waiting to pick them up. Those excursions were the high points of many days.

I was constantly galled, and more than that, infuriated by telephone disagreements with the insurance company over coverage for doctors and medications. Inevitably, those conflicts were followed by irate days or turbulent nights. Because of insurance-related difficulties and a bare-bones budget, our family squeaked by week to week. We'd gone into deep debt with loans and credit cards. We dreaded a car breakdown, an unexpected dental bill, or any unplanned outlay of money. Hard as we tried, we kept falling further behind.

My psychiatrist started me on several new medications that year. They worked well, initially. With rising hopes, I visualized going back to work in a few months, only to be disappointed by the return of mood spells. In some of the worst, I became disillusioned with the whole mental health profession. I didn't believe pills or therapies worked. Every setback eroded confidence in the mental health providers and especially in my ability to handle difficulties.

Because suicide always lurked at the back of my mind, I knew it was imperative to learn how to cope, heal, and rebuild. *To survive will take* more *than meeting with my psychologist and psychiatrist. As helpful as counseling is, and though the medications numb some of the pain, they're not enough. It'll only take a slight turn of events or a harsh comment to knock me down permanently.*

Although my learning efforts were only intellectual knowledge, they enabled me to discuss my past and current situations more productively with Phil, as well as talking more knowledgeably

about medications with my psychiatrist. Having information on pills, side effects, and manic depression gave me more control of my healing. It made me feel less like a passive patient and more like an active partner with them.

Chapter 34

The Forgiveness Process: Finding How to Let Go of Resentments

SESSIONS WITH PHIL MORE THAN VALIDATED the fact that I hadn't had a normal childhood. Our digging into my past enabled me to grieve the loss of what could have been but never was. Resentment over my losses began to surface as I reviewed my youth and adulthood. I realized that if I didn't let go of grudges, every time a future situation evoked those memories, I could sink into a life-threatening depression.

For a long time I'd been reluctant to blame my parents and others for my emotional injuries. To fault them felt like an excuse for *my* inability to overcome "a few hard hits in life." Forgiving and forgetting would be necessary for inner healing to take place. Yet, the sins against us by others *should not* be glossed over. As cathartic as forgiveness is, I learned the danger of pardoning too quickly. Had I granted a hasty, general acquittal like, "I forgive all the sins that Mom, Gram, Dad, Unc, and others have committed against me," I'd have been whitewashing the damage done to me, and short-circuiting the healing process. Exonerating too soon, I believe, would have stuck me in "spiritual denial" of the extent of my wounds, and caused me to bury my pain.

For too long I had blamed myself rather than those who'd injured me. I couldn't begin to forgive until looking squarely at my wounds and reflecting on how those injuries had affected me. Through therapy and reading, I saw the destructive results of having been so mistreated. That pain had followed me through life, impacting me as a man, husband, father, and pastor. Many hurts have healed; some haven't.

I learned neither to excuse nor condone others' destructive behaviors. *They* were responsible for their deeds and words, no matter who or what had influenced them. Forgiveness doesn't mean your abuser was right or that you must excuse someone's wrong behavior. To forgive means choosing to stop holding a grudge, or punishing in some way. Absolution isn't a one-time event. It starts with a decision, but it's a process that sometimes must be repeated over and over until the forgiver is free from all desire to retaliate. Forgiving my parents, relatives, and the church people who'd wronged me took years. After honestly examining the harm done to me, and after much counseling, prayer, and introspection, I chose to begin forgiving them.

Christians are commanded to show mercy, but that doesn't mean we must enjoy or socialize with those whom we forgive. Phil once said, "You can forgive a rattlesnake, but you don't have to eat lunch with it every day." It means that we release our resentment, give up the right to take revenge, and attempt to act in positive — but safe — ways toward the offender. Sometimes our feelings toward the wrongdoer change, but not always.

For most of my life I'd minimized the impact of my childhood experiences: *You didn't have it so bad, Jim. Many have experienced a far worse youth. Your parents were doing the best they could. They were just acting like their parents had toward them. They were incapable of relating any other way. Why blame them?*

I faulted *myself* for our family's problems rather than others: *Jim, you're the cause of your unhappiness. It's been your temper, your lies, your bad choices, your cursing, your obstinacy; you deserved their harsh words.*

It's been a long, difficult process, but I've come to understand Mom, Dad, Gram, and Unc in a new light. I accept them as gifted but tragically flawed people, who tried to contribute to the world and did their best to raise us kids. I grieve at whatever forces in their lives shaped their thinking and made them act in such harmful ways. After years of counseling, I've developed two overriding feelings for them: pity and, strangely, gratitude. I sorrow for them and the battles they fought within themselves. I don't disregard their harmful behavior in any way. *They* are entirely responsible for the vicious words and deeds that scarred my soul. But having faced how their actions have impacted me, I've forgiven them, totally, without reservation. I no longer harbor knee-jerk reactions of anger and resentment. Instead of seeing them primarily as victimizers, I view them as victims themselves.

In addition to compassion for Mom, Dad, Gram, and Unc, I also feel deep gratitude for their positive contributions to my life. Although Gram tore me down publicly, sometimes she affirmed me in ways I never got at home. She, Mom, and Unc modeled for me what it is to help others.

I'm immensely grateful to Dad for teaching me by example to appreciate the small beauties of life: wrens building their nests, cornfields, flowers, geese flying in formation, fresh snowfalls, and more. I owe him for the enjoyment of wrestling, football, boxing, and gymnastics that he exposed me to at Penn State. Despite the endless verbal lashing he got from Mom, I'm grateful for his modeling of longsuffering, regardless of what motivated him. Maybe he knew all along that she was seriously mentally ill; perhaps he was too weak to stand up to her. For whatever reason, he displayed loyalty to her "for better or for worse."

I'd chosen to forgive "the Big Three," Dad, the church members who'd hurt me, and the insurance company's representatives for all the pain they'd inflicted, deliberately or unconsciously. Nonetheless, I had to work at re-forgiving from time to time. Periodically, some incident stirred up an old resentment. It strained me to let go of the desire to strike back. I never forgave perfectly, but I tried. I

needed to repeat the process time and again in the years ahead. I could forgive someone one day, and then a week later a memory of his hurting me would resurface, and the old wound began bleeding again. Each time, I had to reevaluate the circumstance and *choose*, again and again, to let go of resentment so *I* could heal, move on, and begin restructuring my life.

It became clear that resentment and self-pity were a waste of time and hurt me more than people's actions or words. I chose to renew forgiveness for my sake, not others'. Something inside me freed up as a result of letting go of the anger, the desire for retaliation, even though they were all dead except Dad and the insurance people. Now I can honestly say that I feel no anger toward any of them, only sadness and pity.

I came to see Mom, who had once seemed so forceful, as a fragile, helpless person. I accepted her flaws because she was my mother. I'm grateful God used her to birth me, and for what I learned from her: self-sacrifice, generosity, and concern for those less fortunate.

Dad was a socially inept man, yet I appreciate him as a compassionate, sensitive one. In his own way, he was strong, because he hung in there with Mom even when she thrashed him and left him repeatedly. I loved him in spite of his weaknesses, because he was my dad. I'm grateful to God for using him to give me life, and for everything he taught me.

I finally understood Gram, who long ago appeared so domineering, so judgmental, and so spiritual, as a woman who'd been forced to be strong in childhood. She had many shortcomings, but she was my grandmother. I'm thankful for her spiritual influence on me, and for God's using her to give me a broader vision for my life.

I came to view Unc, who'd come across so strong and self-assured, as a man who'd been dominated all his life by Gram. He, in turn, tried to control his wife and sons and others. But in his own way, he also meted out caring and giving and encouragement. He was my uncle, and I loved him in spite of his failings. And I value the positive ways he touched my life.

The Gathering of Men ministry continued to be an exciting challenge, but I was spending an increasing amount of time each week with men in need of career guidance. Finally, the combination of Gathering responsibilities and career counseling grew so burdensome that I began thinking about switching to career counseling only. The national Gathering staff and my board talked at length about it; we decided to form an extension of the Gathering's ministry, offering vocational counseling as another way to reach non-churched men and help struggling Christian men. The new division was called "Career Compatibilities." I became its director. It was an immediate relief to be out from under the Breakfast Ministry pressures. The new part-time ministry took off, and I was soon consulting with clients in our region and from other states.

Besides career guidance, I continued co-leading the weekly mental illness support group and counseling mentally handicapped people and their families. These activities gave me deeper insight into mental illness, and especially recovery principles. Looking back, it's hard to believe all that was accomplished by dogged determination to push through changing moods — clear evidence that God can use anyone, no matter his mental or physical condition, even on his worst days.

By the end of 1995, what I'd learned about medications saved me in two more close calls, both dosage mistakes. Whenever opportunities arose, I shared with others what I'd learned about psychiatric drugs and ways of coping with a mental disability.

Concerned for my ongoing healing, Phil started a support group just for me. He asked me to contact eight or ten people who I thought could be helpful, non-threatening caregivers — a "Jim Stout Fan Club." They called the group *Miqlat,* the Hebrew word for "City of Refuge." At the first meeting, Phil explained the purpose of the group. Then I left, so he could field questions and suggest how they could assist in my recovery.

Phil drove forty minutes each way to the meetings, an investment of time above and beyond his counseling sessions with me. He never charged a cent for his efforts. Talk about genuine Christian

love in action! Because of stress and seemingly never-ending down-turns, I couldn't attend the first six *Miqlat* meetings, but members met monthly with Phil to discuss my circumstances and to pray for me. Individually, they made themselves available to talk whenever I called, they phoned me regularly, sent encouraging notes, and invited me out for coffee and lunches. What an awesome gift!

Every week I received phone calls from several *Miqlat* friends. Sometimes I was too anguished to return their calls, but their patient reaching out gave me enormous boosts during some of my roughest times. In good times, I called "refuge supporters" just to stay in touch, or I huddled with them individually. I also tried to educate them about my illness and how they could best help me. This included sharing tapes and articles on manic depression. Also, we discussed what specific things they could do if I became severely depressed, agitated, or suicidal. And, of course, I shared my latest practical jokes.

When meeting a *Miqlat* person for the first time, I said, "Thanks for getting together with me. Your friendship and encouragement mean a lot. To be most helpful, please don't try to "fix" me by giving advice. Just listen, and tell me you love me and believe in me. That's what I need. I'll try to do the same for you."

The outstanding workbook, *Living Without Depression & Manic Depression*, emphasizes the importance of manic-depressives having a number of supporters they can rely on. One respected survey of bipolars and depressives shows that *three-fourths* of those who were successful at managing their moods were involved in support groups.[116]

From spring through the end of the year, I met periodically with two friends, Dr. Gunnar and Susan Christiansen. In addition to being colleagues in mental illness-related causes, they provided tremendous uplift. Their dedication to reaching out to the mentally disabled inspired hundreds of people, including myself. They infused me with hope and energy to use my experiences to touch others affected by a mental illness.

Chapter 35

Applying the Serenity Prayer and AA's Twelve Steps for Rejuvenating Relationships

MY UNPREDICTABLE UPS AND DOWNS, silent withdrawals, irritability, and manic jabbering took their toll on our family. Many times, Leah said, "Jim, I hope you'll try to understand. The boys and I are not rejecting you. We still love you, but to survive your volatile times, we must occasionally detach ourselves from you emotionally."

My relationship with Jimmy was cordial but strained. I was painfully aware of the injuries I'd caused by my temper and isolation. Both boys were still reluctant to do things with me; they were simply too hurt or afraid to be around Dad much. Not being able to go on adventures or even out for snacks with them hurt badly. It became a burden to think that those troubled relationships were primarily my fault. I loathed myself, but I couldn't do a thing about it.

I tried to patch things up with the boys by initiating all kinds of outings, from a short drive for a Coke, to a movie or a sporting event, to hunting, fishing, and ski trips. "Would you like to...?" I'd ask. Eighty percent of the time I was politely turned down: "No thanks, Dad, I've got plans."

Their rejection stung. Phil's compassionate advice was practical: "Remember, Jim, they're going through their own youthful struggles. Have you forgotten what it was like being a teenager? A college student? No doubt, your hospitalization and illness have affected them. Give them space. Offer to do things with them, but don't pressure. You've been a good father. They'll come around. It'll be hard, but be patient."

That year I became reacquainted with the popular Serenity Prayer, "God grant me the serenity to accept the things I cannot change, the courage to change the things I can, and the wisdom to know the difference."

Saying that simple yet profound prayer helped me to turn my relationships with Leah, Jimmy, and John over to God. I couldn't heal the damage I had caused them, nor could I erase their need to distance themselves from me in self-protection. All I could change was *my* attitude: keep loving them regardless of their responses. It meant trusting God to bring reconciliation and healing in His way, His time.

At best, I did a mediocre job of applying that prayer, but it relieved my regrets and fears, helped me to endure temporary rejections, and gave me a new freedom to accept my sons, whether or not they accepted my offers of companionship.

By the end of 1995, Jimmy had worked through much of his animosity. Perhaps getting away to college had given him a different perspective on his life and his dad. About the same time, though, John began showing signs of anger. His withdrawal was much more obvious than Jimmy's. John didn't want to do anything with me. It was obvious he needed space. I agonized, *Is he afraid of me? Have I said or done things in manic or mixed states that have irredeemably ruptured our relationship? Is he embarrassed to be seen with his mentally ill father? I miss being with him so much. What can I do to heal this breech?*

Part Six

The Promise of Recovery:
Moving onto the Offense

I will build you up again and you will be rebuilt ... Again you will take up your tambourines and go out to dance with the joyful.

— Jeremiah 31:4

Chapter 36

Breaking Free from Needing
the Approval of Others

I'M CERTAIN I WOULDN'T HAVE SURVIVED, let alone made much progress, without Phil's unconditional love. His practical wisdom, biblical insights, and constant affirmations made all the difference. Many times, his words saved me from ending my life.

He also helped me develop greater self-acceptance. I viewed myself as both very gifted and very bad: I had a healthy estimate of my skills and accomplishments, yet hated myself in many ways and was my own worst critic. *Jim, that disappointment happened because you're a failure. Your life is cursed. Your grandmother and mother were right: you're rotten; no one could love you for who you are; the troubles in your life prove it.*

Despite diverse successes, I'd always had low self-esteem. Though a positive visionary, I expected the worst, believing I deserved it. External accomplishments and a mask of self-confidence camouflaged the damaged little boy living inside me. For forty-seven years I'd believed that no matter how much good I did, at my core I was a bad person. Much of what I'd done throughout life was based not only on altruistic motives but also on getting validation from others. Perhaps doing "good things" was a way of proving to myself, others, and God that I really was a "good guy." Believing myself flawed, I sought affirmation through sports, academics, and spiritual leadership.

It's one thing to admit that you have low self-esteem, and quite another to do something about it. A few counseling sessions from the most gifted therapist can't magically change one's self-concept. To move ahead with rebuilding my life, I needed to let go of not only the grudges I held against others but also the ones against

myself. I had to not only accept, but also love my strengths *and* weaknesses. It meant "renewing my mind" by redefining myself only as "Jim" and his *inner* qualities, and not by such achievement-related titles as "pastor," "athlete," "leader," or "counselor."

I read part of Psalm 139 repeatedly: "...you created my inmost being; you knit me together in my mother's womb ... My frame was not hidden from you when I was made in the secret place. When I was woven together in the depths of the earth, your eyes saw my unformed body. All the days ordained for me were written in your book before one of them came to be."[117]

In spring 1996, Bob Long and I met again in North Palm Beach. Besides the relaxing time, I once more overloaded my schedule by having too many meetings with other friends, updating them on my ministry. Spending time with them was rejuvenating, but also siphoned off lots of energy.

I returned home exhausted; it took three weeks to restore my vigor. For the past four years, I hadn't been able to handle more than two appointments a day. When I exceeded that, it tired me to the point of shut-down. Resuming my counseling of men in transition, I improved my stamina, but still found taking on more than two or three appointments a day still overwhelming. Even with pep talks, better planning, or putting myself down for not being able to do more, whenever my schedule went beyond three, I'd nose-dive within a day or so.

Chapter 37

"God Things" That Can Keep You Going

THROUGH MOST OF LIFE, I'D EXPERIENCED very little of God's comforting presence. While always believing in God, I rarely felt close to Him, even after becoming a Christian and a successful pastor. I felt His reassurance primarily through reading the Scriptures, but seldom through prayer.

A child's basic experience of God is through what his parents or primary caregivers are like. Numerous psychology books note that abused children tend to view God as uncaring, unpredictable, and punitive. It seemed that despite my home background and preconceived concepts of God, I was being taken into a deeper understanding of Him.

Historically, when I'd encountered disappointments and couldn't make sense of God's ways with me, I "faithed" it, trusting that He was somehow in the mix and things would work out for the best. In the midst of a crisis, obstacle, or failure, it always seemed that the circumstances "pointed" to a distant, uncaring God who was picking on me, punishing me. Often, I questioned whether He had simply given up on me because I was too bad. Sometimes, when things fell apart, all my biblical theology contributed little relief.

Silently, it dawned on me that God had been trying to tell me all along, "Jim, I'm still here. I haven't deserted you, nor will I ever. I love you, I'm sticking with you, and I still want to use you to mend others and help them to find Me."

Again and again, God consoled, guided, protected, and blessed me in ways that I called "God Things." Before being hospitalized, I'd been too busy with pastoral duties to cultivate a closer relationship with Him. Now, during some of the most trying times of my

life, my relationship with Him was the best it had ever been. Reflecting on the past eight years, I saw myriad "God Things," situations that could only be explained as divine interventions. We were given financial help that enabled us to keep our home, Jimmy received financial aid to attend Brown, Leah got a scholarship to attend Fuller Seminary, and we received scores of communications expressing love. Opportunities arose to share my manic-depressive journey with others, verses from the Bible strengthened my hope, and I found practical special information in libraries, bookstores, and conferences that dealt with mental illness and emotional scars.

Another "God Thing" was the number of simple prayers God answered: prayers for lost car keys, wallets, check books, glasses, watches, and more. To most, these were insignificant, if not childish. To me they were tangible evidence of God's hand still being on my life.

As an athlete I'd exercised my body to develop physical fitness. Now I started to nourish my soul by reading the Bible regularly, as well as books and articles that emphasized emotional healing, recovery, and spirituality. I expanded my daily prayer habits and began worshiping at different churches. Almost every morning I said the Serenity Prayer and thanked God for at least three blessings He'd given me the previous day. Starting the day that way made an astounding difference in my outlook.

Part Seven

Self-Care: Practical Strategies,
Techniques, and Tips for Rebuilding

*Beat your plowshares into swords and your pruning hooks
into spears. Let the weakling say, "I am strong!"*
— Joel 3:10

Chapter 38

The Perils of Sleep Deprivation

HARVARD MEDICAL SCHOOL RESEARCHERS and other scientists have confirmed the necessity of getting enough sleep every night.[118] Disruptions in a manic-depressive's sleep pattern can trigger a manic incident and worsen the illness.[119] In fact, even *one* night of sleep loss or reduction is probably the most significant factor in precipitating a manic episode.[120]

My psychiatrist asked about my sleep habits. "Very poor, Doc. I usually have a hard time falling asleep. My mind won't stop rapid-fire thinking. Sometimes I'm upset over something that happened during the day and I obsess over it. My meds make me get up ten to fifteen times a night to urinate. Half the time, I stay up past one in the morning, watching TV, reading, or driving to an all-night restaurant to read newspapers. Often, I'm so wired that I'm up all night several nights in a row."

"That must be torture, Jim. Don't you know it's crucial for bipolar patients to get adequate sleep? Insomnia can either push you into mania or is already one of the first signs of it. Do whatever it takes to get enough quality sleep."

He prescribed several kinds of sleeping pills but none worked well. I experimented with Tylenol P.M. and Benedryl. They usually put me down within a half-hour, but occasionally I was so manic that they were as effective as firing a BB gun at a charging rhino.

I couldn't do a thing about the frequent bathroom trips caused by lithium, but I worked hard to be in bed by ten. It wasn't easy to turn off a good TV show, put down a book, or shut down the computer, but my evening disciplines improved each week. Better sleep habits definitely helped, because my moods became less jagged.

Jimmy had started out in pre-med, but switched his major to Eastern religions. Leah and I were concerned about Brown's liberal theological reputation, and I'm sure the foundations of Jimmy's faith were often tested to the limit. But we believed God had directed his paths there, so we prayed for him, supported his choices, and encouraged him to stay plugged into Christian groups on campus. He became active with Campus Crusade for Christ and other evangelical organizations. We were thankful for their impact, and especially grateful for the ongoing influence of his St. Andrew's youth group leaders, who called him, wrote to him, and met with him every time he came home.

In 1996, as John enjoyed the tenth grade at Newport Harbor High School, Jimmy thrived in his senior year at Brown and graduated that June. Leah, John, and I flew to Providence, Rhode Island to attend the ceremony. It was thrilling to meet Jimmy's professors and celebrate with him and his friends — a tremendous family event!

John's athletic ability was growing. He did well on the junior varsity volleyball team. Just as Leah and I had relished watching Jimmy's high school track and rowing events, we loved seeing John's volleyball prowess, despite my anxiety about socializing.

While I sometimes received strange looks and condescending comments, I wanted to do my share in educating others about mind disabilities. One way I chose to de-stigmatize mental illness was with a humorous business card I created and passed out whenever appropriate. It also served as a quick, easy-to-use device for diagnosing oneself or a loved one. The front of the card read:

MEMBER AT LARGE

I have Manic-Depressive Illness
Will talk about it!
Have moods; will swing!

Inside the card, I listed the symptoms of clinical depression and manic depression, and four steps to take in getting help. I gave away close to 200 cards that year alone.

In May 1996 I was invited to speak at a mental illness conference workshop hosted by St. Andrew's. Several hundred attended. After sharing my manic-depressive pilgrimage, I handed out dozens of flyers listing the symptoms of bipolar illness and depression, how to help someone living with those brain disturbances, and relevant bibliographies. Apparently, my candidness about the struggles I'd undergone struck responsive chords with fellow strugglers and their loved ones. About forty people came up afterward to ask questions, many with tears in their eyes.

Though plenty of my fellow clergy regarded me as unreliable for pastoral tasks, some considered me an expert on mental illness nonetheless. Later that spring, I shared my bipolar story at another Presbyterian church seminar and with the psychiatric ward patients and staff of a large hospital in Huntington Beach.

In late July I took Dyno with me on a three-day fishing trip to Big Bear Lake, a mountainous spot two hours away. Dyno loved the ride; he stuck his head out the window the whole way. We unloaded our gear at an inexpensive motel a block from the water.

But strange things began happening. I started experiencing troubling symptoms from lithium. I'd brought along *The PDR Pocket Guide to Prescription Drugs* just in case I encountered a problem and couldn't remember all the side effects or signs of overdose.

On the first day, I started having worsening diarrhea. I felt myself moving into a mixed state of increasing irritability and deepening sadness. I became so dizzy the second morning and evening that I could barely walk Dyno. I had ongoing nausea, my eyesight blurred from time to time, and I was urinating every forty-five minutes. I had slept only a few hours the night before. I'd brought along my watercolor paints and brushes and was looking forward to painting some outdoor scenes, but my hands trembled too much to paint a straight line.

By the third morning, my hands shook so badly that I couldn't even bait a hook. I broke down sobbing, stuffed my gear into the tackle box, and headed to the car. Then it hit me: these were symptoms of a toxic overdose of lithium! I re-read the drug book,

and immediately drove to the small community hospital two miles away. I tied Dyno to a long rope under a large tree outside the hospital and walked tipsily to the emergency room.

Though I described the symptoms, the doctor couldn't figure what was wrong. He finally paged the on-call senior physician. He too scratched his head. "What's happening to you sure is unusual."

"I have bipolar disorder and I think I'm having a toxic reaction to an overdose of lithium. How about running a blood test to check my lithium level?"

He did. It took almost an hour for the lab results. Finally, the older doctor returned. "You're right," he said. "Your lithium level is dangerously high. You've got severe lithium poisoning. If you hadn't come here, you could have died in a few days. You've got to stop taking it immediately." I was so shaken that I rushed back to the motel, packed, and headed home with Dyno.

Arriving, I phoned my psychiatrist to tell him what had happened. He scheduled me for an appointment the next day. It sobered me to see the panic in his face as I handed him the hospital lab report.

"I'm so sorry. It must've been very scary. Could you have gotten confused and accidentally swallowed too many pills, Jim? I'm not implying that you were suicidal and trying to kill yourself, but sometimes patients forget they've already taken their day's quota and inadvertently take a double amount. Could you possibly have done that?"

"I don't think so. I keep my medicines in a plastic pill case that's arranged according to the times to take them each day."

"Your knowledge of the side effects probably saved your life, Jim. You've taken lithium for several years, then went off it, and then were put on it again. It's never really stabilized you, and you've always had a rough time tolerating it. No matter what happens, you can't risk going back on it." He wrote a prescription for another drug.

I didn't blame my psychiatrist for the near-lethal overdose. Without a doubt, he and my previous doctors and psychiatrists

were sincerely trying to find the best medicines for me. I think pharmacists did the best they could, too. However, my experience had abundantly proven that doctors, psychiatrists, and pharmacists make mistakes often enough that it would be foolish ever to blindly count on a hastily written prescription or a hurriedly filled pill bottle.

Leaving his office, I renewed my commitment to learn all I could about depression, bipolar disorder, and psychiatric medications. I also wanted to find more information about the most up-to-date counseling methods and the tools successfully used by patients who coped well with their illness or who'd recovered from it. I continued my psychological and pharmaceutical education, attending more conferences and seminars and spending added hours in community, college, and medical school libraries.

Dad had married Alice Warne, his second wife, in 1980. She was a wonderful woman whom he'd known for thirty years. I saw him happy for the first time. It pleased me that he'd finally found someone to love him and ease his loneliness. After twelve years of bliss, however, Alice died in 1992 from some longstanding complications.

Then Dad's health began failing. He'd had prostate surgery in the seventies and periodic bladder cancers removed since then, but I never heard him complain. He maintained his upbeat gratitude for life's small blessings. He never wanted to go into a retirement center. "I don't want to be locked away with old people. I want to stay here in my home where I have people of all ages around me."

That spring, he finally made the painful decision to enter a nursing home. It was a lovely place, nestled in the fertile farmlands bordering State College. Since Betsy and her family lived in Illinois, and Leah and I in California, Bob, who resided in New Jersey, was closest to State College. He drove four hours each way when he visited Dad, and he kept Betsy and me apprised of Dad's condition. I wrote or called Dad nearly every week.

In August 1996, Dad called Betsy, Bob, and me. "Before I sell the house, I want you kids to go through it and pick out anything you want. Betsy arrived and selected some items several weeks

before I did. Afterward, Bob and I met at the house and stayed several nights, going through boxes, drawers, and files.

Each day, we picked Dad up at the nursing home, took him to lunch and then brought him to the house. I could tell it meant a lot to him to be included. I think Dad sensed his days were limited and he just wanted to be with us. He mostly sat and chatted about Penn State's facilities and activities as Bob and I shuffled through old report cards, letters, family photos, childhood toys, stacks of newspapers and magazines, and assorted household wares. The process brought up thoughts of my unhappy childhood, and made me brood about what might have been.

The last morning, Bob and I drove to the nursing home to say good-bye to Dad. He was obviously weak, but in good spirits. I hugged him and, as usual, he kissed me on the head and neck a half-dozen times, saying, "We love you, Jimmy. Take good care of yourself. Leah and the boys need you. We need you. Thanks for coming." That was the last time I saw him.

On November 29, Bob called to tell me that Dad had died. Even knowing that his health was going downhill, Dad's death stunned me. I felt sad, but as much as I wanted to, I couldn't cry. Bob and Betsy and I made some plans about the funeral service. Leah and I made plane reservations, packed, and flew to State College the next day.

Through conversations with the undertaker and greeting friends at the funeral home, I remained numb inside. I looked at Dad's body in the casket we'd selected for him. Dozens of memories returned. *Dad, you've finally found the peace that eluded you most of your life. I hope to see you again in heaven.* Still, like the viewing for Mom years earlier, no tears came.

His funeral was held in the downtown Methodist church. I had the same feelings as at Mom's service. No ache because of having lost a parent. Instead, there came a great sadness that so intelligent a person could live such a tragic, lonely life.

It may seem odd, but I pitied both Dad and Mom. Both bore heavy scars from their upbringing. Each was barely capable of

forming warm, close relationships with anyone, including their children. They tried to parent us the best way they knew. I think they both loved us, however ineptly they showed it. It hurt to think of how much they missed out on in life. They were human tragedies, and I grieved *their* losses as well as mine.

Following the service, forty or more people greeted us. That's when my tears flowed unashamedly. My former scoutmaster hugged me, and former neighbors and family acquaintances muttered words of consolation as they filed past. While shaking hands, listening to their comments, and thanking them for coming, it became clear that most of these dear people had known of Dad's weaknesses for years, yet loved him. They'd come to the service to honor him and to comfort his adult children who had endured so much while growing up.

Though Dad had been overly frugal all his life, in death he made up for it. What financial benefit Betsy, Bob, and I were denied in our youth, we were compensated for, in part, by Dad's will. Leah and I received an inheritance sufficient to pay off a large part of our debts, for which we were extremely thankful.

Our marriage had grown stronger than ever. We wanted to celebrate our thirtieth anniversary in a special way. Leah had always wanted to visit England. With help from Dad's inheritance and a skilled travel agent, we planned the whole trip. Could I stabilize enough to go?

My worst fear was a return of the illness, an apprehension that many manic-depressive patients share. Despite exacting preparations for our vacation of a lifetime, I barely weathered several rugged mood swings before we were to leave. Deep slumps overwhelmed me, eclipsing all hope for our anniversary adventure. It must have devastated Leah to hear, "Honey, I don't think I can pull out of this one. I don't think I'll live to make our England trip."

To relieve as much stress as possible, I'd heightened my watchfulness to avoid criticism, rejection, and over-scheduling, but I wasn't doing well at guarding against resentment, fear, and self-pity. *Are there other things I'm not aware of that are triggering my*

moods? I don't have a clue what else to do to prevent relapses.

I would deal with those questions in the coming years. But right now, to make the trip, I knew internal repairs needed to be made quickly. I was beginning to learn that rebuilding involved a life-long, day-by-day process of adapting and re-adapting. Often, my defeats weren't as bad as they first appeared. In fact, when I seemed to be doing worst, progress was actually happening, because even in defeat, I was learning more about the illness, my limits, and how to develop better coping skills.

Sometimes in the midst of severe mood disturbances, subtle but significant changes were happening. It meant growing beyond the little stressors as well as the seeming catastrophes, finding a new way to live, and taking charge of my life, even though I couldn't completely control the symptoms of my mind illness.

Whenever feasible, I gave Leah, the boys, *Miqlat* members, and others any information that might benefit them personally or help them better understand manic depression. One family member of a manic-depressive shared, "You must learn all you can about your loved one's disorder. Educating yourself is the *key*. Once you understand the symptoms, treatments, and triggers, most of the other things you need to do for yourself and the ill person in your family will come naturally."

Leah's willingness to learn meant a lot to me. She told me how painful it was after having gone through all that she had with me, to then read about and discuss manic depression. It took tremendous courage for her to attend meetings, listen to tapes, and read books and magazines about mental illness.

I discussed contingency plans with her and a few friends in case my condition significantly deteriorated: early signs of impending episodes; what to do if I became suicidal; what to do if I became too agitated to drive; how to limit manic overspending; how to hospitalize me if necessary; our wills; and even funeral plans.

Chapter 39

Reentering Spiritual Kindergarten to Find Help with Attitudes, Habits and Relationships

TWENTY YEARS AGO, A FRIEND HAD GIVEN ME a copy of the Alcoholics Anonymous "Big Book," a fascinating read that teaches a spiritual program based on belief in and dependence on God or a higher power. Its twelve steps for recovering from alcohol addiction include taking an ongoing moral inventory, confessing your personal defects to one other person, making restitution to those you have harmed, and reaching out to help others with similar problems. The "Big Book" alerted me that many of my long-held attitudes and behavior patterns needed to change if I was to recover from bouts of mania and depression.

As I read, it became obvious that some of the *same* stresses that triggered alcoholics to drink also influenced me to overwork and overeat. More importantly, those same stressors seemed to set off my mood shifts. While AA worked for alcoholics, I felt its twelve-step principles could also help manic-depressives like myself to heal and rebuild. Trying to practice the twelve steps in all my relationships marked the beginning of a profound difference in my life, and catalyzed a far deeper spirituality in me. I felt like I was entering spiritual kindergarten, starting all over to trust God with every detail of my life.

Depending on God meant turning over to Him the fears, resentments, and self-hatred that were controlling my life and could precipitate mood swings. Trusting Him involved letting go of my belief that the world was unsafe and against me. It took child-like faith to surrender to God's care and protection, knowing that sooner or later more problems would crowd into my life: side effects from

medications, criticism, rejection, conflicts with the insurance company, and other troubles. I had to accept His supervision of any incident that might come my way. Slowly, I began to let go of my self-defeating mindset and turn it over to God.

Chapter 40

The Risks of Good Stress, Bad Stress, and a Lack of Routine

WHEN A DISAPPOINTMENT HIT, or a dream shattered, I took "mental health" days to watch movies, or attend baseball games. During those revitalization times, I devised new goals and revamped my plans. Somehow, I managed each time to climb out of the pit with the aid of Phil's counsel, reading the Bible and recovery literature, asking for the support of friends, and practicing the twelve steps.

All my life I'd taken care of others; now I began nurturing myself. Stress in any form was "Public Enemy Number One." "Good stress," I discovered, came in varied disguises: meetings, parties, movies, TV shows, exercise, working on home projects, typing at the computer, and making phone calls. When these pursuits lasted late into the evening, no matter how beneficial, they put me at risk of the negative effects of sleep deprivation. If I didn't go to bed early enough, I became over-stimulated, which, in turn, led to poor sleep or not enough of it, and then precipitated a manic attack. "Bad stress" was obvious: being criticized, shamed, rejected, having an over-committed schedule, oppressive deadlines, carrying bitterness, and experiencing disappointment.

Irregularity in a person's accustomed routine can incite mania.

The importance of maintaining a set routine has been confirmed by at least two research studies, which reveal that bipolar patients develop manic symptoms within two months of having their daily schedule rearranged, even temporarily.[121] I found that too many interruptions of my daytime or evening plans kicked off manic disturbances. The more I kept to a regular daily schedule, the calmer I felt. Consistency seemed to protect me.

I'd never before understood the importance of structure in my life. For my birthday, Leah and the boys gave me a saltwater aquarium with six tropical fish. I was responsible for feeding them twice a day. During the most troubled times, I had to force myself to feed those fish, but they, like the water aerobics class, were a great help in handling my ups and downs, giving me a regular schedule to cling to even in emotional turbulence.

I determined to pull myself together for the anniversary trip to England. I curtailed evening activities to get adequate sleep, and cut out caffeine-based stimulants such as coffee, tea, and sodas. To build stamina, I began taking vitamins, and exercised on a treadmill at the "Y" four days a week. By June, I was on top again. Nonetheless, Leah and I had serious concerns about going. We feared my having a bad drug reaction or hitting an emotional snag while abroad. Finally, we decided to go for it. I packed ample pills and asked friends to pray for us.

In August, we took a twenty-four-day trip to England, Ireland, and Scotland to celebrate thirty years of marriage! I joked with friends that it was Leah's reward for putting up with me for so long, but I really meant it. We laughed and gawked throughout the trip, enjoying museums, castles, cathedrals, two plays, a concert, and many historic sites. It was truly the trip of a lifetime — and it proved to be a turning point in our marriage.

On the flight back, I suddenly developed a rash. In an hour it had spread over most of my body. My face flushed and swelled; I itched all over, and became anxious and cranky. I realized that this might be a dangerous, possibly life-threatening reaction to one of the medications. I alerted a flight attendant who returned a

few minutes later and said, "Dr. Stout, the pilot's talked with the airport authorities; a doctor will meet you at the gate."

But as we deplaned there was no physician. Instead, two medics and a police officer stood in the doorway.

"Can we help you? Do you want us to take you to a hospital?"

They were well meaning, but I was terrified. The policeman's presence shocked me; images of being handcuffed and forcibly committed to a Texas mental hospital shot through my mind.

"No, thanks. I'll try calling my psychiatrist from the airport. Thank you for coming."

Waiting for our flight to California, I phoned the psychiatrist but couldn't reach him. When we arrived home, I contacted him and set up an appointment for the next day.

His eyes scanned my puffy face. "What happened, Jim?"

As I described the symptoms, I watched his body language: his eyes widened, his neck and cheeks turned crimson. Seeing his reactions, I panicked, thinking this must be really serious.

"You were doing so well on this medication. I can't understand such a grave reaction. But that sudden rash is a clear danger sign. I've got to take you off your medication immediately. Let's try another. He handed me a prescription. Call me if you have any more problems. I want to see you next week to check how the new one's working."

Happily, the new medication proved the most effective of the thirty-three I'd taken during the past ten years. Still, I couldn't help thinking that most of the other meds had started out well. Would this one develop unsafe side effects too?

I'd worked hard developing the part-time Gathering of Men career-counseling ministry. But the pressures of fundraising wore on me more and more, and wrestling with mood shifts was continually frustrating. A lot of my professional goals seemed unachievable. Finally, I decided to leave the Gathering and set up my own part-time career-guidance practice. I set my official departure date for November 1, 1997. The Gathering staff offered warm encouragement for my new venture. All along, the combination of their belief

in my skills and their practical support had helped me get back on my feet.

Jimmy agreed to let me use his room as my office. I fully believed it would only take a short time to increase my energy and work hours, stabilize my moods, and create a more consistent weekly schedule. At most, I envisioned it taking two years to build up to full-time work. I contracted with a friend to tutor me in using a computer. I kept framed photos of Leah and the boys on my desk. Those graphic reminders fortified me with motivation to rebuild.

Chapter 41

The Medical-Biological Model of Treating Mental Illness:

Medication is the Main Way vs. the Recovery Model

PERIODICALLY, I REMINDED MYSELF, *You can never return to full time pastoring, so you need make the best of your situation. Rebuild your life and make it count. You'll have plenty of opportunities to help others and share your faith with them — only you'll be doing it in different ways and probably with different kinds of people than before.*

The new career-counseling practice progressed slowly. I'd made a detailed business plan that included goals, expenses, incomes, and deadlines. To build income-producing potential, I needed to market aggressively. I knew what to do and how to do it, but my emotional balance and energy levels were still too inconsistent.

Mostly, I counseled many mentally ill people and others who couldn't pay full fees. As a result, I had too few paying clients and too many *pro bono* ones. At the rate I was going, being able to work full-time in two years seemed a long way off.

I had learned that adult children from dysfunctional families need to learn how to nurture themselves. While growing up, my emotional poverty was ignored while I took care of Mom, Dad, Betsy, and Bob. As an adult, I busied myself looking after the needs of Leah, Jimmy, John, and my congregations. I usually shortchanged myself, doing a good job of caring for others and a lousy one of looking after Jim. I guess I'd been programmed to feel selfish for having fun. Now it was time to reconsider. *I ought to develop a new hobby. I love practical jokes and magic. Maybe I can find someone to teach me a few tricks.*

I found a local magician willing to tutor me for a small fee. He explained things very slowly and let me videotape his demonstrations, but grappling with ups and downs prevented me from practicing enough. After several missed opportunities, I canceled the lessons. Filled with self-recrimination for not being disciplined enough to handle the pressure of working on a few simple illusions, I felt so worthless that I slid into a two-month slump.

Although manic depression undoubtedly has a physical-medical basis, there's more to it than that. It's too easy to become fatalistic and shirk personal responsibility, saying, "It's not my fault that I have these mood changes; I'm totally helpless to control them. I'm like a marionette whose strings are pulled by some invisible biochemical, bipolar puppeteer"

Like so many others, I'd started thinking that if my illness had an unalterable biological basis, then it would be useless to try to change. Further study of manic depression confirmed my research, personal experience, and the conversations I'd had with hundreds of people living with depression, bipolar disorder, and other mind disabilities. What I discovered was both a relief and a challenge.

The prevailing "medical-biological model" for treating mental illness focuses almost entirely on giving medications, and advocates

the use of limited psychotherapy primarily to encourage "medical compliance" (pill-taking). Even if meds worked optimally, no amount of them could teach me — or others — how to take disappointment, criticism, and other stresses in stride.

This medical-biological view tends to endlessly continue the idea of being a perpetual victim of a genetic "chemical imbalance." Sadly, the pill-related approach to alleviating mania and depression wasn't working for me or for many other sufferers I knew. When one medication failed, as was often the case, I had no alternative but to try others or simply give up.

The medical-biological concept generally adheres to a deterministic view that *genes alone* control behavior; everything is "set" permanently from conception onward.[122] While genes are involved in manic-depressive illness, it isn't clear how or to what extent.[123] If we knew which individual genes were responsible for psychiatric disease, one's environment wouldn't matter. Hopefully, genetic research will someday provide significant advances in stabilizing or even curing this devastating disease, but research has thus far failed to find the actual genetic cause for *any* serious mental illness.[124] More specifically, no specific genetic marker for manic-depressive illness has yet been found.[125]

Some scientists even believe that the hunt for genes that influence behavior is a waste of time.[126] Others concede that genes along don't control the brain.[127] Research suggests that most mind illnesses are caused by a combination of genetic and environmental factors that interact with each other in complex ways.[128] This means that stress, successes, relationships, attitudes, habits, and other factors also influence initial and subsequent episodes of a mental illness like bipolar disorder.[129] The book, *Breaking the Patterns of Depression*, presents an understanding of the need for both medical and psychological "tools" by encouraging patients to become more than passive pill takers and learn new coping skills.

This news will revolutionize my approach to recovery. My genes might predispose me to radical mood changes, but that doesn't mean I'm helpless. Even though I have a serious, chronic medical condition,

I can be an active agent in my own recovery. I can rebuild my life!

I readily acknowledged that medication was a non-negotiable necessity for me. But I'd observed in counseling others with depression and manic depression that *attitude* made a crucial difference in performance. Indeed, pills are absolutely necessary and make up *25 percent* of the mood war, but *75 percent* of the battles with moods mean developing *stress and life-management skills*. Among other things, the battle between my ears would require cultivating my inner life with God, and deeper, more supportive relationships. It would mean deliberately focusing on positive self-talk when medications failed and people let me down.

As critical as meds are, using pills alone can't keep you at optimum stability. No drug can teach you how to get along with someone, have a stress-free job interview, handle criticism, or overcome disappointment. *To heal, recover, and rebuild successfully will take more than meds; I'll need more people to lean on, and workable strategies and techniques. Where can I find help?*

Wanting to lose weight as part of my restructuring, I attended a number of twelve-step meetings that focused on eating disorders. The sharing of pain, and the honesty and concern for other strugglers, was astounding. Those self-help groups and the addiction-recovery reading I did hooked me on the value of recovery principles in handling life's difficulties.

John made the varsity volleyball team — one of the best in the state and probably in the country. His hard work in his junior and senior high years had paid off. Leah and I proudly cheered at his matches. In June, he graduated Newport Harbor High School, but that day was mixed with celebration and sorrow. Eleven-year-old Dyno had slept in his accustomed place at the foot of our bed. As we awakened that morning, he uttered a loud cry, then gasped. We jumped immediately to his side, but were too late. Dyno was dead. I still mourn his loss.

The summer was a time of major transitions in the boys' lives and ours. In June, Jimmy left to embark on his new calling: an outdoor recreational specialist with the Coalition for Christian

Out-reach, a dynamic ministry to college students in Pennsylvania, Ohio, and West Virginia. He was assigned to work at Geneva College in Western Pennsylvania.

By late August, Jimmy was living in Pennsylvania, and John in Boulder, where he was a freshman at the University of Colorado. He wanted to focus his studies on social work with children.

Now Leah and I were tasting our first experience of the "empty nest." Every day for weeks I walked back and forth between the boys' rooms, staring at the pictures on their walls, photos of high school proms, sports awards, and the things each had collected. Their vacant rooms brought back loving memories, but also were stark reminders of their absence — and of my aging. Gone, too, was Dyno. I ached with loneliness. *How can I fill this emptiness, Lord?*

Something had to fill the quiet at home, so I started reading classified ads for golden retrievers, looking for a successor to Dyno. The search led us to a family in Long Beach whose golden had recently birthed six cute, cuddly, energetic pups. I was smitten by one; we took him home and named him "Ralphie." By week's end, he'd taken over our home and single-handedly solved our empty nest crisis!

That fall, I continued my part-time career practice, doing mostly *pro bono* aptitude testing for friends and for people with mental illnesses. In addition to seeing Phil twice a month, I began seeing a therapist who specialized in sexual abuse issues, and attending the weekly men's group therapy sessions she led. Those individual and group meetings further revealed the damages that the long-ago, seemingly innocuous, abuses had inflicted on me: an isolating sense of secrecy, the self-condemning inner world of smothered self-esteem, and such destructive behaviors as my eating problem and workaholism.

Chapter 42

New Freedom, New Strength from Honest, Supportive Relationships

THERE'S A COMMON SAYING among twelve steppers: "Religion is for people who *believe* in hell; spirituality is for people who've *been* there." Generally speaking, I found laypersons and clergy to have little empathy for the emotional pain, mental illness, or addictions of others. Most of the time, Christians were simply uncomfortable with suffering of any kind. Still, I believe the majority of Christians really mean well. They just don't know what to say or how to act in ways that will be helpful.

I needed honest and accepting relationships, so I decided to visit other kinds of twelve-step meetings to get a feel for those kinds of support groups. I visited meetings sponsored by Overeaters Anonymous, Alcoholics Anonymous, Narcotics Anonymous, and several sexual abuse survivor groups. None was professionally led.

I found people who were willing to listen to me without interrupting, judging, giving advice, or changing the subject. Only in the past few years have I been able to open up and trust more people, primarily in what are called "recovery" groups. What wonderful gifts these people have been. Honest sharing of personal pain was the rule; small talk was the exception, but laughter was frequent. For the most part, I found unconditional acceptance, a place to be and confidentiality — qualities missing from many Christian relationships.

A pastor colleague once said, "We Christians rarely meet; we just bump masks." How sad that our fellowship barely goes beyond exchanging pleasantries or swapping shallow spiritual platitudes:

"Hi. How ya doing?"

"Fine."

"How's work and the family?"

"Great. God is so good."

"That's wonderful. Gotta go now. Catch you later. Have a nice day."

Long before being hospitalized, I realized it wasn't safe to be honest with most Christians (clergy or laity) about my feelings, struggles, failures, and aspirations. I had too often observed how they politely changed the subject whenever anyone disclosed an inner pain, struggle, or success. They guilt-tripped with "shoulds" and "oughts," or gossiped under the guise of "sharing a prayer concern for poor so-and-so." Counseling hundreds of people over the years has shown me that many people experience this kind of "fellowship."

No wonder so many have shunned institutional religion and sought deeper, safer, more caring relationships through groups such as AA. Many people's needs have not been met by organized churches, so they now find help in diverse recovery programs. These support meetings have lovingly reached all sorts of people in pain, and as a result have become the fastest-growing spiritual movement in America. Out of their desperate need for acceptance, love, and encouragement, thousands of Christians, like their secular contemporaries, have gone outside the religious establishment to seek understanding, guidance, and help from non-sectarian self-help groups.

Bible knowledge, solid theology, and unshakable faith in Christ hadn't healed my mood swings or compulsive eating or workaholic tendencies. I had to admit that "spiritual weapons" like prayer and Bible reading hadn't won me many victories. In fact, my batting average stunk!

Although the Scriptures provided the foundation for my faith, they weren't enough. I need others to walk beside me as I tried applying the biblical truths I already knew. The Bible emphasizes that "Two are better than one ... If one falls down, his friend can help him up. But pity the man who falls and has no one to help

him up! ... Though one may be overpowered, two can defend themselves ... Carry each other's burdens ... confess your sins to each other and pray for each other so that you may be healed ... let us consider how we may spur one another on toward love and good deeds. Let us not give up meeting together ... but let us encourage one another ... " [130]

By now, the obvious had become clearer: even with a strong faith, I couldn't recover and rebuild *alone*. I needed to associate daily with positive, non-shaming friends who could encourage me in my struggles, hopes, and plans. Genuine fellowship wasn't an option; it was a necessity.

I read dozens of sources that underscored the necessity of an affirming support system. Ample evidence confirms the biblical teaching on the benefits of supportive relationships, in which people regularly talk about things that are upsetting them. [131] In *Survivors*, Bruno Bettelheim describes his ordeal in a Nazi prison camp. Those who survived banded together to keep each other going. Loners didn't make it.

While the recovery meetings I visited dealt with different problems, all based their teaching on AA principles. After having observed various kinds of support groups, I started regularly attending meetings for eating disorders and sexual abuse survivors. It was like coming home: men and women wrestling with mental illness, severe emotional scars, and addictions were becoming part of my new spiritual family.

These relationships became a doorway to a new life, a more spiritual way of living than I'd ever experienced. How refreshing to hear others sharing their struggles without pretense. At first, I was nervous about being judged or rejected. I'd been a giver all my life, and it was hard to receive. It was extremely difficult to depend on others, and believe that their caring for me was genuine, but gradually, I learned to trust and reach out to people in ways I'd never done before. If I had a stressful day, I did something nice for myself, or called someone to talk about my reactions to the upset.

In conversations with fellow strugglers at twelve-step meetings, I discovered what worked to help people recover. For me, "sobriety" meant maintaining balanced moods and not overeating; "abstinence" meant avoiding activities or attitudes that could cause me to eat improperly or go up or down emotionally. Recovery-based meetings, even those unrelated to my specific problem, kept me out of denial that I had a chronic, life-threatening mental illness and a serious eating disorder. It was too easy to become complacent, believing I was "cured" of either, and could function without medication or the curative support of others.

Chapter 43

A Basic Coping Strategy that Works

IN ADDITION TO MEDICATION and meetings, I needed more spiritual power to cope with and overcome my extreme mood swings and compulsive eating. This meant trusting a power greater than myself, One who could restore me to balanced thinking, who could help me level my moods and rebuild my life. It wasn't easy. I was afraid God wouldn't be there for me, but I kept making dozens of daily decisions to surrender my will and life over to His care as best I could.

The key to this spiritual renewal was the Serenity Prayer. That prayer may sound simplistic, even ritualistic, but when I prayed it as needed throughout the day, I was amazed how those few words re-framed situations, relationships, and stresses! How secure it felt to turn things over to God in ways I hadn't done for years. I implemented a basic coping strategy for difficult situations:

1. Recognize and admit — to myself, someone else, and God — when I'm feeling *any* form of stress.

2. Identify the specific triggering person, place, or emotion.

3. Take immediate action to defuse the stress.

Seeing how vital it was to be alert for triggers that could cause a serious relapse, I adapted my own warning signs from AA's teachings. In their simplicity, they were psychologically profound. I called them "HALTS." "H" warned me to avoid *hunger* — obsessive cravings for food, alcohol, or taking on too much. "A" meant beware of *anger* at others or myself; this included resentments, self-condemnation, and self-pity. "L" cautioned me to avoid situations where I'd feel *lonely*, criticized, or rejected. "T" warned of getting *too tired* from lack of sleep or working too many hours at too fast a pace. "S" was a catchall that alerted me to avoid *stress* in any form: toxic people, places, and situations, as well as deadlines and quotas.

Far more than a list of rules, the twelve steps were a practical formula to follow as I reconstructed my life. I needed to implement the steps as *continuously* as I could, knowing I'd never completely finish them once and for all. They were simply part of a "tool kit" for ongoing use in daily living.

My batting average for applying the steps was spotty at best, but I was taking active responsibility for my own rehabilitation. Since recovery would be a lifelong process, I believed it was really possible to successfully rebuild my life, even though I might face occasional setbacks.

Personal experience had taught me that at least *75 percent* of my mood disruptions were caused by *stress*, not by some mysterious bipolar "cloud" that came out of nowhere. I re-learned that *prevention* was the key to remaining stable. It meant being proactive, catching my symptoms of depression or mania *before* they escalated to extremes.

I watched for incidents that could incite acute mania, depression, or binge eating. I found that the biggest enemies of a mentally

ill person or addict are *resentment, self-pity,* and *fear.* These reactions are not only a waste of time, but are also spiritual poisons, sure setups for emotional upheaval. I'd closed down my emotions for so long that I needed to recognize when my attitude was self-defeating so I could work to change it. I got in the habit of asking myself, *Which of the HALTS is upsetting me right now? What or whom am I obsessing about? Whom can I call to share this feeling? How can I think positively about this? What can I do to take care of myself right now? What helped the last time I slipped into a mood change, self-pity, resentment, or overeating?*

More closely than ever, I monitored the warning signs of oncoming mania, depression, and the HALTS that could cause them. I steered away from faultfinding people, and stopped scheduling more than three appointments a day. It took willpower, but I gradually stopped doing late-night projects, watching 9 P.M. TV movies, and drinking beverages containing caffeine. To reduce stress, I made every effort to avoid any sort of upset or interruption, and stick to familiar routines. Of all the stress-reduction tools I practiced, the most important were:

1. Doing more fun things;

2. Cultivating spirituality;

3. Talking with friends when I was bothered by something;

4. Writing about upsetting events and people.

To build regular structure, I returned to having a morning devotional time that consisted of thirty minutes of reading the Bible, two devotional books, some recovery and nutrition literature, and praying. This centered me, drawing me closer to God, and helped release fears, resentments, and other destructive emotions. It clarified priorities for the day and week. Also, I checked in with at least one person a day to share my thoughts and feelings.

I took my medications conscientiously, and resumed taking vitamins, including fish oil capsules containing omega-3 fatty acids.

When I felt myself going south, I used a Sunnex Lamp (sometimes called a "light box") for fifteen minutes in the mornings, until my mood lifted. I chose to spend time with nurturing people, and took care of myself by slowing down, diverting harmful thinking, and relaxing body and mind.

To do this, I used calming techniques: calling a friend, attending a support group meeting, taking Ralphie for a walk, soaking in the Jacuzzi, reading, writing, watching sporting events, visiting bookstores and sporting goods stores, practicing yoga breathing, and working out on a stationary bike.

It was humbling to admit that I couldn't handle more than a few hours a day of appointments, or deal with certain kinds situations without feeling stressed, but being aware of these limitations helped me set boundaries and reasonable goals.

When it was hard to know which feelings were normal and which were the beginnings of a mood episode, I took my "emotional temperature," asking myself, *Have I been especially energetic and taken on more projects than usual today? Has anyone mentioned that I'm talking faster or more than usual? Am I irritable, angry, or unusually tired? Am I feeling sorry for myself? Am I withdrawing from people?*

Chapter 44

Overcoming Resentment and Self-pity

PEOPLE WHO'VE HAD THEIR LIVES STOLEN by tragedies often can't find closure for the childhood they'll never recover. They rob themselves of happiness, unable to throw away their thick mental notebook of grievances. Their bitter cynicism taints everyone around them. Resentment is a health hazard for anyone, but far more so for those with a psychiatric condition or an addiction. Holding animosity toward insurance company representatives, denominational leaders, churches, and clergy had time and again thrown me into emotional cycling. I could no longer afford the luxury of holding on to resentment; there was too much to lose. For me, nursing indignation over an offense inevitably deteriorated into bitterness and isolation, which led to mood shifts or compulsive eating.

What most convinced me to take action to let go of negative reaction patterns was hearing others in recovery groups share how resentment had repeatedly made them engage in destructive behaviors. I *had* to find a healthy way to deal with my anger at certain individuals.

I checked out what the Bible, the "Big Book," and other literature had to say about getting along with poisonous people, and found page after page of practical suggestions. Also, I found plenty of real-life examples in others' descriptions of their victories over resentment. I experimented with a new way of dealing with my repeating vindictiveness. I adapted my basic coping strategy for difficult situations and applied it to the specific problem of toxic relatives, friends, acquaintances, and strangers hurting or angering me:

1. Recognize and admit, to myself, to someone else, and to God, *how* the resentment and hurt are affecting my attitudes and behavior: *Am I being pushed into a manic agitation or morose self-pity?*

2. Identify the toxic person's *specific* words or actions that are triggering my resentment.

3. Change my thinking, and see the transgressor as a spiritually ill person who is, in his own way, as sick as I am.

4. Ask God for guidance and strength: "Please help me show the same mercy to this person that you've shown me when I messed up."

5. Ask God to bless the person offending me with happiness, well-being, and a closer relationship with Him.

6. Set limits to protect myself from future harm by the individual.

At first, I had to grit my teeth to pray for anyone who'd hurt me. Amazingly, after several weeks the feelings of resentment started to lessen, and I felt a new understanding of the person and his circumstances. The anger didn't entirely disappear forever, but I was learning a whole new way of responding to difficult people.

The "Big Book" also discusses the ruinous effects of self-pity. Much of my life had been eaten up by throwing "poor me" pity parties. Encountering abrasive people, or another torturous medication side effect, mania, or depression, my initial reaction was to feel sorry for myself. Dwelling on how unfairly I was being treated often precipitated bad emotional reactions, sinking or elevating my moods. Getting well would require a change in how I thought about problems. Blaming others or myself was a waste of time. *I can't change anyone, or change my circumstances. All I can alter are my reactions. To get better, I'll have to turn irritating people and situations over to God.*

I began to apply the Serenity Prayer and the twelve steps to dealing with resentment, self-pity, and other damaging mindsets.

Wrestling with these issues made me much more compassionate, and moved me to reach out to those I probably never would have before.

To offset the harmful, I had to focus on the positive. A friend's four-year-old daughter advised, "Jim, you should do the most fun thing you can!" So, I made it a priority to learn to *play* more. In the middle of stressful moments, I pulled practical jokes or undertook new fun-filled activities like going to garage sales, golf, and visiting magic shops.

My work capacities hadn't returned; pre-hospitalization stamina seemed to have evaporated, and my ability to endure stress wasn't there yet. But I kept fighting, hoping for a return of the "good old days," when I could work long hours, and problems just bounced off. I aimed to give the career-guidance practice my best shot, but was prepared to make the most of any limitations I couldn't overcome.

Using the coping skills I'd learned, I functioned better, and wasn't incapacitated by highs and lows. I resolved more issues of resentment and self-pity, and enjoyed deeper friendships. It felt good to be regaining control of my life at last.

Was my successful recovery due to finally finding a medication that worked, or was it the accumulated result of ten years of psychotherapy? Was it due to applying the twelve-step principles, or to my efforts to get up after every defeat and try again? I might never know, but I do know that the loving encouragement from Leah and my friends played a key role. Ultimately, I credit God's intervention through people and medicines. Like the psalmist, I truly believe, "Unless the Lord had given me help, I would soon have dwelt in the silence of death." [132]

In September 1998, a friend and I started another mental illness support group. He was a member of the one that had met in my Newport Beach office. For both accountability and credibility, we wanted to be sponsored by a mental illness organization. I met with founder-psychiatrist Dr. Rick Massimino of the John Henry Foundation. A respected, nonsectarian, nonprofit organization in

Orange County, it seeks to improve the quality of life for people suffering from mental illness. Dr. Massimino was very supportive. Under the foundation's sponsorship, we rented a room in the Costa Mesa Neighborhood Center on Thursday evenings. Our first participants were people who'd attended the other group.

The hour-long meetings drew between four and ten people. Our format was much the same every week: each person would "check in," introducing himself by first name, mentioning his diagnosis or the problem he was struggling with, and sharing his highs and lows (the best and worst experiences he'd faced in the past week). Next, I taught for a few minutes about a tool for recovering or other topic of interest to the group. Our lively conversations were mixed with lots of laughter and sometimes tears.

The discipline of feeding Ralphie and walking him every morning and evening added a healthy routine to my life. I dared not let my furry friend down. Besides, he wouldn't let me. Each morning I awoke to having my arm or foot gently mauled by puppy teeth, telling me it was time to get up and go for a walk. Every evening, like clockwork, he came to my chair, stared at me with his big brown eyes, wagged his tail furiously, and tugged on whatever appendage he could grab. "It's that time again, Dad."

In 1998, in the midst of the Christmas shopping, decorating, and finishing a special holiday gift project, I started dropping, fast. What was triggering it seemed clear: communication mix-ups with my psychiatrist. I'd missed an appointment; then he missed one. I was almost out of pills; he refused to call in prescription refills to the pharmacy. As my supply diminished, I became increasingly anxious that we might not be able to get together in time for him to write a prescription before I ran out. I made numerous calls to remind him, but got no answer. At last, he called, promising to phone the pharmacy for a refill, but there were more delays in getting the medication.

His actions provoked resentment and anxiety in me. *Is this the end of our relationship? Is he angry with me? Has he given up on me? Is he dropping me because I've been so difficult to medicate?* I got

more and more panicked, afraid that I'd run out of pills over the holidays while our family was vacationing six hours away at Mammoth Ski Resort.

I had three panic attacks and was sleeping only a few hours a night. I could feel myself slipping rapidly into a mixed state. The day my main medication ran out, I called one last time, asking him, "Please, phone the pharmacy to refill my prescriptions." Finally, that afternoon the druggist called. "Your psychiatrist just phoned in your renewal." Leah picked it up.

My fear of facing the holiday festivities without pharmaceutical armor dissipated for the moment, but all my trust in that formerly helpful psychiatrist was erased. I was deeply hurt and angry, but stuffed those feelings during Christmas and our family ski trip afterward. But it set me up for six weeks of severe depression.

In December, the Costa Mesa Neighborhood Center and our mental illness support group had scheduling conflicts for the coming year, so we searched and found a church that would let us use one of its rooms rent-free. The first week of January, we resumed on Thursday evenings from 7:30 – 9:00. It was good not to be limited to an hour as before. After some lively discussion, we named our group "Comfort Zone." Attendance averaged twelve to fifteen, with equal numbers of depressives, manic-depressives, and schizophrenics. Our average age was thirty-five.

Then my volatile illness struck again. When Jimmy and John left after the holidays, despair rolled over me like a fifty-foot wave. Recovery techniques helped, but once despondency reached a certain level, all the Bible knowledge, faith, and positive self-talk in the world brought little remedy. In mid-January, unable to reach my psychiatrist in several tries, I left a message saying I was switching psychiatrists and thanking him for all the help he'd been.

Other than continuing leadership of Comfort Zone meetings, I was immobilized. To endure the major dip, I took my medications, but isolated myself, avoiding all twelve-step meetings, worship services, and socializing. I tried everything to distract myself from

hopeless thinking. All I could do was sleep fifteen hours a day, drive aimlessly, or watch movie after movie to escape the unbearable pain of depression.

Chapter 45

How a Crisis of Meaning Can Lead to a New Role in Life —

Hope and Encouragement for the Mentally Ill and Their Loved Ones

THE NEXT TWO MONTHS I MERELY HUNG ON. I sank deeper and faster than ever before. I knew that unless I acted immediately, the descent would become irreversible. I made an appointment with a new psychiatrist, and shared my hopelessness with Phil and several friends. It was a beginning. My life had turned upside-down. The Serenity Prayer and turning my future over to God's care seemed a meaningless exercise. I struggled to find meaning for my losses, realizing that if I couldn't come up with a purpose that could sustain me in the years ahead, the next crisis could put me down permanently.

Hour after hour I studied the Old Testament books of Ecclesiastes and Isaiah, and re-read parts of many books in my library. I scoured stores for newly released books on emotional survival techniques and on finding meaning in suffering.

Without realizing it, I was having the crisis of meaning similar to what many face at retirement. Suddenly they have no title, no work-related colleagues, and no workplace to go to. More than ever, I faced the reality that I wasn't just postponing my career; it

was over. My former self was gone forever; a newly rebuilt person would need to take its place. Now I needed to stop mourning my lost career as a pastor, accept my limitations, and move on to build a new life.

I kept saying the Serenity Prayer and reminding myself that this horrible pain would eventually go away if I could just hold on for Leah and the boys' sakes and for the others who were counting on me. The prophet Isaiah's words comforted me, "... do not fear, for I am with you; do not be dismayed, for I am your God. I will strengthen you and help you..."[133]

Slowly, glimmers of hope arose out of the darkness. Friends continued to phone and leave messages. I knew there were people out there who wanted to help. That, at least, gave me enough perseverance not to give up. Months before this crisis, I'd made a special Valentine's Day lunch reservation for Leah and me at an expensive seaside hotel near San Diego. Canceling it would disappoint her badly. Thinking that our time together might offer some hope to grab onto, I kept our engagement at the hotel, deciding to give life one more try.

I was at low ebb as we drove there. Over lunch, we exchanged cards and small presents. The card Leah gave me had hope-giving words that couldn't have been more fitting; likewise, her gift, a CD, which we played on the way home. One song elicited a steady stream of tears. Those simple well-chosen gifts gave me strength to start over.

Hope has been the key to my survival and ongoing healing. To a clinically depressed person, hope is elusive. You know it has reappeared when you start looking forward to the next couple of hours or the next day. Hope, no matter how fragile, begins to grow when you start planning. Again, hope and love came to me as it had in the past, through Leah, Jimmy, John, Bob Long, Phil Sutherland, and other caring friends.

As important as Scripture has been to me, God's use of people has meant as much. This is what my theology is all about. God reveals Himself and His plan for humanity not only in the Bible,

but also in the person of Jesus Christ. The Bible says, "The Word became flesh and made his dwelling among us..."[134]

God wrote life-giving words that infused optimism and gave direction. He also sent me friends, human messengers, who actually embodied biblical words like "love," "forgiveness," and "grace." While I'd tried my entire ministry to flesh out God's love in my actions and words, it wasn't until the last few years that I experienced these from others.

Man's Search for Meaning and other books discuss the indispensable need for finding a purpose in life that will provide not only a focused direction for living, but also a meaning for suffering. I knew that as long as I had a purpose my life would improve. To rebuild my life, I'd have to move beyond catastrophic illness and find a new purpose. *I'll never get back the six months I spent in psychiatric hospitals, and the decade of suffering that tore up my family and ended my ministerial career, but those losses can be redeemed. I believe God when He says,* "I will repay you for the years the locusts have eaten ... in all things God works for the good of those who love him..."[135]

Paul Abram Constantine, a friend and fellow bipolar, has fought his share of bouts with mental illness. His plans have been interrupted many times, yet he says, "Dreams are never destroyed, only rearranged." His Christian faith has been a support, enabling him to share his journey through word and song. As a result, he's produced two CDs that bring inspiration to those who suffer.

That descent into hell made me reexamine my own concept of "success," which had been based on helping others, achieving spiritual goals, and earning recognition. No longer in the public arena and able to work on a full-time basis in my former occupation, I needed to redefine what it would take to feel "successful" again. I remember the words preached years ago at my ordination service, "Always remember Jim, *who* you are is far more important than anything you'll ever *do*." I'd had my share of success and certainly didn't need to prove myself to anyone. Yet, because of my lost identity as a pastor and the stigma of being "a mental case," I found myself

occasionally dropping names of important people whom I knew, mentioning my accomplishments and "contacts." I hated myself for such insecure egotism. To conquer the temptation to impress others, I had to regularly surrender my reputation to God: *Please help me shut my mouth and let my past accomplishments speak for themselves without words from me.*

Now I see how the agitation and hopelessness I'd contended with for so long had been a necessary prerequisite for understanding, accepting, and redefining the losses in my life. Despite such a traumatic transition, I still believed God was calling me to tell people about his love. *But how can I best use my gifts, given my restrictions? I'll have to reinvent myself and find ways to help others.*

I continued leading Comfort Zone and attending twelve-step meetings, haltingly reconstructing my life. Leah and several friends jump-started my efforts with mega-doses of affirmation. Recovery group members supported me. Each week, people who were hurting called me for counseling, making me feel needed and useful. There were periodic requests to speak about my mental illness journey. I used dozens of recovery tools to help me remain emotionally "sober." Leah's gentle, caring spirit heartened me; she truly was the safe haven I had longed for all my life.

For a long time, life had tasted like a mouthful of ashes. Now, it became an adventure to be enjoyed rather than a torment to be endured. At last, I'd stopped constantly seeing life through the dark glasses of depression or the red lens of manic rage. I began to see manic depression not as a curse but as a *gift*. In place of grudges was sincere *gratitude* — for health, psychological balance, family, friends, nature, and opportunities to be of service. Instead of feeling that God was picking *on* me, I now believed He had picked me *out* to help others with similar mental disabilities. One statement from the Bible imbued me with a fresh outlook for my coming ministry: "God is not unjust; he will not forget your work and the love you have shown him as you have helped his people and continue to help them ... show this same diligence to the very end." [136]

Apart from that brief but brutal downturn, 1997 through 2001 were the best years since I'd hit bottom in 1988. Mood swings still came and went, but I caught them before they got out of control. Lacking the time or energy to pursue the plenteous opportunities to market my part-time guidance practice, I accepted the reality of a limited, flexible schedule. This meant accepting the fact that I'd be using my skills primarily with the mentally ill or with people considering some sort of ministry career.

Since full-time work was too stressful, I carved out hours every week to be available to others' needs. I recommended writing articles and reaching out to friends, other mentally ill individuals and their loved ones, and people in my twelve-step programs.

Coming close to death so many times taught me how precarious life is. I learned why bipolar illness couldn't be cured just by willpower, faith, psychotherapy, or twelve-step recovery principles. Neither could it be treated successfully with medications alone. Rebuilding required using *all* those tools!

Though I didn't always feel God's presence, He let me know His hand was still on my life. Again and again I came across Bible promises like, "Do not be afraid, for I am with you … Forget the former things; do not dwell on the past. See I am doing a new thing! … do you not perceive it? … I am making a way in the desert and streams in the wasteland … For I know the plans I have for you, … plans to prosper you and not to harm you, plans to give you hope and a future … " [137]

I came across a statement in the New Testament that affirmed my past career and the new one about to commence as a volunteer minister-at-large: "Strengthen the feeble hands, steady the knees that give way; say to those with fearful hearts, "Be strong, do not fear… " [138] It was as though God spoke through those words, directing me to reach out to those whom I would never have considered working with: outcasts, the mentally ill, addicts, and their families.

It was humbling to explain what I was doing. When asked why I was wasting my time on people who'd never get better, I shared a story that someone had told me: "Thousands of starfish had washed

up on a beach. It was noon, and the hot sun had killed a lot of them. A little boy was picking them up, one at a time, and throwing them back into the ocean. A businessman walked by and said, "You're wasting your time, son. What difference will saving one or two starfish make?" The boy replied, "You're probably right, mister." Then he held up a starfish and threw it in the ocean. "See that one? It's making a difference to him!"

Some people disparaged my commitment to those with disturbed minds. "I thought you liked working with leaders and athletes, Jim. Can mental patients really be helped? Why don't you use your gifts where they'll make a bigger difference? Those kinds of people can be dangerous. Besides, they aren't church members." Some advised, "You'd better be evangelistic." Others urged just the opposite: "You're not going to get too spiritual and proselytize are you?" This was nothing new. Throughout my previous ministries, both liberals and conservatives had criticized me. Indeed, the person who wants to truly follow Christ is likely to seem a heretic to many.

Fortunately, the stigma surrounding mental illness is changing. But it's requiring courageous efforts to erase the misunderstanding, false information, and fear that blinds so many. It's appalling that we Christians have so badly maltreated the mentally disabled and their families. Faith communities have largely avoided them, as though they didn't exist or have needs like everyone else. In far too many cases, ill-informed clergy and laypersons have harshly judged hurting family members and their mentally ill loved ones.

Yet, I'm confident that followers of Christ can learn about mental illness and how to minister to these valuable people who yearn for acceptance, understanding, encouragement, and genuine love. They desperately need people to reach out to them. Like everyone else, they crave a sense of belonging and being valued for their abilities and experiences. They long for opportunities to serve, for someone to ask them. But for change to happen, it will take openness to learning about mental disabilities from both the Scriptures *and* scientific sources. Individuals must be willing to step out boldly,

sacrificing time and even reputation to start programs in their places of worship as well as in the larger community. To begin with, it will mean listening patiently to the broken hearts and shattered dreams of the mentally injured and their families.

At fifty-seven, I was mindful of having entered the fourth quarter of life. No one could be sure of the long-term effects that medications and past emotional traumas would have on me. Each day was a gift, and I grew ultra-conscious of my use of time, wanting to make the most of every opportunity. Comfort Zone became one of the high points of each week. Almost daily I received calls from mentally ill people, or frustrated family members, needing advice. This led to starting another monthly group — for family members.

Major healing had taken place; I was productive again. While my moods had leveled, I knew that full remission would probably be impossible. The illness is managed, but not cured; my brain would still be vulnerable to it. Though I couldn't hold a full-time job, I was passionate about life. I wanted to use my faith, gifts, and experience to help others. After years of treading water, I was recovering, successfully rebuilding my life, and actively contributing to others in significant ways! What a time of learning, healing, and growing it's been. I'm at peace and happy, and so very grateful to God for giving me a second chance at living — without being controlled by mania, depression, fear, resentment, and self-pity!

Given the choice of suffering all the losses I've experienced, or avoiding them altogether, I'd select a pain-free life, no question. But that option never came to me, so I've played out the hand dealt to me as best I could. In a strange way, I'm *grateful* for all that I've gone through. My manic-depressive diagnosis marked the beginning of a journey to a fuller, more rewarding life. How satisfying it is to live one day at a time, and experience feelings that have been numb for so long.

I've reinvented my life and career, and now am excitedly moving on. Today, I consider myself a "wounded healer." I haven't experienced a serious manic-depressive episode for three years,

and none of the small ones I've had caused a significant crisis. My sense of well-being continues to improve. Much as I hope it won't happen, it's likely I'll have some future mood disturbances. Hopefully, they'll be just minor annoyances. Either way, I'm prepared with up-to-date knowledge about manic depression and medications. Plus, I have a nurturing lifestyle, strategies for coping with stress, many supportive friends, and a simpler, more vibrant faith!

There's no one simple formula for healing and starting over that works for everyone, but the future for those living with depression and manic depression is extremely promising: better tools of healing, recovering, and rebuilding; genetic discoveries; more effective medications, better counseling approaches, and a diminishing stigma surrounding mental illness.

Untold numbers of fine Christians over the centuries have borne unspeakable suffering. They prayed for relief, yet many died, their earnest prayers unanswered. The Bible records what happened to some: "These were all commended for their faith, yet none of them received what had been promised. God had planned something better for us so that only together with us would they be made perfect." [139]

Not long ago someone asked me, "What if you're never healed of your illness? What if you never can work full-time again, or must fight the rest of your life to prevent mood swings?"

I answered, "Living without meds may be possible for some, but probably not me. There's a good chance I'll have emotional swings for the rest of my life. But I'm in a far better position to control the extremes now; I've seen and read about too many instances where a manic-depressive who's had years free from mood troubles suddenly has a serious relapse. It's easy for me to forget that manic depression can be a fatal disease, and think I've got my moods fully and forever under control. But the reality is that even after years of "emotional sobriety," I'll never be cured of this illness; I will *always* be in recovery.

I know my moods cannot be managed alone. I need to depend

on God's love and power as it is mediated to me though people and medication. This means taking my meds and monitoring them, and also applying the biblical principals of AA's twelve steps in all circumstances. Through doing all these things, I'm happily rebuilding my life and new ministry."

How true the saying, "Life is a series of adjustments." Recovering from depression and bipolar mood swings can be rugged, frustrating, and frequently discouraging. It's never easy, but it's often satisfying, even exhilarating. Living with a mental illness or with an afflicted loved one involves courage, creativity, experimentation, forgiveness, and dogged perseverance. I expect to face obstacles, setbacks, and disappointments — they happen to everyone, not just those dealing with brain disorders — but I'm confident I can cope with or overcome them.

As I face a positive yet uncertain future, I fortify myself with the Bible's faith-building pledges: "He heals the brokenhearted and binds up their wounds ... Though you have made me see troubles, many and bitter, you will restore my life ... and comfort me once again." [140] With the psalmist, I'm confident that, "My flesh and my heart may fail, but God is the strength of my heart and my portion forever." [141] Yet whether I ever fully recover or not, I'm looking forward to the time when I'll exchange this afflicted brain for a new, perfect one. Scripture states, "There are also heavenly bodies and there are earthly bodies; but the splendor of the heavenly bodies is one kind, and the splendor of earthly bodies is another ... So it will be with the resurrection of the dead. The body that is sown perishable, it is raised imperishable ... it is sown in weakness, it is raised in power; it is sown a natural body, it is raised a spiritual body."[142] I believe these words refer to my *brain* as well as my body. Therefore, I'm anticipating eternity in heaven where the Bible promises that "God himself will be with them ... He will wipe away every tear from their eyes. There will be no more death or mourning or crying or pain..." [143]

Until I leave this life, though, I yearn to enjoy it and God to the fullest. I want to introduce hundreds more to Him. I passionately

desire to help, heal, and equip scores more to use their experiences and gifts for the world's betterment.

To this end, I continue to do research, take medications, receive counseling, and attend support groups. I still perform occasional pastoral tasks: preach sermons, teach Bible studies, officiate at weddings and funerals, and do career guidance. I counsel those referred to me, and accept occasional speaking engagements for various mental illness groups, seminars, and conferences.

Sometimes it's necessary to cut back on appointments to take better care of myself. I enjoy taking time to appreciate cloudy days, yellow moons, colors, textures, telling jokes, reading newspaper cartoons, flowers, and the myriad little things I seldom took time to notice.

I'll be forever grateful for my family and the close friends who've stuck by me. I should have died years ago, but have been spared again and again. God has given me a brand-new life with everything to live for. I look forward to the years ahead, to enjoying activities with Leah, John, Jimmy and his new wife, Mari, and, someday, my grandchildren. It's uplifting to anticipate seeing some of the fruits of my new ministry. Above all, I'm profoundly grateful to God for giving me firsthand knowledge of the meaning of the remarkable words: "...he restores my soul."[144]

It's been a long war. I'm scarred from the battles, and it's not over. I live in a state of readiness, and long with all my heart one day to say with the great Apostle Paul, "I have fought the good fight, I have finished the race, I have kept the faith." [145]

A story from Winston Churchill's life has inspired me countless times. He struggled with depression and mania most of his life. When he was young, Churchill was kicked out of a private school for boys. Years later, after he'd become Great Britain's Prime Minister, he was invited to speak at that same school's graduation ceremony. He walked up to the podium, and it is reported that he spoke only nine words: "Never give up! Never give up! Never give up!"

If you are struggling through a dark time, never give up! You *can* get better. You *can* live positively, even with your illness. You

can rebuild your life and make it count! You *can* make important contributions! Let Churchill's words sink into the very core of your being. Never give up on yourself. Never give up on your mentally ill loved one. Take courage. Hang on. Fight just one more round. You can do it!

Epilogue

L EAH GRADUATED FROM FULLER THEOLOGICAL SEMINARY in June 2001 with a Master of Divinity degree. She continues to love her work at St. Andrew's Presbyterian Church.

Jim, Jr. married the former Mari Cummings in August 2000. They live in Pittsburgh, Pennsylvania, where he still works with the Coalition for Christian Outreach. Mari does social work in the Pittsburgh area, and is working on a master's degree in biblical counseling.

John is a junior at California State University at Fullerton. His majoring in human services will prepare him for a career in counseling, social work, special education, teaching, or coaching.

And Ralphie persistently rules the roost!

Acknowledgments

SINCERE APPRECIATION TO THE FOLLOWING PEOPLE for their contributions to my life and to this book:

The Minirth-Meier Psychiatric Unit of the Community Hospital of Gardena, and the Las Encinas Hospital of Pasadena, whose talented, caring staffs pulled me through some of my darkest days.

Phil Sutherland, psychologist, beloved friend, and skilled healer, who exudes God's grace.

The other therapists who put balm on my bleeding soul: John Townsend, Henry Cloud, David Stoop, Dae Leckie, Maribeth Ekey, Dan Hartman, and Jane Roschmann.

Dr. Himasiri De Silva, and the other psychiatrists who monitored my moods and medications with great sensitivity and wisdom. That I am alive today is a tribute to their skills.

Bob Long, my best friend, who kept me on my feet, listened patiently, and helped me laugh. No man could ask for a better friend!

Betsy and Bob, my sister and brother, who wrote, phoned, and sent gifts and gags from my earliest hospital days. I couldn't have hung on and kept going without their expressions of love.

John Chandler, Los Ranchos Executive Presbyter, who went above and beyond the call of duty to meet the needs of my family and me while I was in the hospital and afterward.

My twelve-step support groups of friends who provided constant encouragement, guidance, affirmation, and a place to vent.

The *Miqlat* group, who mediated God's love to me in countless ways: Hank and Margaret Weber, Connie Bean, Paul and Ellen Enochs, Jim and Nancy Penney, Fred and Joan Hearn, Jack and May Kline, Dewayne and Rosemary Neufeld, Jim DeBoom, Tom and Karen Taillon, and Susan and Millard Shirley.

John and Anne Huffman, Bill and Christie Flanagan, and Dick Todd of St. Andrew's Presbyterian Church in Newport Beach, for providing socials that stirred up levity and motivation to work at recovering and rebuilding.

St. Andrew's Presbyterian Church, which salaried me through both hospitalizations and long afterward. Its men's breakfast group provided solid encouragement. Thanks for ongoing phone calls, get-togethers, cards, notes, and gifts from special friends: Ed and Sue Egloff, Dan and Jean Ardell, Bob and Rosita Numrich, Bruce and Sharon Corzine, Margie and Larry Smith, Bill Tassio, Ozzie Purdy, Gloria Trefts, Nancy Nelson, Garnet McCulloch, Jex Coons, T. J. and Barbara Abshier, Dick and Ceil Nelson, Dick and Ruth Nelson, Steve Fryer, Larry and Sue Ann Beaty, Bill and Barbara Simons, Ralph and Audrey Jensen, Ron and Barbara Napier, George and Joan Behr, Mac and Gerry Somers, Robert and Patricia Allen, Allen and Terri Hardison, John and Loreen Loftus, Roland and Ruth Lampe, Frank and Phyllis Herman, Len and LaVern Hall, Alex and Pam Metherell, Jim and Vicki Warmington, Barbara (Carr) Freeman and other St. Andrew's friends. You propped up my sagging spirits and helped me believe in myself. Never have I seen such a loving congregation!

First Presbyterian Church of North Palm Beach, Florida, for its generous financial and prayer support of my men's outreach ministries over several years.

Lucky Arnold, Ron Hilliard, Bill Duke, the pastors of First Presbyterian Church of North Palm Beach, its outstanding men's breakfast group, and dear friends like Jake and Alice Swartout, Dick and June Cooper, Jim and Sunny Frevert, John and Ginger Bills, Howard and Lois Wright, Jack and Joyce Brolsma, Bob Schuemann, Dick and Patty Irwin, Paul and Sherrie Reback, Bob and Joan Johnson, Greg and Nancy Adrian, Joe and Bobbie Wise, Jack and Marjorie Dunlap, Bob and Florence Hundemann, Bruce and Donna Sekeres, Forest and Betsy Beaty, Howard and Sue McLean, Jim and Nancy Calhoun, Bob and Joan Kulp, Ed and Terry Elliott, John and Alix Johnston, Lew and Sharon Hayward, Joan Jonson, Amy Johnson, Marianne McCann, Peter Hughes, and others who supported me in every way throughout my long way back.

Good friends from Covenant Presbyterian Church in Sharon, Pennsylvania, who upheld me with love and prayer: Wally and Cy

King, Roger and Nicki Herzog, Karl and Pat Robotham, Rob and Donna Martsolf, Bud and Gerry Charlton, George and Penny Kraynak, and Charlie and Bev Beall.

The executive core group of the South Orange County Gathering of Men, and the board of directors of Career Compatibilities who enhanced my productivity. Some of them were: Fred Pellicciotti, Gary Kruger, Ken Felton, George Fox, Terry Debay, Tom Bazacas, Jack Geerlings, Steve and Bill Lane, Jim Hamilton, Ted Hamilton, Steve Cooke, Dan Rinkin, Bonnie Wilkenson, Dave Blackard, Vic Hausmaninger, Jim Dugan, and Terry Rutledge.

Office volunteers Cathy Dowell and Ellen Enochs, who encouraged, gave sound advice, and labored as loyal co-workers. Bo Derning, for his hilarious cards and letters, and the magic tricks of Brant Glass, which revitalized my humor. Tom and John Bazacas whose Newport Beach Athletic Club provided enjoyable workouts and good fellowship.

Dr. Gunnar Christiansen and his wife, Susan, who inspired me to keep fighting, and provided opportunities to share my story with mental illness groups and conferences. Their example has given me a vision for working with and leading support groups for mentally ill people.

I'm grateful to Danelle McCafferty, who edited the first manuscript. I learned more from her critiques and suggestions than from all my college writing courses combined.

The abilities and efforts of the gifted, dedicated individuals who prepared this book for publication: Cathy Dowell, for her tireless typing of the preliminary draft; Wendy Allee, who tutored me on the computer, repaired my many mistakes, and typed the final drafts; Dr. Himasiri De Silva, Dr. Jim Kok, Wendy Allee, Dr. Gunnar Christiansen, Dr. Phil Sutherland, Connie Bean, Marlene Wessel, Beverly Wells, Kimberly Phillips, and Catherine Wallick, for their proofreading and suggestions; Jean Ardell for her pre-editing and stimulating writing class; and Ruth Helenic for her preliminary copyediting.

I'm indebted to dozens of other people who have been wonderful supports as I've gotten well: Jim and Susan Sabey, Donna and Paul Constantine, Dr. Rick Massimino, John Tolson, Larry and Doug Krieder, Cindy Murphy, Don and Joann Mason, Joe and Margaret Conti, Bill and Louise Lewis, Hap and June Stull, Rich and Charmagne Cesal, Bill and Charlotte Powell, Dean and Sara Sellers, Jim and Marcia Youngblood, Don and Margy Ann Gass, Davis and Gladys Hayden, Tom and Joanne Hayden, Leslie and Rod Opp, Steve Brown, Karen Bush, Linda Krekemeyer, and Bob Scott, who have helped me get well and minister again.

Above all, I am most thankful to God for sparing my life, healing many wounds, stabilizing my moods, and helping me to rebuild. It's my hope and prayer that He will get this book into the hands of those struggling with emotional pain — especially depression and bipolar disorder — and the hands of their loved ones.

Resources

Appendix A

Strategies, Techniques, Tips and Tools for Those Living with Bipolar Disorder and Depression

(These are practical suggestions from a fellow-struggler, and are not meant to be a substitute for the advice of professional health-care givers.)

Living with mental illness takes courage, creativity, experimentation, perseverance, and forgiving others and yourself. Don't expect perfection from yourself. Anticipate obstacles, setbacks, and disappointments; they happen to everyone, including those dealing with mental disorders. Life isn't fair, but you *can* cope with or overcome the difficulties of living with your illness.

Remind Yourself that You Can't Beat Your Illness Alone

You'll need the help of others every step of the way. Seek expert professional advice. Find a psychiatrist and a therapist who specialize in mood disorders. Meet with them regularly. Also, search out and surround yourself with positive, knowledgeable, affirming, supportive people in addition to your support group(s). Meet frequently in person or by phone.

Educate Yourself and Educate Your Loved Ones

Learn all you can about your illness, stress, medications and their side effects, recovery, and coping skills. Teach your family and supporters about your illness and what they can do to help you. Learn from books, magazines, mental illness newsletters, seminars, conferences, lectures, audio/videotapes, knowledgeable laypersons and professionals, and from fellow members of your support group.

Get a Thorough Physical Exam Regularly

Thyroid malfunctions, for example, can sometimes worsen bipolar problems.

Know Your Medications; Monitor Yourself

Never trust your doctor's memory or your pharmacy's computerized system to be 100 percent accurate; your precautions and efforts could save your life!

◆ Each time you get meds from your pharmacy, check the bottle for *your* name. Sometimes, patients' names are mixed up and you might get someone else's pills, which might have serious or fatal consequences. Make sure the *name* of your medication and *dosage* are correct. Even the best doctors or pharmacists can confuse medicines and dosages. Also, note the proper times to take your pills.

◆ Familiarize yourself and your loved ones with the possible side effects and negative interactions with other prescription medicines and over-the-counter drugs. Always get a large- or small-print drug information sheet from your druggist when you pick up your pills. Read the printout. Check other details in a book on medications.

◆ Listen to your body while taking your medication. Are you experiencing any new physical symptoms (dry mouth, rash, frequent urination, sleepiness, etc.), or emotions (agitation, anxiety, depression, etc.)?

- Use your physician's emergency number, your pharmacy's 24-hour hotline, or call 911 if you begin having serious physical or emotional symptoms. Don't wait too long; your hesitation could be life threatening.

- Educate yourself and family about *when* and *how* often you must have lab tests (blood work, etc.) done. Put dates in your DayTimer/calendar. Remind your doctor.

- Be patient, but report to your doctor *any* strange symptoms you're having. Remember: no one medicine works the same for everybody. You and your doctor might need to try a number of meds until you find one that works.

Know the Early Warning Signs of Your Illness

Don't delay taking preventive action in order to prevent a serious negative episode. Teach your family and friends about the signs of oncoming depression or mania.

Have a Plan in Case You Ever Need to be Hospitalized

Develop a rescue plan in case you get severely depressed, agitated, fearful, or suicidal. Discuss with your family and close friends the conditions under which you might need to be hospitalized, your hospital of choice, and the treatments you prefer and oppose. Make a written plan of action that your loved ones can follow should you need to be hospitalized.

Get Adequate Sleep

Sleep deprivation can trigger mania and other problems. Discipline yourself to stop all activities so you can get to bed at your normal time.

Know Your Limits

Don't bite off more than you can chew: discuss with your family and supporters your action plans, schedule, and deadlines. Ask for their feedback.

Nurture Yourself as Needed

Treat yourself like a king or queen! Write down activities that you can do when you begin to feel overwhelmed, fearful, angry, depressed, or manic. Take a hot bath, see a movie, call a friend, or do something else you'll enjoy.

Practice Positive Thinking

Read books and articles, and listen to tapes that will encourage you and improve your outlook. Avoid "toxic" people.

Develop an Attitude of Gratitude

Try thanking God (or your Higher Power) each morning for three blessings you received the previous day.

Become Aware of Dangerous Triggers That Can Precipitate a Relapse

Remember the *enemies* of most mentally ill people: Hunger, Anger, Loneliness, Tiredness, Stress (HALTS). Do all that you can to avoid people, places, and things that could subject you to the negative consequences of the HALTS. Avoid shaming your relatives, friends and other people if possible, but set clear-cut boundaries to protect yourself.

Tell them, "Please don't give me advice unless I ask for it. Don't try to fix/cure me. Just listen to me and tell me I'm OK and that you love me."

Meet With a Weekly Support Group

Find a group like "Comfort Zone," or a twelve-step group, a small church group, or some other cluster of people who can comfort, guide, and encourage you.

Initiate Peer Counseling with a Friend

You share for twenty or thirty minutes without being interrupted. Then your friend does the same. After each of you has shared, the other may give feedback if asked.

Force Yourself Out of Isolating Any Way You Can

Get involved in church / community activities. Reach out to others; don't wait for them to contact you. Force yourself to be with people. Make appointments to socialize with friends.

Volunteer in Activities That Help Others

Church, Little League, Scouts, YMCA, Red Cross, museum, library, and other service organizations.

Set Measurable Goals and Make Specific Plans

Discuss these with your family and friends. Write them down and monitor your progress. Give yourself an "A" if you achieve 50 percent, "B" if you do 40 percent and so forth.

Try to Accomplish at Least One Thing Every Day

A sense of accomplishment, no matter how small, is a great confidence builder. Wash the dishes, plant some flowers, write a letter, call a friend or do something else that will give you a feeling of satisfaction.

If You're Tempted to Medicate Yourself with Alcohol, Drugs, Food or Sex, Join a Twelve-step Support Group, like AA, NA, SA, OA

Seek help from its members and from mental health professionals.

Develop and Maintain Meaningful Contact with God (or your Higher Power)

Make time each day to relax, meditate, pray and read spiritually enhancing literature. This will give you a break from daily pressures and help you focus on your real priorities rather than momentary deadlines, pressures, and fears. Check out worship services and formal teaching sessions on spiritual topics.

Try Hobbies, Old and New: gardening, sports, plays, concerts, reading, whatever you enjoy.

Have Fun with a Pet: a dog, cat, fish, parakeet, or other "companion."

Develop Your Sense of Humor: read joke books, tell jokes and play tricks on friends.

Keep a Journal: write about things that happen and especially about your *feelings*.

Exercise: a half-hour a day or more, three to five days a week. Start slowly and build up.

Work to Build Structure / Routine into Your Daily and Weekly Schedule: set regular times for hygiene, spiritual reading, pet care, meetings with friends, house chores, and other activities.

Develop a "People-helper Kit"

Collect mental illness literature, tapes, and resources that you can use to share with others struggling with similar problems.

**Share with Others What You Learn
About Living with Your Illness**

Reach out to help others *each week:* make phone calls, write letters or notes, give gifts, take a person out for coffee and encouragement, or perform other acts of caring and helpfulness.

Appendix B

Simple Ways You Can Give Help and Hope to a Mentally Ill Person or His Family

THE MENTALLY ILL AND THEIR FAMILIES often feel estranged from, or judged by, relatives, friends, and faith communities. Clergy are usually too busy or uncomfortable to meet these people's needs. Mind-damaged individuals and their families desperately need caring friends who will accept, love, and believe in them. You may know very little about mental illness, but you can provide simple caring gestures.

Several surveys asked people living with mental illness, "What's been the greatest help to you in coping with or recovering from your disability?"

Overwhelming Response: "What helped the most has been people who accepted me despite my problem, who believed in me, and who demonstrated simple, practical caring love for me in their words and actions."

The Biggest Needs of Mentally Ill People and Their Families:

◆ Practical information about mental illness.

◆ A welcoming, accepting atmosphere at worship and faith community activities.

◆ Simple, tangible expressions of caring and love.

◆ *Hope* that they will get well and lead purposeful, productive lives.

◆ Having others believe in them; believe that things will get

better, and that they can use their abilities and experiences to make valuable contributions in the faith community and the world at large.

◆ *Faith* that will help them find meaning and purpose for their struggles. Share encouragement and teaching, so their faith can comfort, sustain, and strengthen them amid difficulties and relapses by answering two key questions: "Why has God let this happen to us?" and "Now that we have this mental illness, what can we do to cope, to overcome it, so we can live happily and productively?"

◆ Being needed for their skills and experience.

◆ Often, by phone or in person, tell a mentally ill person, "I love you, whether you're up or down, whether you can work or not, whether you attend worship or not."

◆ Ask, "Is there anything I can do for you? Can I drive you to the doctor, pick up groceries for you, pray for a specific need you have?"

◆ Compliment them on an accomplishment, their courage to keep struggling, or a positive character trait.

◆ Phone regularly. Don't get discouraged if your calls aren't returned for a month or more; keep calling and leaving messages: "Hi Sam/Susie! I've been thinking of you. I know you're fighting tough battles. I admire your courage. I believe you're going to get better. Hang in there. I care very much for/about you. Whenever you feel up to talking or whenever you just want someone to listen, I'm here for you. Please call me when you're able."

◆ Offer to attend religious, cultural, or sporting events, a mental illness support group, or educational meetings with your friend (or his family member).

◆ Send an occasional card, note, letter, flowers, anonymous money

gift, or other expression of care.

◆ Educate *yourself* about your loved one's mental illness: its causes, symptoms, and treatments.

◆ When appropriate, hug or touch.

◆ Share inspirational books and tapes that you've found helpful.

◆ Pray with and for your friend(s).

◆ Recruit them for volunteer tasks in your faith community or town.

◆ When appropriate, share quotes from spiritual/inspirational literature that have been meaningful to you.

◆ Offer to help with lawn work, housework, transportation, budgeting, or provide other assistance they might need.

◆ Send a cartoon or joke with an encouraging note.

◆ Invite your friend for coffee, lunch, shopping, a walk on the beach, a movie, play, ball game, or any fun activity.

Appendix C

Practical Things Your Faith Community Can Do to Help the Mentally Ill and Their Families

- Give them a sense of belonging rather than avoiding them or spouting spiritual platitudes.

- Provide a room for meetings.

- Worship suggestions:

    1. Balance fast, "peppy" praise hymns with slower hymns (depressed people often can't identify with fast-paced hymns, but can with slower ones).

    2. Preach sermons on issues dealing with mental illness: "Is mental illness God's punishment for sin?" "Is mental illness caused by demons or lack of faith?" "How can I apply my faith to find comfort, meaning, and guidance in my suffering?"

    3. Include the mentally ill and their loved ones in Pastoral Prayers.

    4. Use the personal testimonies of mentally ill people and family members in worship services.

    5. In a nearby room after each worship service, offer prayer for those who wish to be prayed for.

- Several times a year, offer seminars, workshops, and classes on various aspects of mental illness, suffering, and strengthening faith.

- Find mental health professionals or trained laypersons to organize and lead weekly or monthly support groups for mentally ill individuals and their families.

- Recruit people with mind disorders for volunteer work: stuffing envelopes, computer work, office tasks, committees, and other areas of service.

- Have clergy or a visitation person visit members who are in psychiatric hospitals.

- Have a Stephen Minister or lay visitor assigned to meet regularly with mentally ill people and their families.

- Put $100–10,000 in your faith community's budget for speakers, teachers, literature, and the emergency needs of people affected by mental illness.

- Set up and maintain a "clothes closet" with shoes, socks, suits, dresses, coats, ties, etc.

- Add to the training curriculum for official lay leaders and Stephens Ministry volunteers a lecture on "Mental Illness: Causes, Symptoms, and Treatments." Use testimonies of mind-injured persons.

- Encourage the Mission Committee or other groups to sponsor an annual mental illness project: collecting clothes, helping in a board-and-care residence, providing a Christmas party in the worship building or in a psychiatric facility.

- Encourage Stephen Ministers and other caregivers to send occasional cards and notes to mentally ill people and their families.

- Recruit people to offer counsel on finances, insurance, disability, conservatorship, housing, and legal matters.

- Sponsor a "Hot Line" or "Prayer Line" for people undergoing a life crisis.

- Have a group pray regularly for those affected by mental problems.

- Alert and train greeters to relate to the mentally ill and their loved ones.

- Organize and maintain a "Mental Illness Information" table to be displayed each week before and after worship services. Place fliers, brochures, books, and tapes about mental illness (causes, symptoms, treatments, testimonies) in visible areas. When appropriate, also have political action literature relating to mental illness available to influence legislation on local, state, and national levels.

- Several times a year, offer "Ask the Clergy," or "Ask the Mental Health Professional," or "Question and Answer" sessions dealing with life issues and/or mental illness.

Appendix D

Support, Information and Advocacy Organizations

INTERFAITH ORGANIZATIONS

THESE REACH OUT TO FAITH COMMUNITIES to equip them for meeting the needs of the mentally ill and their families. These organizations also offer spiritual support, information, and training, and act as advocates for mental illness causes.

Faithnet NAMI

Offers audio and videotapes, a newsletter, speakers, and assorted information relating spirituality to mental illness issues.

Faithnet NAMI
621 South B Street, Suite B, Tustin, CA 92780
Tel: 714/544-8488 *or* 916/567-0163
Web site: www.faithnetnami.org

Pathways to Promise

Has informational booklets, manuals, curricula resources, bulletin inserts, and videotapes designed to be used by faith groups on national, regional, local, and congregational levels. Some written materials are available in Protestant, Roman Catholic, or Jewish versions.

Pathways to Promise
5400 Arsenal St.
St. Louis, Missouri 63139
Tel: 314/644-8400

OTHER KEY ORGANIZATIONS

National Alliance for the Mentally Ill (NAMI)

An information, advocacy, and support organization dedicated to improving the lives of those with serious mental illness and of their families. Has over 1,200 local and state affiliates around the U. S., with more than 210,000 members who offer support group meetings and a wide range of resources. NAMI also coordinates national advocacy efforts, which include lobbying on national and state levels, publishes a monthly newsletter, the *Advocate,* and makes available numerous publications.

NAMI

Colonial Place Three
2107 Wilson Blvd., Suite 200
Arlington, VA 22201-30421
703/524-7600
Web site: www.nami.org
NAMI Help line: (800) 950-NAMI (6264) Offers emotional support, information and referrals to local organizations.

NAMI California

Provides services similar to national NAMI.

NAMI California
1111 Howe Avenue, Suite 475
Sacramento, CA 95825-8541
Phone: 916/567-0163
Fax: 916/567-1757
Web site: www.namicalifornia.org

NAMI Orange County

Supplies services similar to national NAMI and NAMI California. Has a fine newsletter and regular informational meetings.

NAMI Orange County
621 South B Street, Suite B
Tustin, CA 92780
Phone: 714/544-8488
Fax: 714/544-0791
Web site: www.NAMIOC.org

National Depressive and Manic-Depressive Association (DMDA)

DMDA has 275 chapters and 260 support groups, and is guided by a sixty-five member Scientific Advisory Board. DMDA offers literature and audio and videotapes on a wide variety of topics. It is active in advocacy and lobbying efforts involving the rights of those with depression and manic depression, including insurance, housing and job discrimination. Publishes a quarterly newsletter.

DMDA
730 N. Franklin Street, Suite 501
Chicago, Illinois 60610-3526 USA
Phone: 800/826-3632 *or* 312/642-0049
Fax: 312/642-7243
For free educational materials, call national DMDA's toll-free information line: (800) 826-3632.

DMDA of Orange County, California

Provides services similar to national DMDA. Has an excellent newsletter and regular informational meetings.

DMDA, Orange County
P.O. Box 223
Tustin, CA 92781
For information call: 714/744-8718

Bipolar Resource Center (of Orange County, California)

Offer seminars and other information for patients and families.

Bipolar Resource Center
St. Joseph's Hospital
Sister Elizabeth Building, 2nd Floor
P.O. Box 5600 / 1101 W. Stewart Dr.
Orange, CA 92863-5600
714/744-8718

John Henry Foundation (JHF)

Serves the community with programs for those suffering mental illness, runs several consumer-operated businesses, and provides support groups, counseling, information, housing, and lectures.

John Henry Foundation
12821 Garden Grove Blvd.
Garden Grove, CA 92843
Tel: 714/539-9597 or 714/404-3315

National Mental Health Association (NMHA)

Offers patient and family support services through Mental Health Associations across the United States. Also furnishes educational and community outreach materials, including speakers for schools, businesses, and local organizations. Its catalog contains lists of materials available from NMHA Information Center.

National Mental Health Association
1021 Price Street
Alexandria, Virginia 22314
800/969-6642 (Hotline); 703/684-7722 (Office)

Mental Health Association of Orange County
(Provides services similar to the national organization.)

Mental Health Association of Orange County
822 W. Town and Country Road
Orange, California
Tel: 714/547-7559

Bipolar Network

Publishes a newsletter, *Bipolar Network News,* which describes up-to-date studies and treatments for bipolar disorder.

Bipolar Network News
C/O NIMH
10 Center Drive
Bldg. 10, Room 3S239
Bethesda, MD 20892
Tel: 800/518-SFBN (7326); Fax: 301/402-0052
Web site: www.bipolarnetwork.org
Email: stanley@sparky.nimh.nih.gov

Notes

1. David B. Peters, *A Betrayal of Innocence* (Dallas, TX: Word, Incorporated, 1986), 17; Beverly Engel, MFCC, *The Right to Innocence* (Los Angeles, CA: Jeremy P. Tarcher, Inc., 1989), 23, 34; Susan Forward, Ph.D. and Craig Buck, *Betrayal of Innocence* (New York: Penguin Group, 1988), 75, 76.
2. Lee W. Carlson, *Child Sexual Abuse* (Valley Forge, PA: Judson Press, 1988), 11.
3. Ibid., 11.
4. David A. Sack, M.D., *No More Secrets No More Shame* (Washington, D.C.: PIA Press, 1990), 13.
5. Kenneth M. Adams, Ph.D., *Silently Seduced* (Deerfield Beach, FL: Health Communications, Inc., 1991), 8–14; E. Sue Blume, M.S.W., *Secret Survivors*, New York: Ballantine Books, 1991), 8, 9.
6. Beverly Engel, MFCC, *The Right to Innocence* (Los Angeles, CA: Jeremy P. Tarcher, Inc., 1989), 28, 29; E. Sue Blume, M.S.W., *Secret Survivors*, New York: Ballantine Books, 1991), 84.
7. Elizabeth Loftus, Ph.D. and Katherine Ketcham, *The Myth of Repressed Memory* (New York: St. Martin's Press, 1994), 49–54, 65, 264–269.
8. David A. Sack, M.D., *No More Secrets No More Shame* (Washington, D.C.: PIA Press, 1990), 22, 25, 26; Robert M. Post, M.D., *Bipolar Network News*, Volume 4, Issue 4 (Bethesda, MD: Stanley Foundation Bipolar Network, December 1998), 10.
9. Lee W. Carlson, *Child Sexual Abuse* (Valley Forge, PA: Judson Press, 1988), 29.
10. Sack, *No More Secrets,* 36.
11. Engel, *The Right to Innocence,* 30, 37, 38.
12. Mark Laaser, Ph.D., *Faithful & True* (Grand Rapids, MI: Zondervan Publishing House, 1992), 51, 115.
13. *Family News From Dr. James Dobson* (Colorado Springs, CO: Focus on the Family, August 1988, Issue Number 8), 2; Ed. Rev.

Karen L. Kiser, *The Southern California and Hawaii Presbyterian* (Los Angeles, CA: The Synod of Southern California and Hawaii Presbyterian Church (U.S.A.), spring 2000), 6.

14. *Family News From Dr. James Dobson* (Colorado Springs, CO: Focus on the Family, Aug. 1988, Issue Number 8), 2.

15. Ed. Rev. Karen L. Kiser, *The Southern California and Hawaii Presbyterian* (Los Angeles, CA: The Synod of Southern California and Hawaii Presbyterian Church (U.S.A.), spring 2000), 6.

16. Ibid., 6.

17. 1 Corinthians 10:12

18. Romans 9:2

19. 2 Corinthians 1:8, 9

20. Psalm 142:4; 88:3–5

21. Hebrews 13:5

22. Psalm 50:15

23. Lamentations 3:17, 18, 2, 3, 5–8

24. Job 7:16; 30:15–17, 20, 25-27

25. Psalm 77:2–4

26. National Depressive and Manic-Depressive Association, *Living with Bipolar Disorder: How Far Have We Come?* (Chicago, IL: National Depressive and Manic-Depressive Association, 2001), 3, 4.

27. Ibid., 4, 6.

28. Kay Redfield Jamison, Ph.D., *Night Falls Fast* (New York: Alfred A. Knopf, 1999), 246–248; Carol Tavris, Ph.D., *Los Angeles Times* (Los Angeles, CA: May 7, 1999), B-15.

29. Jamison, *Night Falls Fast*, 246–248; Michael Gitlin, M.D., *The JOURNAL of the California Alliance for the Mentally Ill*, Volume 6, Number 2 (Sacramento, CA: The California Alliance for the Mentally Ill, 1995), 7.

30. Kay Redfield Jamison, Ph.D., *Touched with Fire* (New York: Free Press Paperbacks, 1993), 46; Jamison, *Night Falls Fast,* 210, 211.

31. Jamison, *Night Falls Fast,* 190.

32. William Potter, M.D., *Manic Depression: Voices of an Illness* (New York: Lichtenstein Creative Media, Inc., 1992), 19.

33. Jamison, *Touched with Fire*, 250.

34. ˋFrank Kiefer, *The CAMI Statement*, Volume XIX, Number 1 (Sacramento, CA: California Alliance for the Mentally Ill, January/February 1999), 1.

35. Jamison,, *Night Falls Fast,* 46.

36. Ibid., 114, 115.

37. Curtis B. Flory and Rose M. Friedrich, *The CAMI Statement,* Volume XVII, Number 3 (Sacramento, CA: NAMI California, May/June 1997), 1, 3.

38. Susan Brink, *U.S. News & World Report* (New York: U.S. News and World Report, Inc., Dec. 20, 1999), 62; Susan Brink, *U.S. News & World Report* (New York: U.S. News and World Report, Inc., Jan. 19, 1998), 64; Stewart D. Govig, *Strong at the Broken Places* (Louisville, KY: Westminster/John Knox Press, 1989), 52.

39. Michael A. Glueck, M.D., *Los Angeles Times, Daily Pilot* (Newport Beach and Costa Mesa, CA: Tribune Publishing Co., May 11, 1999), 2.

40. Ronald R. Fieve, M.D., *Moodswing* (New York: Bantam Books, 1994), 210.

41. Mary Ellen Copeland, M.S., *The Depression Workbook* (Oakland, CA: New Harbinger Publications, Inc., 1992), 11.

42. David Segarnick, Ph.D., *The JOURNAL of the California Alliance for the Mentally Ill*, Volume 1, Number 4 (Sacramento, CA: The California Alliance for the Mentally Ill, 1990), 5.

43. Frederick K. Goodwin, M.D. and Kay Redfield Jamison, Ph.D., *Manic-Depressive Illness* (New York: Oxford University Press, Inc., 1990), IX, X.

44. Jamison, *Night Falls Fast,* 110.

45. Ibid., 197, 198, 292, 294, 120, 121, 87–94, 101,102.

46. Gitlin,, *The JOURNAL of the California Alliance for the Mentally Ill,* 8.

47. Jamison, *Touched with Fire,* 16; Robert Sapolsky, *Newsweek* (New York: Newsweek, Inc., April 10, 2000), 68.

48. Henry Mulder, M.D., *Pine Rest Today* (Grand Rapids, MI: The Marketing Department of Pine Rest Christian Mental Health Services, Spring, 1995), 1; Robert Sapolsky, Ph.D., *Newsweek*

(New York: Newsweek, Inc., April 10, 2000), 68; Dean Hamer,
Ph.D., *Time* (New York: Time Inc., April 27, 1998), 61.

49. Frederick K. Goodwin, M.D. and Kay Redfield Jamison, Ph.D.,
Manic-Depressive Illness (New York: Oxford University Press,
Inc., 1990), 725, 729; Jamison, *Night Falls Fast*, 252, 253.

50. Henry Mulder, M.D., *Pine Rest Today* (Grand Rapids, MI: The
Marketing Department of Pine Rest Christian Mental Health
Services, Spring, 1995), 3.

51. Robert M. Post, M.D., *Manic Depression: Voices of an Illness* (New
York: Lichtenstein Creative Media, Inc., 1992), 8.

52. Jamison, *Night Falls Fast*, 87–89; Selina I. Glater, M.A., R.M.T.,
The JOURNAL of the California Alliance for the Mentally Ill,
Volume 6, Number 2 (Sacramento, CA: California Alliance for the
Mentally Ill, 1995), 22, 23.

53. Ibid. 87–89.

54. Ibid. 87–89.

55. Robert M. Post, M.D. and Gabriele S. Leverich, M.S.W., Bipolar
Network News, Volume 5, Issue 1 (Bethesda, MD: Stanley
Foundation Bipolar Network, March 1999), 10.

56. Jamison, *Night Falls Fast*, 114, 88–94.

57. Jamison, *Touched with Fire*, 194.

58. Demitri Papolos, M.D. and Janice Papolos, *Overcoming Depression*
(New York: HarperCollins Publishers, Inc., 1992), 71; Dean
Hamer, Ph.D., *Time* (New York: Time, Inc., April 27, 1998), 61.

59. Jamison, *Night Falls Fast*, 88–94; Sheri Johnson, Ph.D., *The
JOURNAL of the California Alliance for the Mentally Ill*, Volume
6, Number 2 (Sacramento, CA: California Alliance for the Mentally Ill, 1995), 22, 23.

60. 2 Timothy 1:16

61. U.S. Department of Health and Human Services Publication ADM
#90-1470

62. Lori Holman, *CAMI Statement*, Volume XIX, Number 2 (Sacramento, CA: California Alliance for the Mentally Ill, March/April,
1999), 2.

63. Jamison, *Night Falls Fast*, 190.

64. William Styron, *On the Edge of Darkness* (New York: Doubleday, 1994), 78.

65. Psalm 38:11

66. Lori Altshuler, M.D., *The JOURNAL of the California Alliance for the Mentally Ill*, Volume 6, Number 2 (Sacramento, CA: California Alliance for the Mentally Ill, 1995), 17.

67. 1 Corinthians 11:17

68. Psalm 31:11

69. Gunnar E. Christiansen, M.D., *The JOURNAL of the California Alliance for the Mentally Ill*, Volume 8, Number 4 (Sacramento, CA: California Alliance for the Mentally Ill, 1997), 5.

70. Ibid., 5.

71. Jennifer Shifrin, *The JOURNAL of the California Alliance for the Mentally Ill*, Volume 3, Number 4 (Sacramento, CA: California Alliance for the Mentally Ill, 1992), 14.

72. Edward E. Cooper and Patty Cooper, *When Even the Devil Deserts You* (Ft. Lauderdale, FL: Dream Again Press, 1992), 64.

73. Jeremiah 15:18

74. Avery Comarow, *U.S. News & World Report* (U.S.A.: U.S. News & World Report, Inc., November 29, 1999), 82.

75. Gitlin, *The JOURNAL*, 7; Goodwin and Jamison, *Manic-Depressive Illness*, 127–142.

76. Gitlin, *The JOURNAL*, 7.

77. Proverbs 3:5

78. Isaiah 1:18

79. Mark 12:30

80. Lamentations 3:33

81. Isaiah 55:8; Romans 8:28

82. 2 Corinthians 12:7, 8

83. John 16:33

84. Matthew 5:45

85. 1 Corinthians 12:3

86. Proverbs 17:22

87. Al Siebert, Ph.D., *The Survivor Personality* (New York: The Berkley Publishing Group, 1996), 231–233.

88. Psalm 56:9

89. Isaiah 43:1, 2, 5

90. Jamison, *Night Falls Fast*, 252.

91. Job 4:4

92. Frieda Eastman, *NAMI Advocate*, Volume 19, Number 1 (Arlington, VA: National Alliance for the Mentally Ill, July/August 1977), 1.

93. Robert M. Post, M.D., *Bipolar Network News*, Volume 4, Issue 1 (Bethesda, MD: Stanley Foundation Bipolar Network, March 1998), 2, 9; Jim McNulty, *NAMI Advocate*, Volume 20, Number 1 (Arlington, VA: National Alliance for the Mentally Ill, August/ September 1998), 13.

94. Goodwin and Jamison, *Manic-Depressive Illness,* 681; Demitri Papolos, M.D., and Janice Papolos, *Overcoming Depression* (New York: HarperCollins Publishers, 1992), 46.

95. Barbara Perry, M.D., *On the Edge of Darkness* (New York: Doubleday, 1994), 161.

96. Robert M. Post, M.D., *Bipolar Network News*, Volume 4, Issue 4 (Bethesda, MD: Stanley Foundation Bipolar Network, December 1998), 10.

97. Ibid., 10.

98. Ved P. Varma, Ph.D., *Managing Manic Depressive Disorders* (Great Britain: Cromwell Press Ltd., Melksham, Wiltshire, 1997), 166, 176; Mary Ellen Copeland, M.S., *Living Without Depression & Manic Depression* (Oakland, CA: New Harbinger Publications, Inc., 1994), 1–3; Agnes B. Hatfield, Ph.D. and Harriet P. Lefley, Ph.D., *Surviving Mental Illness* (New York: The Guilford Press, 1993), 164, 165, 168.

99. Jamison, *Touched with Fire*, 58.

100. Ibid., 41.

101. Frank Kiefer, CAMI STATEMENT, Volume XIX, Number One (Sacramento, CA: California Alliance for the Mentally Ill, January/February, 1999), 1, 3.

102. Joe Graedon and Teresa Graedon, Ph.D., *The People's Pharmacy* (U.S.A.: St. Martin's Press, 1998), 219, 221; Jay S. Cohen, M.D., *Over Dose* (New York: Jeremy P. Tarcher/Putnam, 2001), 21, 22, 29.

103. Jay S. Cohen, M.D., *Newsweek* (New York: Newsweek, Inc., December 6, 1999), 97.

104. Cohen, *Over Dose*, 2; Cohen, *Newsweek*, 97.

105. Graedon and Graedon, *The People's Pharmacy*, 6.

106. Susan Brink, *U.S. News & World Report* (U.S.A.: U.S. News & World Report, Inc., December 20, 1999), 62.

107. Cohen, *Over Dose*, 8; Graedon and Graedon, *The People's Pharmacy*, 37, 46, 60, 61, 221.

108. Cohen, *Over Dose*, 6.

109. Graedon and Graedon, *The People's Pharmacy*, 8, 37, 57; Cohen, *Over Dose*, 13, 8, 6.

110. Graedon and Graedon, *The People's Pharmacy*, 38.

111. Anne Underwood, *Newsweek* (New York: Newsweek, Inc., March 27, 2000), 81; Graedon and Graedon, *The People's Pharmacy*, 7.

112. Graedon and Graedon, *The People's Pharmacy*, 7.

113. Paul Meier, M.D., Stephen Arterburn, M.Ed. and Frank Minirth, M.D., *Mood Swings* (Nashville, TN: Thomas Nelson, Inc., 1999), 91.

114. Jamison, *Night Falls Fast*, 109, 110, 127, 128, 259.

115. 2 Corinthians 1:3, 4

116. Mary Ellen Copeland, M.S., M.A., *Living Without Depression & Manic Depression* (Oakland, CA: New Harbinger Publications, Inc., 1994), 23.

117. Psalm 139:13, 15, 16

118. Bruce Bower, Ph.D., *Science News*, Volume 157 (Washington, D.C.: Science Service, April 2000), 233; Jamison, *Touched with Fire*, 252.

119. Papolos and Papolos, *Overcoming Depression*, 201, 202; Goodwin and Jamison, *Manic-Depressive Illness*, 738; Jamison, *Night Falls Fast*, 201.

120. Bower, *Science News*, 233.

121. Ibid., 233.

122. Robert Sapolsky, Ph.D., *Newsweek* (New York: Newsweek, Inc., April 10, 2000), 68.

123. Jamison, *Night Falls Fast*, 253.

124. Arthur Allen, *Family Therapy Networker* (Washington, D.C., Family Therapy Network, March/April 1998), 48.

125. Gitlin, *The JOURNAL,* Volume 6, Number 2, 9.

126. Allen, *Family Therapy Networker,* 49.

127. Dean Hamer, Ph.D., *Time* (New York: Time, Inc., April 27, 1998), 61; Sapolsky, *Newsweek*, 68.

128. Sharon Begley, *Newsweek* (New York: Newsweek, Inc., March 27, 2000), 64.

129. Stephen P. Hersh, M.D., *On the Edge of Darkness* (New York: Doubleday, 1994), 37.

130. Ecclesiastes 4:9, 10, 12; Galatians 6:2; James 5:16; Hebrews 10:24, 25

131. Hatfield, *Surviving Mental Illness*, 22, 23, 126, 127, 138, 165, 185; Henry Cloud, Ph.D. and John Townsend, Ph.D., *Boundaries* (Grand Rapids, MI: Zondervan Publishing House, 1992), 37, 137, 224, 225, 259, 278; Henry Cloud, Ph.D., *Changes That Heal* (Grand Rapids, MI: Zondervan Publishing House, 1992), 45-87; Dean Ornish, M.D., *Love and Survival* (New York: Harper Collins Publishing, Inc., 1977), 23-71.

132. Psalm 94:17

133. Isaiah 41:10

134. John 1:14

135. Joel 2:25; Romans 8:28

136. Hebrews 6:10, 11

137. Isaiah 43:5, 18, 19; Jeremiah. 29:11

138. Isaiah 35:3, 4

139. Hebrews 11:39, 40

140. Psalm 147:3; 71:20, 21

141. Psalm 73:26

142. 1 Corinthians 15:40, 42–44

143. Revelation 21:4

144. Psalm 23:3

145. 2 Timothy 4:7